THE ARCHITECTURE OF FRANK LLOYD WRIGHT

The MIT Press
Cambridge, Massachusetts,
and London, England

THE ARCHITECTURE OF FRANK LLOYD WRIGHT

A Complete Catalog

William Allin Storrer

January 1975

This book was designed by Lauri Rosser.
It was set in IBM Univers at The MIT Press, printed on R and E Satincote by Eastern Press, and bound in G.S.B. Bahama Brown by Colonial Press, Inc., in the United States of America.

Library of Congress Cataloging in Publication Data

Storrer, William Allin.
  The architecture of Frank Lloyd Wright.

  1. Wright, Frank Lloyd, 1867-1959. I. Title.
NA737.W7S83 1973   720'.92'4   73-11300
ISBN 0-262-19097-4
ISBN 0-262-69046-2 (pbk.)

To all those who,
like Frank Lloyd Wright,
recognize an organic way of life,
a beautiful life,
as the most desirable alternative
to ecological disaster.

FOREWORD

It is thirty years since *In The Nature of Materials,* the book that Frank Lloyd Wright had me prepare covering his work of the previous half century, appeared. A reprint is now available, but the coverage remains very incomplete. In the years since the last war, during which Mr. Wright continued in active production, the chronological limitation of *In The Nature of Materials* has become increasingly distressing to me and even more, surely, to the new generation of students, for they were at least as much interested in the then current work of the "Master" as in what he had produced in their grandparents' and their parents' time.

Publications by and about Wright did not and have not ceased to appear. On the contrary, they have proliferated, so that the preparation of a complete bibliography of Wright and his work would be a very difficult, and even, since publication still continues, an unending, task. Grateful as we must be for the many existing reprints of early writings by and about Wright, not to speak of studies dealing more especially with his drawings and with his work in relation to that of his Middle Western contemporaries and followers, the present book is what has long been most needed. Here, for the first time, everything is included from the earliest houses for whose design the young Wright was responsible while in the employ of Sullivan to the semiposthumous buildings carried to completion by the Taliesin Associated Architects from Wright's extant designs since his death in 1959. With indefatigable assiduity Mr. Storrer has tracked down and photographed every structure there is good reason to believe was designed by Wright, even visiting the sites of demolished buildings. For the first time the entire Wrightian *oeuvre,* from his own house of 1889 in Oak Park, which still stands, though it has often been remodeled by him and others, to what survives across the Pacific in Japan. Graphic material, most particularly plans, could not be brought together to the same degree, as access to the Taliesin holdings has become, as is well known, all but impossible.

However thoroughly one may previously have known the work of Wright over the years—and I have had some familiarity with his work for forty years— there are innumerable surprises here, not merely as regards the work since the last war, never brought together before, but even for the early decades, the "classic" years of the Prairie house before World War I and the less productive years that immediately followed.

Mr. Storrer has performed an inestimable service not only in what he has amassed here but also in opening the way to a renewed study of the entire canon. I do not doubt that other young scholars will soon be following up clues that Mr. Storrer recurrently provides. His entries, in addition to giving present locations and describing the actual condition of extant buildings, include in many cases identification and analysis of later changes. Above all, the additional information he has brought together in several crucial instances will certainly affect understanding of the sequence of Wright's development. On the basis of the factual information and photographic imagery made available here, new interpretations of the immense variety in the seventy years of Wright's architectural production should emerge. When, eventually, what is offered here can be collated with the surviving graphic material, of which so little has been accessible thus far except when shown in special exhibitions, knowledge of Wright's work will exceed that of any other American architect.

Now, characteristic whole interiors by Wright are entering the collections of museums as well as single pieces of furniture—the living room of the Little house from Deephaven, Minnesota, in the Metropolitan Museum in New York and the Kaufmann Office from Pittsburgh in the Victoria and Albert Museum in London. Mr. Storrer's compilation has the great advantage of directing attention not merely to the particular qualities such interiors illustrate but to Wright's buildings as total architectural entities, from the smallest Usonian houses—one example of which, the Pope-Leighey house, is now preserved on a new site in Virginia by the National Trust—to the belatedly completed large-scale governmental buildings for Marin County in California. Finally, though Mr. Storrer disclaims the intention of providing any concerted critical consideration of Wright's work, the extent of his firsthand knowledge, unrivaled by that of any other scholar of his or an older generation, lends the innumerable decisions he has had to make a special authority. No one writing about Wright henceforth can afford to ignore what may be called the connoisseurship that has gone hand in hand with the accumulation of factual data and visual documentation. Although at one time I doubtless knew more of Wright's work of the period before 1940 than anyone else, I have been recurrently struck by refinements of the dating of well-known works here and the many minor structures, hitherto ignored, that are here included.

This is not primarily a picture book, filled though it is with pictures. Yet it should stimulate other photographers working in various regions to renewed attempts to produce with the camera images that for most students have remained those of the old Fuhrmann photographs, which have been so frequently reproduced over the past sixty years. This book represents the conclusion of Mr. Storrer's ambitious project, but it should also provide scholars the incentive to restudy critical aspects of the total Wright story that have unfortunately acquired the dubious authority of accepted myths.

Henry-Russell Hitchcock

ACKNOWLEDGMENTS

The author gratefully acknowledges the assistance
of the following individuals:
Bruce Brooks Pfeiffer
  of the Frank Lloyd Wright Foundation
Henry-Russell Hitchcock
Ben Raeburn
Bradley Ray Storrer
Denis C. Schmiedeke
Pete Pantaleo and Tom Moore, darkroom assistants
Rick Grabish
Raku Endo
Lloyd Wright
Eric Wright
John H. Howe

INTRODUCTION

To have seen every work of Frank Lloyd Wright that stands today is like having heard every work of Beethoven, not just the masterpieces. It occasions new thoughts on the opus of America's best-known architectural genius. Falllingwater is a completely unique architectural creation, opening new vistas to architects willing to reach for the horizon, yet one would hardly call it typical of Wright's work. What is typical? Is there some ideal work that could be drawn from the masterpieces known to every architectural student of our century—Fallingwater, the Robie house, the second Jacobs house (the solar hemicycle), La Miniatura, Ward Willits' residence, Hollyhock house, to name some of the most popular? No one of these looks vaguely like any of the others here named.

Wright's output was so varied over the years that to try to define any underlying principle would be presumptuous. Possibly the principle of "organic architecture" is a fair solution, but then many would have expected some "style" to have emerged in Wright's designs. Though several styles did emerge, they correspond to changes in the architect's life-style as much as to any other factor.

Wright's earliest work is largely eclectic. Even so, given real freedom of choice, he could still design a Winslow residence that was unlike any of its neighbors and distinctly "modern." The Prairie School style appeared in Wright's work when, in his own studio and as his own boss, the architect received enough commissions to gather a staff, many of whom later became well-known Prairie School architects on their own. Wright's move to Taliesin brought further changes, coupled with commissions on the West Coast. The start of the Taliesin Fellowship in the Depression (with Wright's first student, William Wesley Peters, now continuing the work of the Fellowship as vice-president of the Frank Lloyd Wright Foundation) brought about the Usonian house as part of Broadacre City. Many later works that Wright called "Usonian," such as the Pappas residence, bear little visual resemblance to the first of the Usonian houses, the first Jacobs residence, so we cannot even rely on Wright for stylistic terminology.

Accordingly, even though stylistic terms are used in the text, it has been my practice to employ them only in obvious cases or where historical precedent so dictates. The reader may make his own decisions about "styles" as he chooses.

I have tried to avoid drawing too many conclusions in this text, though I certainly have developed strong ideas while traveling 78,000 miles in search of every extant architectural work of Wright. It is the facts derived from my search that I wish to present, those facts about the structures themselves that seem incontestable. What constitutes a Wright building, and what does not? I have visited every building listed in this text that is not marked "demolished," and even for those buildings I have visited the sites. Photographs were made, though not without some difficulty. Several houses are so surrounded as to prevent a good foliage-free view. Although I should have liked to photograph each structure as Wright envisioned it in his presentation drawing, this too was largely impossible, if only due to a decade's tree growth since the last of Wright's projects was designed.

The basic starting point of my search was published lists of Wright's work—Bruce Radde's list in *Frank Lloyd Wright; Writings and Buildings,* edited by Ben Raeburn and Edgar Kaufmann; Bruce Brooks Pfeiffer's list in Olgivanna Lloyd Wright's *Frank Lloyd Wright, His Life, His Work, His Words;* as well as Henry-Russell Hitchcock's *In The Nature of Materials,* Grant Carpenter Manson's *Frank Lloyd Wright to 1910: The First Golden Age,* and hearsay from Wright homeowners, friends, and scholars. Buildings long since thought destroyed appeared (two buildings of the Como Orchard project), and many listed as built were simply not there. The Frank Lloyd Wright Foundation also has its own list of projects, which is based on plans in their archives, and and I have used this as a further guide. Where disagreement between my list and the Foundation's appeared, my own personal knowledge of the structure from my visit plus discussion with various architects and Wright scholars resolved the conflict to my satisfaction. (One example is the W. Irving Clark house in La Grange, Illinois. Hitchcock attributes this house to Wright's draftsman, Turnock, on the authority of Wright's own words.)

The important point I am making here is that no study of Wright can do the architect full justice if it ignores any of Wright's work. Yet nowhere has Wright's architectural opus been published *in toto.* Surely, we do discuss Attic Greek tragedy "with authority," though we possess not even forty complete works of the thousands that may have been written. To discuss Beethoven or Shakespeare, it is not necessary to know all their work, but it is helpful and may avoid costly error. The works of Wright that have been published over and over do constitute a fair cross section of his opus, particularly of the early years, but the later work is poorly represented in print.

This book documents all of Wright's architectural work. In an attempt to eliminate confusion about the "names" of Wright's buildings, the simplest possible system of personal identification is used. In almost all residences, the client's name suffices. In some instances only a line drawing and the name of the city or town where the house is located identifies the building. The names of the owners and the street addresses do not appear because we were unable to persuade the owners to join with us in producing this first complete catalog of Wright's work. For most nonresidential structures, the type of building is included as part of the identification. The boldfaced part of each entry in this volume is that part of the total name of each work that is needed for unique identification of the building. Although there is no standard term for residential works, if Wright's drawings can be taken as evidence of his own choice of terms, *residence* is preferred to any other identification; and this term has been used in the titles for the text listings, with other terminology employed in the body of the text for variety.

The book also identifies each extant project (though not every building within a project) by a photo or, in cases where foliage or the client's desire for privacy interfere, by a drawing. The photographs tend to show full views of each of the houses. Often achieved only by the use of ultrawide-angle lenses to overcome limitations of surrounding foliage, these photographs are as consistent as seems practical with Wright's own expression of the buildings as rendered in his presentation drawings. Wright carefully designed privacy into his residences, and the photograph or drawing here presented keeps this intent in mind, even when a less than satisfactory view is the result. Where suitable photographs or drawings of demolished buildings were made available to me, they are included with the text. The catalog lists the earliest known date for Wright's concept of the project, client, type of building, and, where it seems appropriate, such matter as the materials used in construction, some background on the client, the nature of the site, and supervision of the project. (Where a more consistent picture of the chronological development of Wright's designs may be obtained, the construction date, representing all changes in the original design, is given instead of the concept date.) Beyond this outline, no standard format is followed in the text, any more than Wright had a specific formula for designing a house.

The question of supervision of projects is worthy of a whole book unto itself and is therefore given little space in this volume. It does raise a further question, that of authenticity of structures. Wright disowned structures built from his plans but slightly modified in construction—for example the boards of the second level of the George Spencer residence were laid vertically, although Wright "always" specified horizontal siding; however, such works are listed as by Wright in this study. Supervision was largely of three types—by Wright himself, by a builder whom Wright trusted implicitly from earlier work, or by a Taliesin Fellow. From the Depression on, Wright had one of the students of the Taliesin Fellowship live on the site of each project throughout the duration of construction. Occasionally the work of this Fellow bears comment for his later individual accomplishments or his significance to the Frank Lloyd Wright

Foundation. Any project supervised by Wright, builder, or Taliesin Fellow is considered authentic. Any project built from Wright's plans but not supervised in one of these three ways, yet listed in the text, is so noted.

Projects are numbered in their order of appearance in their basic listing in the catalog. This order is largely chronological, but, as there is insufficient information to determine the exact order in which Wright conceived his project or obtained the commissions, no attempt has been made to give the works more than general chronological listing or numbering. Boldfaced numbers have been assigned to all buildings for which a photograph or drawing appears, while lightfaced numbers indicate that there is no illustration of this project.

The question of how many numbers should be applied to a project might be raised. A group of apartments built at one time as a contiguous group on a level site—Munkwitz or Richards are examples—is given a single project number. Three originally identical cottages—Mrs. Gale and Duplicate I and II—are individually numbered, since Wright located each on its site to take advantage of the lakeshore and sun position with respect to surrounding foliage.

The one possible deviation from this system might be in the numbering of additions to projects. Only those additions of Wright's design, of course, are considered. Where such additions to a project are for a client other than the original one, they are numbered under that client's name. Additions for the original client are usually not given a separate number; generally, the altered project in these few instances— McCartney is a fine example with its three closely spaced additions—remains so organically organized as to defy separation of the parts by even a well-trained eye. Such additions are noted by a letter suffix to the project number. Additions by the architect himself to his own residential "complexes"— his first home/studio, Taliesin, and Taliesin West—are separately numbered where they are sufficiently distinct units or where they mark steps in the continuous construction of the project.

Though a builder could have "pirated" a Wright plan, this

text lists no such works. In Wright's work, the design considered site shape and placement; site and house are one. Even today, when the Frank Lloyd Wright Foundation releases a Wright design to a new client, such release depends upon approval of a site suitable to Wright's original concept. A house not placed on the site in accordance with organic architectural principles would likely deny the creator's intention and therefore cannot qualify as authentically Wright. For this reason, pirated designs are not herein listed.

Nor are any of Wright's designs being built in the seventies listed. This category poses a problem to any specialist; these are Wright's by design, but how true to his conception is the current realization? If built on the same site as Wright intended and without other alteration, there would be little doubt as to authenticity. The designs are, however, available for different sites, and they are altered for modern appliances. Early Wright structures have been modernized, particularly in the kitchens and for the addition of air conditioning, and still command listing as Wright's work. Since none of these structures is complete at this writing, none is yet listed, though some may qualify as entries to the listing at a later date if Wright's concept of interior space remains unaltered. The 1959-designed Lykes house, though altered by John Rattenbury (in a manner I feel Wright would have approved of), for late-1960's construction, is the latest work listed.

Neither does this catalog include Wright's minor contributions to the work of other architects in whose offices he was employed. Manson mentions some possibilities, mostly connected with Wright's work in Silsbee's office, and there are some details in works of the office of Adler & Sullivan as well. These works belong properly to the office; only where Wright was entrusted with the entire project—the Charnley and Sullivan summer residences, for example—is it considered suitable for listing in this text.

Much information is left to the indexes, maps, and plans. Here the location information is more specific than in the text, giving geographical insights that may not be otherwise apparent, allowing quick checks on clients or building types (all buildings being listed according to Wright's/clients' intended use), and freeing the catalog to be organized in chronological fashion so that the photographs provide the reader with the greatest amount of comparative information.

The book cannot possibly exhaust the approaches to Wright's work or supply all the information everyone would like to find in it. It does, for the first time in history, list every Wright work that was built and identify in photo or drawing the extant constructed projects. It should give everyone interested in Wright's work—architect, student, or amateur enthusiast—the basis for expanding his knowledge of the infinite variety of architectural themes that constitutes three-quarters of a century's designing. Even the most careful scholar may find an aspect of Wright's work not before known to him.

William Allin Storrer

CATALOG OF FRANK LLOYD WRIGHT BUILDINGS

1 Nell and Jane Lloyd Jones, **Hillside Home School I** (1887)
Spring Green, Wisconsin
Demolished, 1950

Wright's aunts, Nell and Jane Lloyd Jones, taught in this
private school for many years. Eventually, a larger, more
complex structure was erected in 1903 (69).

2, 3 **Frank Lloyd Wright Residence** (1889), **Playroom Addition**
4 (1893), and **Studio** (1895)
Oak Park, Illinois

The oldest extant house by Wright is surfaced with wood
shingles. In the interior space the architect defines door
tops with string courses rather than the more common architraves. To the rear of the house is the studio of brick,
wood shingles, and stone, added in 1895. Because Wright
was his own client, his expression was not reserved; ornament became one with architecture, structure and design
one with each other, and the whole and its parts could not
be separated. The octagon, one of Wright's favorite geometrical forms during the earlier years, appears in the plan of
the library. Eventually Wright moved to Taliesin. The studio was first altered, then remodeled and restored, by Clyde
Nooker (405) in 1956. The house is now open during the
warmer months of the year to visitors.

Playroom Addition and Studio

5, 6 Louis Sullivan Summer Residence and **Stables** (1890)
Ocean Springs, Mississippi
Stables demolished, 1942

Located directly on the Gulf Coast, this house was part of a group of Wright-designed buildings on adjacent lots (5-8). Its high-pitched roof is characteristic, not of Louis Sullivan, but of the young Wright to whom the "Lieber Meister" had delegated the work. In 1970 a new dining room was added to the east half of the south facade, permanently altering Wright's T plan. There are many other alterations, mostly from restoration in the 1930s, but the woodwork in several rooms remains in fine condition.

7, 8 James **Charnley Summer Residence** and **Guesthouse** (1890)
Ocean Springs, Mississippi

The main structure is a very large version of the neighboring
Sullivan house (5) and was preferred by Wright to the
"Lieber Meister's" residence. Its T plan features bay windows of octagonal geometry, and the guesthouse (at the left
in the photograph) originally was a large octagon divided
by a single wall into two rooms. The building was restored
in the 1930s and later altered. The northeast porch has
been considerably enlarged, both side porches enclosed,
and the wood front steps replaced with brick. Otherwise,
this structure is in remarkably good condition.

9 James **Charnley Residence** (1891)
Chicago, Illinois

While Sullivan was busy with larger commercial works,
Wright gained the opportunity to do some of the office's
domestic commissions, including the Charnley house. It was
a statement far beyond its time in terms of the simplicity of
the ornamentation and in the way the exterior reflected interior space. Although the house was originally symmetrical
about an east-west axis, a later addition (cropped from the
photograph) squared off the dining room bay window on
the south facade.

10 W. S. **MacHarg** Residence (1891)
Chicago, Illinois
Demolished
Even while gaining some of Sullivan's domestic commissions, Wright was working at night on commissions of his
own, unknown to the firm of Adler & Sullivan and against
the express provisions of his five-year contract with them.
The MacHarg (or possibly, McHarg) house is the first of
nine of these that were constructed in this manner.

11, 12 Warren **McArthur Residence** (1892), **Residence Remodeling**
13 (1900), and **Stable** (1900)
Chicago, Illinois

In the McArthur residence, another of Wright's moonlighted projects, Roman brick is used up to the window sill, and plaster above. The stable has been remodeled since Wright's work. To the immediate south is the Blossom residence (14) and garage (133). The McArthur family was an important Wright client. E. E. Boynton (147) learned of Wright through McArthur. In the mid-twenties Wright's collaboration with McArthur's son Albert on the Arizona Biltmore Hotel (221, 222) may have been the initial step to the eventual establishment of Taliesin West as winter home for the Fellowship.

14 George **Blossom Residence** (1892)
Chicago, Illinois

With this house, Wright demonstrated that, had he so chosen, he could have been one of the greatest of academic architects. The work is a fine example of academic Colonial Revival. With the exception of the rear extension to the conservatory, visible in rear view photograph, the plan is symmetrical. The house is of clapboard siding, and the dormers are a later addition. This is another of the moonlighted, or "bootlegged" (to use Grant Manson's term), houses.

15 Robert G. **Emmond** Residence (1892)
LaGrange, Illinois

Another moonlighting venture while Wright was with Adler
& Sullivan, the Emmond house is the most elaborate of
three houses using the same T plan, in each case set sideways to the street. The Emmond, though, is symmetrical
about a north-south axis, while the Thomas H. Gale and
Parker (located only three lots apart in Oak Park) are
turned onto east-west axes. All three were originally clapboard structures, but the Emmond has been resurfaced with
brick on its lower story; the terraces have also been enclosed,
and the house otherwise considerably altered. The Emmond
dwelling is across the street from the Goan residence (29).

16 Thomas H. Gale Residence (1892)
Oak Park, Illinois

Though a copy in plan of the Emmond (15) and Parker (17) houses, the Thomas H. Gale residence apparently pleased Mrs. Gale. She had two designs by Wright built in the first decade of the 1900s, a cottage (88) and a home (98).

17 R. P. **Parker** Residence (1892)
Oak Park, Illinois

Before the porch was destroyed, the Parker house was identical in plan to the Emmond and Thomas H. Gale residences. In the photographic background to the Parker house is the Walter Gale dwelling (20).

18 Allison **Harlan** Residence (1892)
Chicago, Illinois
Demolished, 1963

Of the many houses Wright moonlighted while with the
firm of Adler & Sullivan, this stands out both in design and
as the one that probably caused Wright's separation from
the firm. The facade is not broken by an entryway; rather,
that is placed on the side facing south (left in the photograph), as in the McArthur (11) and later Heller (38) residences, and is reached via a walled walkway. The living
room, though it was later altered at Dr. Harlan's insistence,
originally spanned the full width of the facade. Full-width
terrace and second-story balcony further emphasize the horizontal aspect of the structure. The demolition of this and
two other South Side Chicago works designed by Wright
came about under curious circumstances. All three were designed in the early 1890s. The Harlan house was demolished
first, then the Albert Sullivan dwelling (19), and the Francis
Apartments (32) last. Each was destroyed without any adjacent buildings being damaged. In the early seventies, both
the Harlan and Albert Sullivan lots were still vacant while
the original neighbors remained. A year after the demolition
of the Francis Apartments, the lot remains vacant, while
old neighbors remain.

19 Albert Sullivan Residence (1892)
Chicago, Illinois
Demolished, 1970

The facade of this row-house design of two floors and basement reveals Sullivanian tracery in its detail. Louis Sullivan, Wright's "Lieber Meister," lived here some four years before his brother occupied the quarters. This and other Louis Sullivan (5, 6) and James Charnley (7, 8, 9) buildings could all be attributed to the "Lieber Meister" on the principle that all originated from his office, and Wright designed in Sullivan's manner, not as he would have had the commissions been his own.

20 **Walter M. Gale** Residence (1893)
Oak Park, Illinois

Although Sullivan gave Wright several projects in Ocean
Springs (5-8) and the Charnley project in Chicago (9),
Wright moonlighted other works of this period. Most reveal
but little of the Wright work that was to come in the year
this house was designed. The clapboard Walter M. Gale
house has lost its front terrace but otherwise appears much
as constructed. It is located immediately west of the Parker
house (17).

21   Robert M. **Lamp Cottage** (1893)
Madison, Wisconsin
Demolished

Though living in Oak Park at this time, Wright maintained
contact with his native area around Madison, Wisconsin.
Two works were designed for Madison in 1893, but photographs of this project have not been found. Wright also designed a residence for Mr. Lamp eleven years later (97).

22 Madison Improvement Association, **Municipal Boathouse**
(1893)
Madison, Wisconsin
Demolished, 1928

In May of this year Wright won a competition for design of
the Municipal Boathouse. Its large arch, facing the lake (at
the left of the photograph), may also be seen as a design
feature of later lakeside structures, such as the Jones house
(83) and the George Gerts Double House (77).

23 Francis **Wooley** Residence (1893)
Oak Park, Illinois

South of the Thomas H. Gale house (16) is the Wooley residence. Probably originally built of clapboards, it has been
resurfaced with an imitation brick siding.

24, 25 William H. **Winslow Residence** and **Stable** (1893)
River Forest, Illinois

The Winslow residence, designed for the publisher of *House Beautiful*, was Wright's first independent commission after he left the offices of Adler & Sullivan. Already one may note stylistic characteristics that were to stay with Wright throughout his life; a stylobate-like foundation that firmly sets the house on the earth, living quarters that dominate the structure, broad overhanging eaves, and, in two-story structures, a second story that is like a gallery, never dominating the first floor. In the Winslow house, Roman brick and stone, with a terra-cotta frieze above the entryway and broad, overhanging roof, are treated to a foliage ornament in the manner of Sullivan. This is the only one of Wright's "modern" designs in which double hung windows appear. The porte-cochere on the north was balanced in Wright's plan by a pavilion on the south, of the architect's ubiquitous (in early years) octagonal geometry. It was never built. The southeast corner porch (not visible in the photograph) was enlarged and enclosed by architect Norman Steenhof in 1962.

Stable

26 Robert W. **Roloson Apartments** (1894)
Chicago, Illinois

The first of Wright's "apartment" projects, this complex is actually his only executed example of city row houses. The stone work is abstract, not Gothic. The northernmost unit has been painted over its brown brick. Roloson was a son-in-law of Edward C. Waller (see 30, 31, 47, 65, 66).

27   H. W. **Bassett** Residence **Remodeling** (1894)
Oak Park, Illinois
Demolished
No records are available to indicate the nature of this re-
modeling for Dr. Bassett.

28   **Frederick Bagley** Residence (1894)
Hinsdale, Illinois
Many of Wright's early houses reflect the eclectic tastes of
the clients. The Frederick Bagley dwelling reveals the influence of J. L Silsbee on Wright and, perhaps, also of H. H.
Richardson. It is of stained wood shingles, now painted a
lighter color. The veranda is of stone, and the northern
structure, the library (at left in the photograph), is octagonal in plan.

29 Peter **Goan** Residence (1894)
LaGrange, Illinois

Wright never expressed any love of clapboard in his later years; board and batten, laid horizontally, were his clear preference in wood construction. Here we see them in the Goan house, which, over the years, has lost a full-width front terrace and second-story porch, which added to the horizontal character of the structure in a manner similar to the Harlan residence plan (18). Located directly across the street from the Emmond house (15), it is also near the first Hunt residence (138) and is the last of the designs Wright moonlighted while with the firm of Adler & Sullivan.

30 Edward C. Waller, **Francisco Terrace Apartments** (1895)
Chicago, Illinois

Edward C. Waller, neighbor of William H. Winslow (24, 25)
in Auvergne Place, was one of Wright's more important
early clients, and Waller's son commissioned the Midway
Gardens (180). In 1895 Waller built two sets of apartments
at the corner of Francisco and West Walnut streets. Francisco Terrace is the more original of the two, reaching deep
into its allotted space, with a half-circle archway forming
the entrance to the interior court. All but the street-front
apartments open on this courtyard, much like a mid-
twentieth-century motel. The second-story balcony is of
wood, and there are back porches, also of wood. General
neglect and vandalism have rendered the building but a
shell, and demolition seems imminent.

31 Edward C. **Waller Apartments** (1895)
Chicago, Illinois
Partially demolished

The Waller Apartments, five units planned for Jackson Boulevard and Kedzie Avenue, were not supervised in construction by Wright. Entry detail varies, but plans do not. The fifth unit from the east is shown in the photograph; the fourth has been demolished. The others, like Francisco Terrace around the corner, are threatened with the same fate already suffered by the Francis Apartments (32), demolition due to urban blight.

32 Terre Haute Trust Company, **Francis Apartments** (1895)
Chicago, Illinois
Demolished, 1971
The ground floor of this four-story structure was surfaced with a geometrical pattern in the manner of Sullivan. Upper floors had eight apartments of four to five rooms each. The north wing on the ground floor contained four shops. This photograph shows the Francis Apartments shortly before demolition.

33 Chauncey L. **Williams** Residence (1895)
River Forest, Illinois

With its steeply pitched roof, articulation of plaster between eaves, and Roman brick below the sill line, this dwelling creates a colorful impression. It has undergone some interior remodeling. Wright made several designs for the dormers, at least two of which have been used at separate times.

4, 35 Nathan G. **Moore Residence** and **Stable** (1895)
Oak Park, Illinois

This Roman brick house, which is intentionally Tudor in character, was built in 1895, then rebuilt above the first floor in 1923 after a 1922 fire. Located directly north of the Hills residence (51), which Moore executed for his daughter, it is also across the street from the Heurtley house (74). The stable is at the far left in the photograph.

36 H. R. **Young** Residence **Alterations** (1895)
Oak Park, Illinois

Wright contributed only alterations, particularly at the main level, to this structure. It is located only half a block from the Mrs. Thomas H. Gale house (98).

37 Nell and Jane Lloyd Jones, **Romeo and Juliet Windmill** (1896) Spring Green, Wisconsin

In Romeo and Juliet, the plan reveals a diamond interlocked with an octagon. This supposedly suggests Romeo and Juliet, Shakespeare's lovers, clutching each other. Construction was in the fall of 1897, about a year after the idea for the windmill was probably first conceived. The *Weekly Home News* of Spring Green suggests 1897 as both the conception and construction date. In 1939 (right photograph) the original wood shingles were replaced with horizontal boards and battens.

38, 39 Isidore **Heller Residence** and **Stable** (1896)
Chicago, Illinois
Stable demolished

The Heller house is essentially an I plan of rectangular interlocking spaces. The living room has a north-south orientation that crosses the long rectangle of the primary east-west
axis through the entry hallway to the dining room. This
dining room maintains the east-west orientation but is offset south of the prime axis. Space flows freely and draws
one from the entry to the larger living and dining quarters.
The exterior is of Roman brick, with the third story decorated in sculptured figures (not nude, as some texts suggested, but draped) by Richard Bock. The downspout in
the photograph is a later addition. Considerable evidence
suggests that the stable may not have been built.

40 Charles E. Roberts Residence Remodeling and
41 Stable Remodeling (1896)
Oak Park, Illinois

Wright's work on the two Charles Roberts structures seems
to have been limited to remodeling. In the house, work was
confined to two main floor rooms and the stairwell and
perhaps a southwest upstairs library. String courses, not
architraves, define door tops, and the woodworking is well
preserved. There is some evidence that final remodeling of
the stable did not take place until 1929.

Charles E. Roberts Stable Remodeling

42 H. C. **Goodrich** Residence (1896)
Oak Park, Illinois

Were it not for the porch, this house would be quite symmetrical. The clapboards are original, but the once-open porch has been enclosed and the interior altered.

43 George Furbeck Residence (1897)
Oak Park, Illinois

The George Furbeck house no longer appears as originally
constructed. The brown brick and wood trim remain, but
the porch has been enlarged and enclosed, altering Wright's
proportions.

44 **Rollin Furbeck** Residence (1898)
Oak Park, Illinois

The cruciform plan of the Rollin Furbeck house is slightly
altered by the entry porch and by a porte-cochere, which
has since been removed. The light tan brick and colored
wood trim are part of a three-story facade articulated in
both surface and color. The house was built in 1898; the
plans may date from a much earlier year.

45 George W. Smith Residence (1896)
Oak Park, Illinois

This is one of the last houses Wright designed during his
first decade as an architect. The roof is very steeply pitched,
while the wood-shingled exterior walls are the first of his
to slope inward as they rise; this battered wall construction
becomes common in Wright's later work. The similarity
between the roofline of this house and that of the 1889
Catherine M. White house in Evanston, Illinois, suggests that
Wright may have assisted Myron Hunt in the design of the
White house. The double hip of the Hills residence (51),
which was built a year after the White house and which also
resembles the house by Hunt, makes Wright's assistance
even more apparent.

46 Joseph **Husser** Residence (1899)
Chicago, Illinois
Demolished

The Husser dwelling takes several strides forward toward
the soon-to-emerge Prairie house style. Wright apparently
never liked "cellars." He eliminated them altogether in the
Usonian house principles; in the Prairie house he raised living quarters above ground level. In the Husser residence, the
basement was at ground level, and the house rose yet two
floors higher, thereby affording a magnificent view of nearby Lake Michigan. This design innovation may also be seen
as a means of avoiding flooding of living quarters. Octagonal elements appear in the plan, breaking the monotony of
rectilinearity. A favored plan of Prairie style dwellings, the
cruciform, appears in the west-east extensions of a basically
north-south structure in the entryway stairwell and the dining room overlooking Lake Michigan. The surface ornamentation is reminiscent of Sullivan.

47 Edward C. **Waller Residence Remodeling** (1899)
River Forest, Illinois
Demolished

Though Wright produced many designs for Edward C.
Waller, few—principally, only two apartment projects (30,
31)—came to fruition. This remodeling of a large house in
Auvergne Place across the street from William Winslow (24,
25) included the dining room and other interior work. In
1899 Wright kept a Chicago office in the Rookery Building
(113), managed by Waller. Winslow was another Rookery
tenant at that time.

48 William Adams Residence (1900)
Chicago, Illinois

Little is known with certainty about William Adams
(Addams?), who may have been one of Wright's builders.
His house is of brick and plaster, which shrubbery often
obscures.

49, 50   S. A. **Foster Residence** and **Stable** (1900)
Chicago, Illinois

Though Wright had not yet visited Japan, the roof lines of
this dwelling, curved and rising toward their extremities,
suggest an Oriental influence. Perhaps the source is Wright's
extensive knowledge of Japanese prints. Wright's first visit
to Japan was in 1905.

51 E. R. **Hills** Residence (1900)
Oak Park, Illinois

The Hills house is primarily a remodeling, but its plaster-
and wood-trimmed exterior with broad overhanging roof
suggests a step toward the soon-to-emerge Prairie style
house. It was executed by Nathan Moore for his daughter;
Moore's own Wright-designed dwelling sits on the lot immediately to the north (34).

52 B. Harley **Bradley Residence**, "Glenlloyd," and
53 **Stable** (1900)
Kankakee, Illinois

In Glenlloyd the influence of Japanese prints on Wright becomes quite apparent. Because of the porte-cochere, which extends the wing on the left in the photograph, the cruciform plan shows clearly in the exterior. Plaster with wood trim and leaded-glass windows articulate the surface. It was built for Mrs. Bradley, sister of Mrs. Charles Roberts (40, 41) and Warren Hickox (56). Located on the right bank of the Kankakee River, this large residential structure with stable has been converted into a restaurant, "Yesteryear," and gift shop. To the immediate north is the Hickox house (56), which may have been used as the builder's office/house while Glenlloyd was being constructed.

54 Ward W. **Willits Residence** and
55 **Gardener's Cottage with Stables** (1901)
Highland Park, Illinois

Ward Willits's house is of cruciform plan, on the line of
Glenlloyd (52). The Willits residence, however, has a
hipped, not gabled, roof. Its wood stripping no longer suggests Tudor half-timber but articulates a Prairie style house
in wood and plaster. The raised living area, above ground
level, is also typical of Prairie style. The cottage has been
remodeled.

56 Warren **Hickox** Residence (1900)
Kankakee, Illinois

When the wood members of this type of house become less structurally obvious in the Tudor half-timber sense, as they do in the Henderson residence (57), the house becomes a Prairie style structure. The Hickox residence is located just north of its client's brother-in-law's residence, the Bradley house (52).

57 F. B. **Henderson** Residence (1901)
Elmhurst, Illinois

Both Hickox and Henderson share the same T plan, set
sideways to the street in the former (the latter is on a corner lot). The Hickox has a gabled roof and octagonal bay
windows, while the Henderson has a hipped roof; it is one
of the first of the Prairie style houses. A covered, second-
story porch has been added, over the original terrace, at
the living room (to the right in the photograph), but in
1972 the house was being structurally corrected to Wright's
design. This house was done in collaboration with Webster
Tomlinson, the only "partner" Wright ever accepted in his
office.

58 William G. **Fricke** (Fricke-Martin) **Residence** (1901) and
59, 60 **Emma Martin Alterations** (1907) and **Garage** (1907)
Oak Park, Illinois

Several elements—masonry-like treatment of plaster walls,
lack of clarity in plan, among them—suggest a date earlier
than is generally given this structure. The building permit
was issued in 1901. Like the Heller (38), Husser (46), and
Rollin Furbeck (44) houses, it is a three-story dwelling.
The house was a collaboration with Webster Tomlinson.
Six years after its construction, alterations were made for
Emma Martin, and a garage, in the style of the house, added
(visible at far left in photograph). For many years it was
known as the Emma Martin house.

61 W. E. Martin Residence (1902)
Oak Park, Illinois

The plaster and wood trim of this three-story dwelling for
W. E. Martin, brother of Darwin D. Martin—see E-Z Polish
Factory (114) and other Martin listings (100-102, 225,
226)—is not too unlike that of the Fricke residence (58).
Yet it is closer to the Prairie ideal, as typified by the Willits
Residence (54), being much clearer in plan. The building
had been, for several years, subdivided into three apart-
ments when, in 1945, it was restored to single-family usage.

62, 62A **River Forest Golf Club** (1898) and **Addition** (1901)
River Forest, Illinois
Demolished

This building was a single-story structure of horizontal
board and batten construction, originally of T plan. In
1901 it was considerably enlarged in the top of the T by
extension and addition of an octagonal lounge. The photograph shows the original structure, before enlargement.

63   Universal Portland Cement Company, **Buffalo
      Exposition Pavilion** (1901)
      Buffalo, New York
      Demolished
      Though the Universal Portland Cement Company never
      commissioned a permanent building from Wright, it did
      commission this work for the 1901 Pan American Exposi-
      tion in Buffalo and an exhibition in Madison Square Garden
      in 1910 (163). Neither photographs nor plan seem to have
      survived the structure.

64   T. E. **Wilder Stable** (1901)
      Elmhurst, Illinois
      Demolished
      This building is known only through records at Taliesin,
      and it is not known to have been photographed.

65, 66   Edward C. **Waller Gates** and **Stables** (1901)
      River Forest, Illinois
      Stables demolished
      All that remains of the work done for Edward Waller by
      Wright are his two apartment buildings (30, 31) and these
      gates to Auvergne Place, where he was neighbor of William
      Winslow. The house in Auvergne Place that Wright remod-
      eled for Waller has been demolished. Of the gates, the stone-
      work remains, but lighting fixtures and ironwork are gone.

67 Frank **Thomas** Residence, "The Harem" (1901)
Oak Park, Illinois

A Prairie style house of wood frame originally surfaced with plaster, the Thomas residence has been resurfaced with shingles. Done in collaboration with Webster Tomlinson, the house was built for James Rogers, who presented it to his daughter and son-in-law, Mr. and Mrs. Thomas, upon completion.

68 E. Arthur **Davenport** Residence (1901)
River Forest, Illinois
This is a straightforward two-story, gable-roofed, stained-
wood board and batten structure, with plaster under the
eaves. A front terrace has been removed. The house was
done in collaboration with Webster Tomlinson.

69 Nell and Jane Lloyd Jones, **Hillside Home School II** (1901)
Spring Green, Wisconsin

Hillside (the school building proper is on the right in the
photograph) has gone through many transformations. The
first building, dating from 1887 (1), was demolished in
1950. The second school was built in 1903 for Wright's
aunts. With the formation of the Taliesin Fellowship in
1933, the school became a part of that complex. It has
since undergone considerable remodeling and the left
section (in the photograph) dates from these more recent
times. The interior is of H plan, and materials include native
limestone, oak, and plaster.

The remodeling of the building since 1933 is listed as part
of a separate project: Frank Lloyd Wright, **Taliesin Fellowship Complex** (228).

70 Francis W. **Little** (Little-Clarke) **Residence I** and
71 **Stable** (1902)
Peoria, Illinois

The first Little residence is a brick home of T plan with a separate, large stable. Additions were completed by Wright in 1909 for Robert Clarke (152). The porch has since been enclosed with glass. The Littles also built a "Northome" in Minnesota a decade later (173).

72 Susan Lawrence **Dana Residence** (1902) and
73 **Lawrence Memorial Library** (1905)
Springfield, Illinois

The Dana residence, of cruciform plan, incorporates an earlier house into its Prairie style brick structure. It is the first example of Wright's work to feature a two-story-high living room. Sculptor Richard Bock and the Linden Glass Company, regular collaborators with Wright in this period, contributed to the design. Though the designs for details are abstract patterns, they derive largely from prairie sumac. The Lawrence Memorial Library (at the left in the photograph) is connected to the main structure by a raised walkway.

74 Arthur **Heurtley Residence** (1902)
Oak Park, Illinois

In 1902 Arthur Heurtley commissioned two works, a home half a block away from Wright's studio and a cottage in northern Michigan (75). In this home Roman brick is laid so that, at a distance, it suggests board and batten. The plan is square, and living quarters are above ground in typical Prairie fashion. It has been remodeled into two apartments.

75 Arthur **Heurtley Summer Residence Remodeling** (1902)
Marquette Island, Michigan

The Heurtley cottage was only a remodeling. Exterior walls lean inwards, much as the George Smith house (45). Horizontal siding, originally stained, is now painted. The large living room and its dominating fireplace are clearly Wrightian touches. The building is one of many cottages on the properties of Les Cheneaux Club. It has been altered with glass in place of screen, and a balcony has been added on the south side of the western facade (side opposite to that shown in the photograph). Below the hillside lakefront retreat is a boathouse with similar exterior treatment, perhaps by Wright but not authenticated.

76 E. H. Pitkin Residence (1900)
Sapper Island, Desbarats, Ontario, Canada

Wright built several cottages in this period. The Pitkin residence, one of the first, is near the Heurtley cottage by boat, though some distance via Sault Sainte Marie and ground transportation. Designed as a "Swiss chalet," it is located on the westernmost promontory of Sapper Island. Pitkin visited the area on a summer cruise, apparently expecting to find a thriving colony of vacationers. Few were there, but on a side cruise he found this lovely location with an incomparable view of northern sunsets. Many nearby cottages reveal the influence of this Wright work in their copying of roof lines and board and batten construction. The cottage has been altered over the years, mostly, it seems, on the exterior. The living room and stone fireplace retain their Wrightian character.

77 George Gerts Double House, "Bridge Cottage" (1902)
Whitehall, Michigan.

Birch Brook flows under the bridged loggia of this T-plan
(double-L) cottage and fifty yards farther empties into
White Lake. South Shore Drive is well above the cottage,
which is entered halfway down a steep hill. Once a wall
divided the T into two Ls. Each L had its own fireplace,
though they shared a common chimney. Now, with the
wall removed, they are back to back and jut into the top
of the T somewhat anachronistically.

78 Walter Gerts Residence (1902)
Whitehall, Michigan
Mostly demolished

This structure has been relocated on the lot, resurfaced, and gutted. The original was a single-story board and batten structure of rectangular plan, with centrally located fireplace.

79 Henry **Wallis** (Wallis-Goodsmith) **Summer Residence** (1900)
80 and **Boathouse** (1897)
Lake Delavan, Wisconsin
Boathouse demolished

Five summer residences (79, 81, 82, 83, 87), all part of a
Delavan Lake group, may have been designed and built in
fewer years than the dates commonly assigned to them
indicate. Wright was supervising construction of at least the
Fred Jones (83) and A. P. Johnson (87) structures at the
same time. The Wallis cottage was unsupervised and sold
upon completion to H. Goodsmith. Horizontal board and
batten siding has been mostly resurfaced.

81 George W. Spencer Residence (1902)
Lake Delavan, Wisconsin

Wright supposedly disowned the George Spencer cottage
when, during construction, it was altered so that the boards
on the second level were laid vertically.

82 Charles S. Ross Residence (1902)
Lake Delavan, Wisconsin

The Charles Ross cottage is a cruciform-plan, board and batten, Prairie style structure, originally stained dark, now painted yellow. The first-story veranda has been enclosed and the second story extended and enclosed. This latter alteration considerably increased upper floor space and made that story symmetrical about two axes, modifying its original T plan.

"Penwern" (1903)
Lake Delavan, Wisconsin

This is the most extensive of the Delavan Lake Projects. The arches at the porte-cochere and front veranda distinguish it from all the other lakeside cottages. The main house has a living room the width of the lake facade, and the stair therein leads to a balcony that opens over living, dining, and other rooms. It features a large Roman brick fireplace; rooms and new woodwork have been added. Exterior is board and batten siding. The gate lodge is directly on South Shore Road, and the boathouse sits so that only the roof rises to the brow of the hill. The work was only partially supervised by Wright.

Fred B. Jones Boathouse

87 A. P. Johnson Residence (1905)
Lake Delavan, Wisconsin

It is said that when Wright, approaching on horseback via the
the dirt driveway to supervise final stages of work on this
Prairie style tongue-and-groove-sided house, saw it painted
white, he rode away, never to return. As of 1970, restoration of the house, which still retains its fine leaded windows
and Roman brick fireplace, by owner Robert Wright (no relation to the architect) was underway. By 1971, when this
photograph was taken, landscaping had been considerably
improved, and modernization of the kitchen was completed.
The building is to be given a darker exterior and may then,
for the first time in its history, look as its architect intended.

88
89, 90

**Mrs. Thomas H. Gale Summer Residence,
Summer Residence Duplicate I and II (1905)**
Whitehall, Michigan
Duplicate II mostly demolished

Another board and batten cottage, this summer house has an almost flat roofline. The dating is not certain, and the work was unsupervised. Two other nearly identical units were erected on lots nearby, each set differently to take advantage of its site. Only one duplicate remains in good condition, and it was renovated in 1970-1971. The original is dark green, Duplicate I dark brown, and Duplicate II white.

91 J. J. **Walser**, Jr. Residence (1903)
Chicago, Illinois

This Prairie style house of wood with plaster surface now stands in rather cramped quarters, between apartment buildings. There have been alterations to the rear of the structure.

92   **W. H. Freeman** Residence (1903)
Hinsdale, Illinois
Demolished

This house and a house designed by another Prairie school
disciple, William Drummond, once stood on opposite cor-
ners. Only the Abbott house by Drummond survives.

93   Larkin Company Administration **Building** (1903)
Buffalo, New York
Demolished, 1949-1950

The Larkin Company was a mail-order business. Among
the firsts of the Larkin Building are use of air conditioning
and plate glass. Also, the furniture was of metal. Wright
entrusted the working drawings of the project to William
Drummond, many of whose own designs were constructed
near Wright works, often causing the casual viewer confusion about which is which (see Isabel Roberts, 150, and
Coonley residence, 135). Larkin Company cofounders were
John Larkin and Elbert Hubbard (one of whose sisters was
Mrs. Larkin). All the Wright homeowners in Buffalo were
involved with this enterprise in some manner. Darwin D.
Martin (see 100-102, 114, 225, 226) replaced Hubbard on
the latter's retirement. Alexander Davidson (149) was a
Larkin Company advertising manager. W. R. Heath (105)
was an attorney for the Larkin enterprise. George Barton
(103) married Martin's daughter.

94 Scoville Park Fountain (1903)
Oak Park, Illinois

In an article by Donald P. Hallmark in the Second Quarter 1971 *Prairie School Review*, this work is identified, not as "with sculpture by Richard Bock," but as by Bock "with the help of Wright." As Bock's work, it is known as the Horse Show Fountain and was dedicated on July 24, 1909. This listing, however, attributing the work to Wright from a much earlier year, agrees with the records of the Frank Lloyd Wright Foundation. The current work is a replica of the fountain, with new sculpture that is an interpretation of Bock's original work.

95 Reverend Mr. Jenkin Lloyd Jones, **Abraham Lincoln Center**
(1903)
Chicago, Illinois

The original project, for All Souls Church, had more of
Wright's signature on it than this construction. The first-
floor lobby reveals the imprint of Wright, but the building
may be largely attributed to, and was entirely executed by,
Dwight Heald Perkins. John Lloyd Wright claims the original design to have been his father's first architectural work
and dates it 1888. Intended for use as a community center,
it was built in 1903 in Perkins's altered form.

96 Unity Church (1904)
Oak Park, Illinois

Unity Church is the first significant American architectural statement in poured concrete. Wright's use of concrete is truly original, making no obeisance to earlier French experiments in this material. With its exposed pebble surface, the Unity monolith introduced reinforced-concrete construction to America on a grand scale. Its use was dictated in part by the need to keep costs of the structure low; only $35,000 was available to house a congregation of 400 persons. Unity Church is composed of what Wright called Unity Temple—the north section (on the left in the photograph), whose plan inscribes a Greek cross in a square, used for religious services—and Unity House, the parish house to the south. The prime mover in the building committee that chose Wright as architect was Charles Roberts (see 40, 41). The working drawings were prepared by Barry Byrne, who, after leaving Wright's office, became one of the more successful and imaginative of Prairie School architects. Renovations, begun in 1962, have continued over the years, although they are limited by available funds. Visitors' donations help the work progress. The church is open daily to the public.

Robert M. **Lamp Residence** (1904)
Madison, Wisconsin

At one time this was a simple rectangular brick structure
bearing some semblance to Unity Church (96) in principle.
A third story, totally out of keeping with Wright's concept,
has been added, and the brick painted white. Had the brick
been concrete, the relationship to Unity Church and also to
the Mrs. Thomas H. Gale Residence (98) would be more
apparent.

98 Mrs. Thomas H. Gale Residence (1904)
Oak Park, Illinois

If the date on a perspective drawing is good evidence, this design dates from 1904 or earlier, before the Robie house (127) and approximately the same time as Unity Church (96) and the Lamp residence (97). The commonly accepted date, 1909, is that of construction. Roughly square in plan, with concrete originally envisioned as the construction material, this plaster-surfaced, wood-trimmed Prairie house is often suggested as the spiritual progenitor of Fallingwater (230). In its use of cantilever design, it does anticipate Fallingwater, yet the Gale house is itself the offspring of the 1902 Yahara Boat Club Project, which gave birth to nearly all the flat-roofed Prairie houses by Wright. The Yahara landmark in Wright's inventive thought was never built.

99 Burton J. **Westcott** Residence (1904)
Springfield, Ohio
Dating of this house is not certain, although in Springfield
it is put at 1904. It is one of the larger of the square-plan
Prairie style wood houses with plaster surface.

Darwin D. Martin Residence, Conservatory, and
Garage (1904)
Buffalo, New York
Garage and Conservatory demolished

Darwin D. Martin was a brother of W. E. Martin (61); they
were partners in the E-Z Polish Factory (114). In Buffalo
Darwin Martin assumed Elbert Hubbard's administrative
duties when that cofounder of the Larkin Company (93)
retired. This house, with its conservatory and connecting
gallery, was originally the largest expression of the T plan
in a Prairie style house. Primary construction materials are
russet Roman brick and oak. Orlando Gianinni, often associated with Wright in this period, did the glass work. Garage
and conservatory with gallery have been demolished, and
apartment buildings now crowd the lot.

103 George **Barton** Residence (1903)
Buffalo, New York

Mrs. Barton was the sister of Darwin D. Martin, and the
Barton dwelling was built on space immediately adjacent to
the north limit of the Martin residence (100) as originally
constructed with gallery and conservatory. The cruciform
plan is articulated on the main floor by western dining and
eastern living rooms, northern kitchen, and southern entry
and veranda. The house is being restored by Eric Larrabee
and his architect wife, Eleanor Larrabee.

104 Edwin H. **Cheney** Residence (1904)
Oak Park, Illinois
This is a single-story house in brick with wood trim. A brick
wall encloses its terrace. Mamah Borthwick Cheney, wife of
Edwin Cheney, accompanied Wright to Europe when the
architect left America for a year in 1909; she later died in a
fire that destroyed Taliesin.

105 W. R. **Heath** Residence (1905)
Buffalo, New York

Although 1905 is the year of Wright's first visit to Japan,
the effect of what he saw there is not apparent in this work.
The Heath dwelling is a dark red brick Prairie style structure
with large eastern porch and a living room opening to the
southern sky that breaks the rectangle into a stubby T plan.
Mr. Heath was attorney to the Larkin Company (93), and
his wife was a sister of Elbert Hubbard, cofounder of the
Larkin mail-order enterprise.

106 Harvey P. **Sutton** Residence (1905)
McCook, Nebraska

Wright's only work in Nebraska, the Sutton residence is a plaster-surfaced, wood-trimmed Prairie style structure. The building housed a doctor's offices in the early 1970s.

107 Hiram **Baldwin** Residence (1905)
Kenilworth, Illinois

A Prairie style house, which has been remodeled extensively inside, the Baldwin residence is located on a large north corner lot.

108 Mary M. W. Adams Residence (1905)
Highland Park, Illinois

This is a plaster-surfaced, wood-frame Prairie style house located on a southeast corner lot near Lake Michigan. Its best face (left side in the photograph) is turned away from public view.

109 W. A. **Glasner** Residence (1905)
Glencoe, Illinois

Situated on a brow of a ravine, this house defies simple designation as to plan type, though its major axis is east-west and all spaces flow from this spine. It features organization of spaces similar to later Usonian designs in that no separate room was planned just for dining. Although the original plan included a bridge over one part of the ravine, that extension was never built. Like many Prairie style houses with horizontal board and batten exteriors, the wood is rough sawn in finish. Many remodelings of Wright houses wrongly use smooth lumber under the mistaken notion that this original rough wood was used for economy; in fact, it was often preferred by the architect. The Glasner dwelling was renovated in 1926 and 1938 and is undergoing restoration by Dr. and Mrs. Henry Fineberg in 1972-1973. The west porch has been enclosed, and the east library (left in the photograph) was enlarged, one side eliminating the octagonal plan, in an earlier renovation.

110 Charles E. Brown Residence (1905)
Evanston, Illinois

A compact rectangle, with open front porch, in horizontal
board and batten, the Charles Brown house also has plaster
under the eaves and between top-story windows.

111 Frank L. Smith Bank, First National Bank of Dwight (1905)
Dwight, Illinois

The cut-stone exterior conceals the Wrightian delineation of
interior spaces. The building was completely renovated in
1970. It is open during regular banking hours.

112 E. W. **Cummings Real Estate Office** (1905)
River Forest, Illinois
Demolished

All that is known of this building is that it was built, probably in 1907, in River Forest, and has since been demolished.

113 Rookery Building Entryway and Lobby **Remodeling** (1905)
Chicago, Illinois

In the late 1890s Wright, the American Luxfer Prism Company (which contracted lighting fixtures designed by
Wright), and William Winslow (24) all had offices in this
building, which was under the management of another
Wright client and patron, Edward C. Waller (see 30, 31, 47,
65, 66). Wright remodeled only the entryway and lobby in
this 1886 skyscraper by Burnham and Root. There have
been further alterations since Wright's work. The building
is open during regular business hours.

114 Darwin D. Martin and W. E. Martin, **E-Z Polish Factory** (1905)
Chicago, Illinois

This building, designed for the Martin brothers (see 61, 100-102) as a polish-making factory, now serves other commercial uses. Upper floors were rebuilt after a 1913 fire, and most of the windows have been bricked in. One painted mural survives on the main office floor.

115 Thomas P. **Hardy** Residence (1905)
Racine, Wisconsin
It seems that few people view the Hardy house as Wright envisioned it (as shown in a penned drawing in Japanese style
from his own, or Marion Mahony's hand) from the Lake
Michigan shoreline. The photograph here published reveals
that lakeside aspect. The terrace is one story below street
level, and the living room, with its upper-story balcony,
opens the entire living quarters to the Lake Michigan view.
None of this is apparent from the street (western) approach.

116 W. H. **Pettit Mortuary Chapel** (1906)
Belvedere, Illinois

The chapel is a T-plan, one-story, plaster-surfaced, wooden "Prairie Mortuary Chapel"; the Belvedere Cemetery is open at all times.

117 P. A. **Beachy** Residence (1906)
Oak Park, Illinois
Of brick and plaster with wood trim, the Beachy residence, like the 1902 Dana house (72), incorporates an earlier house into its structure. Barry Byrne was involved in preparation of working drawings and supervision.

118 Frederick **Nicholas** Residence (1906)
Flossmoor, Illinois

A stained, lapped wood siding cube, the Nicholas house was not supervised by Wright during construction.

119 River Forest Tennis Club (1906)
River Forest, Illinois

On this horizontal board and batten project, Charles E.
White and Vernon S. Watson were associated with Wright.
Watson later added to and otherwise altered the structure.
It was moved from its original site in 1920. Today it re-
veals but little of Wright's contribution.

120 P. D. **Hoyt** Residence (1906)
Geneva, Illinois

A square-plan, Prairie style house, the Hoyt residence has a plastered surface and stained wood trim. Mrs. Hoyt was a daughter of Colonel George Fabyan (129).

122 A. W. **Gridley Residence** and **Barn** (1906)
Batavia, Illinois
Barn demolished
This Prairie style house of plastered surface and stained
wood trim is of cruciform plan on the ground floor and T
plan at the second story, which has no upper level at the
long, open porch.

123 Grace Fuller Residence (1906)
Glencoe, Illinois
Demolished

The second house designed by Wright in Glencoe (after the Glasner, 109), this was a design of two-story square plan, the lower floor extended by a wing. This small Prairie house was plaster surfaced and wood trimmed.

124 C. Thaxter **Shaw** Residence **Remodeling** (1906)
Montreal, Quebec, Canada
Demolished
Although Wright designed a residence for Shaw, the only
work by Wright that was completed for this client was a
small amount of remodeling in a row house complex. Continual alterations have totally obscured Wright's work.

125 K. C. **DeRhodes** Residence (1906)
South Bend, Indiana
The wood-trimmed, plaster-surfaced Prairie style DeRhodes
residence now houses a club. The main floor features an
immense living room, now an assembly room, that spans
the entire length of the building. The side entryways turn
this otherwise plain rectangle into a cruciform plan.

126 George Madison **Millard** Residence (1906)
Highland Park, Illinois

This is a two-story, cruciform-plan, board and batten Prairie style structure. Seventeen years later, Mrs. Millard built "La Miniatura" in Pasadena, California (214).

127 Frederick G. **Robie** Residence (1906)
Chicago, Illinois

One of the U.S. government's declared national architectural landmarks, the Robie house is Wright's best expression of the Prairie masonry structure. It is of Roman brick with living quarters raised above ground level. Living and dining rooms are in line, separated only by the fireplace-chimney block. Sleeping quarters are yet another floor above. The garage and surrounding high wall have been altered. Construction was begun in 1908 and completed the following year. The building's local nickname, "The Battleship," has never gained currency among Wright scholars. The building may be visited by appointment.

128 F. F. **Tomek** Residence (1907)
Riverside, Illinois

This Prairie plan has a small, second-story square centered over a large, main-floor L plan. Supports to the terrace roof are later additions. Barry Byrne drew the working drawings and was involved in construction supervision.

129 Colonel George **Fabyan** Game Preserve **Remodeling** (1907)
Geneva, Illinois

For Wright, one client invariably led to another. Wright designed the Hoyt house (120) in 1906, and this led to the Gridley commission (121, 122). While Wright was supervising construction of these two works, he met Colonel Fabyan, father of Mrs. Hoyt, who commissioned remodeling of two structures on his game preserve, one for a Fox River Country Club and the other a residence in the preserve (shown here), overlooking the Fox River. Remodeling included details of the main-floor living room, the north room of the second story, and some exterior work.

130 Fox River Country Club Remodeling (1907)
Geneva, Illinois
Demolished

This, like the Game Preserve remodeling for Colonel Fabyan (129), was a reworking of an existing structure on the estates of the Colonel. It was destroyed by fire only a few years after the remodeling was completed.

131 Pebbles & Balch Shop (1907)
Oak Park, Illinois
Demolished

This is actually a remodeling of a building on Lake Street for Pebbles and Balch, interior decorators. It reveals the influence of Wright's visit to Japan in both interior and exterior. Inside, natural woods, oiled paper for glass, and plain surfaces were seen side by side with lighting fixtures of geometrical forms used by Wright for over a decade. Wright also designed a home for O. B. Balch (168).

132 Larkin Company, **Jamestown Exhibition Pavilion** (1907)
Jamestown, Virginia
Demolished

The Jamestown Tercentennial celebration brought little
that was new to the South, except this building, which was
geometrical and comparatively plain except for some sculptures that gave it a vertical dimension not again seen until
similar sculptures appeared at Midway Gardens (180). These
sculptures suggest that it was Wright who taught Alfonzo
Iannelli his design ideas, even if Iannelli carried out the
actual work of making the sculptures for the Ravine Bluffs
(185-192) and Midway Gardens projects.

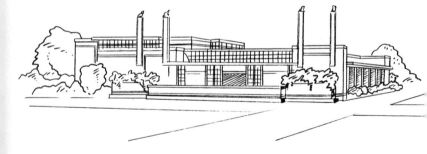

133 George **Blossom Garage** (1907)
Chicago, Illinois

To the rear of the Colonial Revival Blossom house (14) is the much later Prairie style garage in Roman brick with wood trim. Here Wright obviously ignored the original house and designed in his then current Prairie style.

134 Andrew T. **Porter** Residence, "Tanyderi" (1907)
Spring Green, Wisconsin

Tanyderi—"under the oaks" in Welsh—was built for Wright's
sister Jane and brother-in-law on the grounds of Taliesin.
Siding is of shingles. Stylistic evidence suggests a design date
of 1901 or earlier, with construction being delayed until
1907, the date generally accepted for this work. By this
later date, Wright would have provided a design more in
keeping with Prairie style ideas; perhaps this explains why
the architect on occasion denied that the design was his.

Avery **Coonley Residence** (1907), **Gardener's Cottage**
(1911), and **Coach House** (1911)
Riverside, Illinois

The Coonley residence provides the first example in Wright's
work of the zoned plan. Living quarters are raised, in typical Prairie fashion, and a pavilion links various spaces. Inlaid
tiles form a geometrical pattern in the frieze on the plaster-
surfaced, wood-trimmed house. Published plans (actual
working drawings were by Barry Byrne) include the cottage
and coach house, originally a stable, so their design date
might also be set at 1907, but construction was well after
the 1909 completion of the main residential structure. The
entire project has been somewhat altered, the residence
being converted into three separate apartments. The coach
house and contiguous sunken gardens are now a separate
plot. Remodeling of the stable into the coach house was the
late 1950s work of Arnold P. Skow for Carolyn and James
W. Howlett. On the corner opposite the former Coonley estate is "Thorncroft," one of the finest examples of Prairie
school architecture by an early Wright apprentice, William
Drummond.

Coonley Gardener's Cottage and Coach House

138 Stephen M. B. **Hunt Residence I** (1907)
La Grange, Illinois

This is the best-constructed example of "A Fireproof House of $5000" from the April 1907 *Ladies Home Journal*. Originally planned for construction in concrete, which would have made it fireproof, it is a square-plan, Prairie style building in wood and plaster. The terraces have been enclosed. Restoration over the past decade has been undertaken by Edward M. Marcisz. The Tiffany brick fireplace and oak woodwork have been fully restored. (Photograph courtesy of Edward M. Marcisz.)

139 G. C. **Stockman** Residence (1908)
Mason City, Iowa

The Stockman house is Wright's first extant work in Iowa.
Its design is basically that of the "Fireproof House of
$5000" (138).

140 Robert W. **Evans** Residence (1908)
Chicago, Illinois

From a basic square, this Prairie structure extends into a cruciform plan, with porch on the south (left in photograph) balancing porte-cochere on the north. It has been resurfaced with a stone veneer and otherwise altered.

141 Browne's Bookstore (1908)
Chicago, Illinois
Demolished

The placement and limited height of bookshelves created
alcoves around tables, each with four Wright-designed
chairs, providing the cosy atmosphere desired in the bookstore setting.

142 L. K. **Horner** Residence (1908)
Chicago, Illinois
Demolished
Published photographs reveal a strong kinship between the
Horner and Mrs. Thomas H. Gale (98) residences.

143 Willard Ashton, **Horseshoe Inn** (1908)
Estes Park, Colorado
Demolished

Little is known of this structure, though it is likely of the
same genre as the Como Orchard Summer Colony project
(144, 145).

144 Como Orchard Summer Colony, including
145 Bitter Root Inn (1908)
Darby, Montana
Inn demolished, Summer Colony mostly demolished
One small Land Office building (shown in top photograph)
and one altered cottage are all that remain of the Como
Orchard (Land Company) Summer Colony project for Uni-
versity of Chicago professors and other vacationers.

146 E. A. **Gilmore** Residence, "Airplane House" (1908)
Madison, Wisconsin

The small porches of the Gilmore residence represent a break with Wright's rather consistent rectangular and octagonal modules.

147 E. E. **Boynton** Residence (1908)
Rochester, New York

A very elongated T plan of Prairie style surfaced with plaster and wood trim, the Boynton residence has been kept in good condition. Porches emphasize the elongation of the top of the T. Boynton knew of Wright through Warren McArthur, his partner in the Ham Lantern Company (see 11-13, 221, 222). Wright often visited the site during the year of construction, taking great care with details. He designed all of the furniture for the house and required that 28 elm trees be added to the plot. Barry Byrne, often entrusted with major projects such as Unity Church (96), prepared the working drawings.

148 Meyer **May** Residence (1908)
Grand Rapids, Michigan

The details in the May house, particularly the leaded ceiling
windows, are most worthy of note. Roman brick is used
throughout, including the 1920 rear extension that emphasizes the T plan. Window detailing is copper sheathed. Terrace and second-story porch are now enclosed.

149 Alexander **Davidson** Residence (1908)
Buffalo, New York

A Prairie style structure whose two-story living room faces
east, the Davidson house is of cruciform plan. Davidson was
the advertising manager appointed by Darwin Martin at the
Larkin Company (93).

150 **Isabel Roberts** (Roberts-Scott) Residence (1908)
River Forest, Illinois

This is a Prairie style house with a two-story-high living
room, designed for Isabel Roberts, a bookkeeper of five
years' standing in Wright's Oak Park Studio and daughter
of Charles E. Roberts (40, 41). The original structure was
of wood with plaster surface and, like the Baker (151) and
Davidson (149) houses, of cruciform plan. It is a "split-
level" dwelling, with living room at ground level, sleeping
quarters a half-level above, and work spaces a half-level
below. Wright remodeled the house for Warren Scott in
1955. Resurfacing was with brick veneer (as shown in the
photograph), and blonde Philippine mahogany was used
throughout the interior. The living room clerestory (center
of photograph) starts only after an interrupting section of
wall next to the floor-to-ceiling front windows (at left).
The south porch is built around a tree that rises through
the roofing. Immediately to the south and across the street
are houses by a Prairie school disciple, William Drummond,
who prepared the working drawings for the Isabel Roberts
house.

151 Frank J. **Baker** Residence (1909)
Wilmette, Illinois

A Prairie style wood house with plaster surface, the Baker
dwelling also features a two-story-high living room. Its once-
open porches are now enclosed. The Baker living room
clerestory starts immediately from the floor-to-ceiling front
windows. The ground floor is cruciform, the second story
L plan, with no second story over either east or west porch.

152   Robert **Clarke Additions** to the **Little Residence I** (1909)
Peoria, Illinois

The Clarke additions elongated the original T plan of the
first Little residence (70). Published plans show the house
as enlarged.

153   Oscar **Steffens** Residence (1909)
Chicago, Illinois
Demolished

The Steffens residence was a two-story, cruciform-plan
Prairie style structure, with a two-story-high living room;
it was located near Lake Michigan.

154 Thurber Art Gallery (1909)
Chicago, Illinois
Demolished

Two long panels of leaded glass lighted the Thurber Art Gallery on sunny days and concealed the indirect lighting that lighted the gallery at other times. As in other "shops" of this time, such as the Pebbles & Balch Shop (131) and Browne's Bookstore (141), Wright took great care in achieving interesting interior spaces.

This bank and the Park Inn hotel behind it are now so thoroughly altered by store window fronts cut into the lower
wall and other ''modernizing'' alterations as to disguise the
once-elegant quality of these works. The project was nearly
two years in construction and was completed by William
Drummond during Wright's 1910 absence from America.
J. E. E. Markley, whose eldest daughter had been a student
at Wright's aunts' Hillside Home School I (1) in Spring
Green, Wisconsin, probably brought Wright the commission.
Had Wright not run off to Europe, Markley's business partner, James E. Blythe, might have become the kind of client
that so often failed to materialize for the architect, one
with many commissions at his command. Blythe and
Markley were involved in the 1912 Rock Crest-Rock Glen
project, designed by Walter Burley Griffin. Blythe built a
Griffin-designed house and commissioned several others,
including one for Arthur Rule of the law firm of Blythe,
Markley, Rule and Smith. Wright had also designed at this
time a house similar to Isabel Roberts's for J. C. Melson;
Melson built a Griffin design. William Drummond and Barry
Byrne also designed houses that were built in or near the
Rock Glen area. But as these former Wright students were
becoming independent of their master, the master himself
was breaking free of his own past and looking westward in
the second decade of the century for his future in architecture.

W. H. **Copeland Residence Alterations** and **Garage** (1909)
Oak Park, Illinois

The Copeland residence remodeling includes three main-story rooms and the stairwell. Wright replaced architraves with string courses. The garage, to the rear of the residence, reveals external Wrightian Prairie characteristics.

Copeland Garage

160 George C. **Stewart** Residence (1909)
Montecito, California

The first of the California houses, the Stewart house reveals
Wright's use of Midwestern Prairie concepts on the Pacific
Coast—two-story living room, broad overhanging roof, and
raised living quarters. The two-story-high living room is the
main feature of the structure. The living room and the
house plan suggest a board and batten reworking of the
Isabel Roberts house (150). Additions, not by Wright, have
been made to the west facade (on the right in the photograph).

161 J. Kibben **Ingalls** Residence (1909)
River Forest, Illinois

This square-plan Prairie style house of plastered surface and painted wood trim is Wright's last extant work in River Forest.

162 Peter C. **Stohr Arcade Building** (1909)
Chicago, Illinois
Demolished

This building was located at the Wilson Avenue Station of
the Chicago "El." Most of it was under the "El" tracks—the
structure incorporated stairs to the ticket booths and rail-
way—but where it ducked out from under this obstruction,
it rose to three stories. The main-level row of shops extended the predominantly horizontal motif from the three-
tiered section.

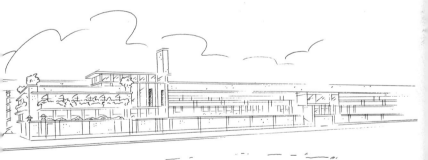

163 Universal Portland Cement Company, **New York City Exhibition** (1910)
New York, New York
Demolished

The Universal Portland Cement Company never had Wright design them a permanent structure. He did, however, design two works, both for public fairs. The first was for the Pan American Exposition in Buffalo in 1901 (63), and the second was this New York City Exhibition, held in Madison Square Garden.

164 Reverend J. R. **Ziegler** Residence (1909)
Frankfort, Kentucky

Wright's only work in Kentucky, a square Prairie style structure, this building was not supervised during construction
by the architect. It is located a short distance from the state
capitol building.

165 E. P. **Irving** Residence (1909)
Decatur, Illinois

This dwelling and the Amberg (166) and Mueller (167) were
supervised by Herman V. Von Holst and Marion Mahony
(later Mrs. Walter Burley Griffin) while Wright was traveling
outside America. How much of these houses is by Wright,
and how much by Mahony (who was the primary designing
influence in Wright's office during his absence) is not defi-
nitely known. In the Irving house, it would appear that the
exterior and plan are by Wright, with much of the interior
work by Mahony. The furniture for the three houses (165-
167) was by George M. Niedecken, long an associate of
Wright's in these matters.

166 David M. **Amberg** Residence (1909)
Grand Rapids, Michigan

Though the final plan, finished while Wright was away from
America, states this as a design of Von Holst and Mahony,
Wright claimed the design as his. The proportions of the
building suggest his hand in the plan and basic exterior design, while the handiwork of Marion Mahony is clearly evident in the interior treatment of living and dining spaces.
The house is now divided into three apartments.

167 Robert **Mueller** Residence (1909)
Decatur, Illinois

This house, immediately east of the Irving residence (165),
bears the imprint of both Wright and Marion Mahony.
Wright probably did the preliminary sketches, then Mahony
altered the plan to satisfy specific requirements of the client. Only when viewed next to the Irving house does it look
too tall for a true Wright design, and the alterations to
Wright's idea by Mahony become apparent.

168 O. B. **Balch** Residence (1911)
Oak Park, Illinois

The current orangish tint of the wood trim and the gray
plaster provide contrast with the usual dark brown on white
of Wright's plaster-surfaced, wood-frame Prairie houses,
which was the original color pattern for this dwelling.
Wright also designed a shop for interior decorator Balch
(131).

169 Herbert **Angster** Residence (1911)
Lake Bluff, Illinois
Demolished

A Prairie house of plaster surface and wood trim, this building was so densely surrounded by trees that good photographs were impossible to achieve. The George Madison Millard residence (126) is located on a similarly wooded site. Mrs. Angster was a sister-in-law of Sherman Booth (187).

170 **Banff National Park Pavilion** (1911)
Alberta, Canada
Demolished, 1939

A very long, basically board and batten structure, this pavilion was similar to the River Forest Tennis Club (119). Wright worked in association with Francis C. Sullivan, a Canadian architect.

171 Arthur L. Richards, **Geneva Inn** (1911)
Lake Geneva, Wisconsin
Demolished, 1970

This project was not completed as designed. A Prairie style structure of wood frame as constructed, the main lobby featured a large Roman brick fireplace. Dining and entertainment facilities were west of the entry, guest rooms in an east wing. Plain and identical, these rooms could have allowed indefinite extension of this wing to accommodate any number of guests. They faced south, to the sun and Lake Geneva. A new high-rise apartment building of no distinction stood on the lot in mid-1971.

172 Frank Lloyd Wright, **Taliesin I** (1911)
Spring Green, Wisconsin
Demolished, 1914

Living quarters were destroyed by fire; other quarters survive in today's Taliesin III (218). Taliesin I was built on
land of Wright's mother, Anna Lloyd Jones Wright, who
lived for many years in Taliesins I and II. Taliesin I provided a haven for son Frank and Mamah Borthwick Cheney,
wife of a former client (104), with whom the architect had
gone to Europe in 1909.

173 Francis W. **Little Residence II**, "Northome" (1912)
Deephaven, Minnesota
Demolished, 1972 (living room to be reconstructed at
Metropolitan Museum of Art, New York City)

Wright's first building in Minnesota used its site most effectively. Overlooking Robinson Bay of Lake Minnetonka, the
55-foot living room, perhaps Wright's most spacious domestic interior from this Prairie period, opened its secondary
view inland. Sleeping quarters were also on the main and
upper floors, opposite the living room and over the dining
space which nestled in a hilly depression. Two adjacent
buildings, though of Prairie board and batten style, were
not done by Wright. Purchased in 1972 by the Metropolitan Museum of Art in New York City, the building was dismantled. When reconstructed, its living room will be a permanent part of the museum's American wing.

Little Residence II Living Room

174 Avery **Coonley Playhouse** (1912)
Riverside, Illinois

A post-Prairie symmetrical cruciform plan, this building has been significantly altered by the glass enclosure of wing spaces and removal of a small front flower-box wall. The clerestory windows, in many-colored geometrical designs by Wright, would deserve a detailed note if all were still intact.

175 Park Ridge Country Club Remodeling (1912)
Park Ridge, Illinois
Demolished
Wright both added to and altered an existing building in his
remodeling of the clubhouse of the Park Ridge Country
Club.

176 William B. **Greene** Residence (1912)
Aurora, Illinois

Familiar elements are present here: plaster surface, wood
trim, hipped roof. Harry Robinson, Wright's draftsman, was
involved in the original drawings and supervision of construction and was called upon in 1926 to add a dining room
and master bedroom wing (on the right in the photograph).
The old screened porch was removed, and an enclosed,
heated porch added in 1961 by Robert Mall, for William A.
Greene, son of the original client.

177 Florida Cottage (1912)
Palm Beach, Florida

Designed as a single-story, asymmetrical H-plan structure,
this cottage may not have been built. Although at least one
Florida newspaper has published articles seeking the location of this cottage and identification of the original client,
no one has come forth with any building that looks like
Wright's sketch or that matches the plan.

178 M. B. **Hilly** Residence (1913)
Brookfield, Illinois

A one-story, square-plan, board and batten bungalow, the building is thought to have been designed for Brookfield but may have been a cottage constructed on the eastern shore of Lake Michigan. The building has not been located in Brookfield. It may have been a summer cottage designed for Hilly while he was living in Illinois and built in southwest Michigan, where many Chicago-area residents vacationed.

179 Harry S. Adams Residence (1913)
Oak Park, Illinois
This large brick structure is Wright's last work in Oak Park.

180 Edward C. Waller, Jr., **Midway Gardens** (1913)
Chicago, Illinois
Demolished, 1929

Prohibition was but one of the many factors that destroyed
the Midway Gardens pleasure palace. Only two years after
being opened, it was purchased by the Edelweiss Brewing
Company and converted to serve the needs of a clientele
hardly accustomed to its refined surroundings. The richness
of architectural expression, in patterned concrete block and
brick, was exceptional. An entire city block was enclosed
by the structure, while the interior court was open to the
elements yet separated from the harshness of urban life.
Sculptures by Alfonzo Iannelli adorned the work, and John
Lloyd Wright, a son of the architect, assisted in construction supervision. Of the major nondomestic works of Wright
completed prior to the Johnson Administration Building
(237)—The Larkin Company Administration Building (93),
Midway Gardens, the Imperial Hotel (194), and Unity
Church (96)—only the last-named exists today.

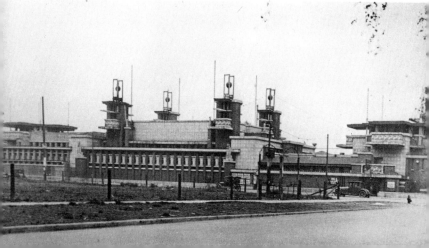

181 **Mori Oriental Art Studio** (1914)
Chicago, Illinois
Demolished

The southeast corner room on the eighth floor of the Fine
Arts Building on Michigan Avenue is quite large with a high
ceiling. Wright decorated this interior for use as an art studio, much along the lines of other small commercial enter-
prises, such as Browne's Bookstore (141), the Pebbles &
Balch Shop (131), and the Thurber Art Gallery (154). The
characteristic feature of Wright's work was the geometrical
lighting fixtures, of which similar types can be seen in the
interior photographs of Browne's Bookstore and the Pebbles
& Balch Shop and also the Rookery Building Remodeling
(113). Though the Fine Arts Building still stands, Wright's
work has long since been removed.

182 Frank Lloyd Wright, **Taliesin II** (1914)
Spring Green, Wisconsin
Demolished, 1925

Only living quarters were destroyed by fire, while other
quarters remain today from Taliesin I (172).

183 A. D. **German Warehouse** (1915)
Richland Center, Wisconsin

This warehouse, still in use today, is an imposing cube of
brick and cast-in-place concrete.

184 E. D. **Brigham** Residence (1915)
Glencoe, Illinois

One of seven houses in Glencoe designed by Wright during this year, this is the only one not part of Sherman Booth's concern (185-192). Wright did not supervise construction, and many alterations in both materials and design details were made without his consent.

185-192 Sherman M. Booth, Ravine Bluffs Development

185, 186 Ravine Bluffs Development Sculptures and Bridge (1915)
Glencoe, Illinois

Sherman M. Booth commissioned a complete plan for a housing development just west of a Glencoe ravine. Six homes, including his own, were built. Additionally, there are several sculptures (one of which is shown here) in poured concrete. These were probably executed by Alfonzo Iannelli, collaborator with Wright in the early part of this decade on several projects, including the Midway Gardens (180). The northeastern entrance to the development is by way of a bridge over the ravine from which the project takes its name. Three lots south is the honeymoon cottage for Sylvan Booth, relocated from its original location near the Sherman Booth house (187), and once claimed by a Chicago newspaper to be by Wright. It is not listed here for lack of sufficient evidence of authenticity.

Ravine Bluffs Development Sculpture

Ravine Bluffs Development Bridge

Ravine Bluffs Development

187 Sherman M. **Booth Residence** (1915)
Glencoe, Illinois

Booth was Wright's lawyer at this time. He commissioned
the Ravine Bluffs Development, but his own house is not as
extensive or fanciful as that first planned by Wright. That
idea included a bridge spanning the ravine to the Sylvan
Booth honeymoon cottage, which has since been relocated.

Ravine Bluffs Development

188 Charles R. **Perry** Residence (1915)

Glencoe, Illinois

The Ravine Bluffs Development included five houses for rent. Each is here named for the first known independent owner. All are of plaster surface, with wood trim, and none were supervised by Wright. All may be variants of designs prepared for Edward C. Waller, Sr. (30, 31, 47, 65, 66), and Jr. (180), for Waller Estates in River Forest.

Ravine Bluffs Development
189 Hollis R. **Root** Residence (1915)
Glencoe, Illinois

This house appears to have survived with little need of upkeep.

Ravine Bluffs Development
190 William F. **Kier** Residence (1915)
Glencoe, Illinois
An essentially square-plan house, the Kier residence is
topped by a hipped roof.

Ravine Bluffs Development
191 William F. Ross Residence (1915)
Glencoe, Illinois
The porch (at left in the photograph) is not by Wright.

Ravine Bluffs Development
192 Lute F. **Kissam** Residence (1915)
Glencoe, Illinois
The original timbers show weakening in the open porch
extension of the main square of the house.

193 Emil **Bach** Residence (1915)
Chicago, Illinois

Here Wright employed cantilever design to allow the second story to overhang the first. The brick is unchanged, but wood and plaster are now painted.

195 **Imperial Hotel** (1915) and **Annex** (1916)
Tokyo, Japan
Hotel demolished, 1968 (entrance lobby to be recon-
structed at Meiji Village near Nagoya, Japan)
Annex demolished, 1923

Wright's major work in Japan, the Imperial Hotel made lib-
eral use of Oya stone, a soft lava block. The hotel's floating
foundation permitted it to survive, almost undamaged, the
great earthquake of April 1922. It was employed, and altered, by the American army following World War II. Apparently Wright was offered the opportunity to remodel
the structure at this time but refused. As downtown-Tokyo
land values rose, it became more feasible to tear down the
building than to renovate it. Japan's tradition of beauty,
however, would not allow the building to vanish completely; the entrance lobby was dismantled and stored near
Nagoya. It is to be reconstructed on the western reaches of
the Meiji Village architectural shrine about 1976.

196 F. C. **Bogk** Residence (1916)
Milwaukee, Wisconsin

A post-Prairie house in Roman brick and of square plan, the Bogk residence facade is most strikingly ornamental.

197 Ernest **Vosburgh** Residence (1916)
Grand Beach, Michigan

Wright designed three houses in Grand Beach, and only the Vosburgh remains essentially as built. It is a Prairie gem of cruciform plan with a two-story-high living room, set near a creek that flows through the woods to nearby Lake Michigan.

198 Joseph J. Bagley Residence (1916)
Grand Beach, Michigan

Leaning over the precipice that leads down to Lake Michigan from a knoll considerably above street level, the Joseph Bagley summer home spreads into several one-story wings from its single two-story unit. It has been extensively remodeled, with much glass added and metal replacing wood trim.

199 W. S. Carr Residence (1916)
Grand Beach, Michigan

This cottage, now winterized, sits on the edge of the high
bluffs leading down to Lake Michigan. Originally of plaster
with wood trim, it has been added to, resurfaced, and extensively altered throughout.

200 Arthur **Munkwitz Duplex Apartments** (1916)
Milwaukee, Wisconsin

These are four apartment buildings symmetrical in pairs
about their common entryways.

201 Arthur L. **Richards Duplex Apartments** (1916)
Milwaukee, Wisconsin

These are four separate buildings, each with upper and lower apartments. Originally all were of plaster surface with wood trim; two have been resurfaced. All are from American System Ready-cut prefab plans of 1911, and all have been somewhat altered. None were supervised by Wright during construction.

202 Arthur L. **Richards Small House** (1916)
Milwaukee, Wisconsin

Just east of the Richards Apartments (201) lies this small,
single-story flat-roofed house. It is from American System
Ready-cut prefab plans.

203 Arthur L. **Richards Bungalow** (1916)
Milwaukee, Wisconsin
Next to the Richards Small House (202) is this bungalow,
now resurfaced with stone veneer. In its original form, it
looked much like the second Hunt residence (204).

204 Stephen M. B. **Hunt Residence II** (1917)
Oshkosh, Wisconsin

This building follows the same basic plan as the Richards Bungalow (203).

205 Henry J. **Allen** Residence (1917)
Wichita, Kansas

In his fiftieth year of fruitful life, Wright began moving
west, pausing on his way for this, his first building and only
house in Kansas. Although on initial inspection the Allen
house looks like a brick Prairie type, it actually encloses a
garden court from the noise of passing autos. In this detail
it breaks with Prairie principles and tends toward Japanese
forms. The house and grounds were completely restored for
A. W. Kincade in 1971-1972.

206 Aizaku **Hayashi** Residence (1917)
Tokyo, Japan

Wright did not do complete plans for this structure but apparently made only sketches, the details being filled out by the craftsmen involved in its construction. Oya stone (soft lava block) is trimmed with wood. The living room, which is the part of this structure most characteristic of Wright's style, faces south over an open field to what is now the Komazawa Olympic Park. Hayashi was general manager of the Imperial Hotel (194). As of 1972 the building was owned by the Dai-ichi Advertising Company of Tokyo.

207 **Fukuhara** Residence (1918)
Hakone, Japan
Demolished
All that is known of this structure is the surname of the client and the general location of the house. It was destroyed by an earthquake.

208 Aline **Barnsdall Hollyhock House** (1917),
209 Little Dipper **Kindergarten** (1920),
, 211 **Studio Residence A** (1920), and **B** (1921)
Los Angeles, California
Kindergarten and Studio Residence B demolished
Commanding the western view as the major structure in Barnsdall Park, Hollyhock House, so named for its ornamental forms, suggests a Mayan temple. Its exposed poured-concrete structure was built about 1920. Earliest sketches of this building as it appears in constructed form may be dated as early as 1913. Hollyhock House was given to the city of Los Angeles in 1927. The Olive Hill Foundation—Barnsdall Park of today was the former Olive Hill—reconstructed the building in 1947. Then it became part of the Los Angeles Municipal Art Museum and, after early 1970s reconstruction, is now open to the public. The only other part of the Wright-designed Barnsdall Park complex that remains today, the Studio Residence A, reveals some imprint of R. M. Schindler, who supervised its construction, then went on to fame of his own in southern California. It is now used as a classroom-studio space by the Los Angeles Parks and Recreation Department. Landscaping of Olive Hill was designed by Lloyd Wright, but it has been altered during various reconstructions and recent additions to the grounds.

Barnsdall Studio Residence A

212 **Yamamura** Residence (1918)
Ashiya, Japan

This house is perched on a promontory above the left bank of the Ashiyagawa River, facing south to Osaka Bay. Four stories lift it up the hillside, and one 120-degree bend takes it around its eastern slope. Oya stone and Lauan (Philippine mahogany) are the prime construction materials. Owned in 1972 by the Yodagawa Seiko (Yodagawa Steel Company) of Osaka and used as a company dormitory, the structure may yet be saved from a scheduled 1975 demolition.

213 Jiyu Gakuen Girls' School (1921)
Tokyo, Japan

This school is known to many in English as the "School of the Free Spirit." L-shaped, single-story wings jut out from the central, two-story rectangle of this Oya stone and wood structure. The living room is of two stories, with interior balcony. Construction was supervised by Erato Endo, a practitioner of organic architecture whose son is a former Taliesin Fellow and successful Japanese architect. These two architects are largely responsible for the new Jiyu Gakuen School in the countryside west of Tokyo. Wright's "old" Jiyu Gakuen School remains a school for girls, and permission may be obtained from the headmistress to visit its interior.

214 Mrs. George Madison **Millard** Residence,
"La Miniatura" (1923)
Pasadena, California

This is the first of four textile-block houses designed by
Wright in 1923 for the Los Angeles area. It is also possibly
the most romantic of the four, its high living room dropping
a full floor from the entry level into a lush garden terrace.
The patterns for these textile-block houses are all different,
and each is worth inspection. The method of construction
was called at this time "knit block." Concrete blocks three
or four inches thick were made by pouring concrete into
molds. Blocks were then placed next to and on top of one
another with no mortar separating them. The thin sides had
concave hollows, through which steel rods were run vertically and horizontally, "knitting" the whole together; grouting filled the remainder of the hollow. Two walls were usually constructed, knit together by steel rods, the air space
between walls providing insulation. After the Second World
War, this knitting process gave rise to the term commonly
employed today, "Wright textile block." This and the three
other California houses (215-217) were supervised in construction by Lloyd Wright, eldest son of the architect. Lloyd
Wright also provided complete landscaping and designed the
1926 studio addition to La Miniatura.

215 John **Storer** Residence (1923)
Hollywood, California

This is the second of the four Los Angeles area textile-block houses. Its lowest story contains a variety of work spaces, but the second (public entrance) floor features a two-story-high living room, textile block throughout. One side opens from the hillside perch to a full view of Hollywood, Los Angeles, and the San Bernardino Valley. The other looks onto a courtyard, sunk into the rising hillside. The Storer house was supervised during construction by Lloyd Wright, who also designed the landscaping.

216   Samuel Freeman Residence (1923)
Los Angeles, California

Still owned and occupied by the client at this publication,
this third of the California textile-block houses clings to the
Hollywood foothills of the Santa Monica Mountains. Living
room, kitchen, and garage are on the entry level, and sleeping quarters and terrace are one story below. Eucalyptus,
common pine painted redwood red, and both plain and patterned textile block are the materials employed in construction. The project was supervised by Lloyd Wright, who also
did the working drawings and landscaping; and one of the
architect's students, R. M. Schindler, designed the Freeman's furniture.

217 Charles **Ennis** Residence (1923)
Los Angeles, California

The last of the four Los Angeles textile-block houses, the
Ennis is the most monumental. Anywhere along Vermont
Avenue, looking north, one sees it completing its ridge on
the southern reaches of the Santa Monica Mountains. Its
views are to both Griffith Park, on the north, and the Los
Angeles metropolitan area, on the south. The textile block
pattern is almost symmetrical about the diagonal of its
square surface. While in the Freeman house (216) blocks
are paired, one mirroring the other, here they usually are
given the same orientation, and in the Arizona Biltmore
Hotel and Cottages (221, 222) the pattern is complete only
when the blocks are paired. Lloyd Wright supervised construction, prepared the working drawings, and designed the
landscaping.

219 Frank Lloyd Wright, **Taliesin III** (1925ff) and **Dams** (1945)
220 Mrs. Frank Lloyd Wright, **Enclosed Garden at Taliesin** (1959)
Spring Green, Wisconsin

"Taliesin" is the name of Wright's home in Wisconsin. It is from the Welsh for "the shining brow"; Taliesin does not sit on a hill but rather clings to its brow above the left bank of the Wisconsin River, looking north and east. Actually there have been three Taliesins, the first built in 1911 (172), the second in 1914 (182). There is also a Taliesin West (241), plus perhaps even a "Taliesin the Third" as the Hotel Plaza Apartment Remodeling (381) was known. The current Taliesin was rebuilt in 1925 after destruction by fire. As in 1914, only living quarters were destroyed, and much of Taliesins I and II remains in Taliesin III. Constructed mostly of native limestone, wood, and plaster surfacing, it has been continually altered in keeping with the needs of the Wrights and the Taliesin Fellowship. The dams in the valley have created a small lake that is used for recreation as well as to control water flow through the farm land. The garden design, Wright's last sketch, was built for Mrs. Wright in the summer of 1959. (Upper photograph next page supplied by Bradley Ray Storrer.)

Taliesin III

221 Warren McArthur, **Arizona Biltmore Hotel**
222 and **Cottages** (1927)
Phoenix, Arizona

Both hotel and cottages are Wright's work. Though attributed by some to Albert McArthur, son of Warren McArthur (11-13), who had begun work in Wright's Oak Park studio in 1908, the younger McArthur's major activity in this project was preparation of the working drawings. The hotel is perhaps the largest textile-block design by Wright. The cottages come in both T and rectangular plans, single- and two-story. Entrance to the Biltmore grounds is at 24th Street and Missouri Avenue, and the hotel is open during the fall, winter, and spring.

Arizona Biltmore Cottages

223 **Beach Cottages, Dumyât, Egypt** (1927)
Demolished

These cottages were prefabricated structures designed to be disassembled each year and stored during the spring flood season.

224 Frank Lloyd Wright, **Ocatillo Desert Camp** (1928)
Chandler, Arizona
Demolished

Wright's association with Dr. Alexander Chandler was for the most part unfruitful. Projects never realised from this year and for this client alone included San Marcos-in-the-Desert (a resort hotel), San Marcos Hotel alterations, San Marcos Water Gardens, a simple block house, and a residence for Owen D. Young. The Ocatillo Desert Camp, constructed of wood and material much like the later Taliesin West (241), was a temporary residence for Wright during the period in which these designs for the Chandler, Arizona, area were in progress.

225 **Darwin D. Martin Residence, "Graycliff" and**
226 **"Graycliff" Garage** (1927)
Derby, New York

Graycliff was built as a summer home for Darwin D. Martin. It sits a scant 25 yards from the gray cliff whose precipice drops directly to Lake Erie. The residence structure, probably originally of plaster surfacing with wood trim and stone fireplaces and chimneys, has been resurfaced. In the early 1970s it was serving as a residence for the Piarist Fathers. The garage may have been started in 1926. Wright did not supervise the construction of either building.

Graycliff Garage

227 Richard Lloyd Jones Residence, "Westhope" (1929)
Tulsa, Oklahoma

Wright's first project in Oklahoma was for his cousin,
Richard Lloyd Jones, founder of the *Tulsa Tribune*. No
one view reveals the true dimension of this accomplishment
in glass and textile block. The dwelling, two stories high for
only a third of the plan, encloses a raised inner courtyard
with swimming pool. Built on a five-foot module, it employs
concrete blocks inside and out that are one-third by one-
fourth of the module in surface dimension. The structure
has been modified for modern conveniences such as air conditioning (with vents concealed behind the grillwork of the
cut-out Mayan-design blocks), and kitchen and master bedroom have been enlarged by combining earlier smaller
rooms. Three decorative extensions of the interior space
(one shown in the photograph) were originally aviaries but
now serve as miniature greenhouses.

228 Frank Lloyd Wright, **Taliesin Fellowship Complex** (1933ff)
Spring Green, Wisconsin

The Great Depression left Wright with few commissions,
but instead of retiring in 1932 at the age of sixty-five, he
entered a whole new era of creativity. He founded the
Taliesin Fellowship (two of the first apprentices were
William Wesley Peters, now a Frank Lloyd Wright Foundation vice-president, and John H. Howe), remodeled the
Hillside Home School II (69) including Hillside Playhouse
(burned, rebuilt in 1952) for use by the Fellowship, and
began work on his concept of a Broadacre City and then
the Usonian home. His scheme for a truly American city
was realized on a grand scale in models and in a few scattered works—for example, the Affleck house (274), Suntop
Homes (248), and Lindholm Service Station (414)—but
never in the way Wright wanted, in a complete city or in a
new concept of American city planning universally applied.

229 Malcolm E. **Willey** Residence (1933)
Minneapolis, Minnesota

The Willey house, the latter of two designs by Wright for the client, is of dark red sand and paving bricks, with cypress trim. It is a single-story structure located on a former bluff above the Mississippi River, which was disfigured in the 1960s by the intrusion of Interstate Highway 94. With its central work space—Wright's term for a kitchen plus utilities core—directly adjoining the living-dining room (center in the photograph), it represents the major bridge between the Prairie style and the soon-to-appear Usonian house plan. The radiator floor heating in this house is a direct forerunner of the gravity heating characteristic of the Usonian home. The elimination of servants' quarters is also typically Usonian.

230 Edgar J. **Kaufmann**, Sr., **Residence "Fallingwater"** (1935),
232 **Guesthouse** (1938), and **Guesthouse Alterations** (1948)
Ohiopyle, Pennsylvania

Aside from his own Taliesin Fellowship Complex, Wright
had seen only two of his projects constructed over a period
of almost eight years, from 1928 to 1935. Then, when the
architect was sixty-nine, came Fallingwater, the Johnson
Administration Building, and the Usonian home concept all
in one year, and Wingspread a year later. Fallingwater is perhaps the best-known private home for someone not of royal
blood in the history of the world. Perched over a waterfall
deep in the Pennsylvania highlands, it seems part of the rock
formations to which it clings. Reinforced-concrete cantilever
slabs project from the rock band to carry the house over the
stream. From the square living room, one can step directly
down a suspended stairway to the stream. Immediately
above, on the third level, terraces open from sleeping quarters, emphasizing the horizontal nature of the structural
forms; "the apotheosis of the horizontal" it has been called.
Three years separated design of the main house and the
guesthouse, seen through dense foliage from a north terrace
of Fallingwater (in the photograph), with the covered walkway circling upwards on the left. The Western Pennsylvania
Conservancy conducts guided tours during most of the year,
except the cold winter months; reservations are advised.

Kaufmann Guesthouse

233 Edgar J. **Kaufmann**, Sr., **Office** (1937)
Pittsburgh, Pennsylvania
Dismantled and stored (to be reassembled in the Victoria
and Albert Museum, London)

Paneling and furniture for the Kaufmann Office are typical
of design features built in to the Usonian houses, which
form the bulk of Wright's domestic work in this period.

234 Herbert **Jacobs First Residence** (1936)
Madison, Wisconsin

This is the first truly Usonian house. The structural characteristics of a Usonian home as here established are a concrete-slab floor providing gravity (radiant) heating, a masonry core, and for most of the remainder, "dry wall" construction. As Wright used the term, "dry wall" usually meant a sandwich type of construction with three layers of wood boards screwed together. The center layer, or core, was commonly plywood and eliminated the conventional two-by-four studs. In this L-plan structure, the first of two Wright-designed residences for Herbert Jacobs, brick is the masonry, and the dry wall uses sunk redwood battens—this reversal of Prairie board and batten is common in Usonian construction.

235 Paul R. **Hanna** Residence, "Honeycomb House" (1936)
Stanford, California

Wright called this a wooden house. Though it clearly uses
common wire-cut San Jose brick inside and out, many of
the walls are solid laminated wood (dry wall). The ease
with which these walls could be assembled or disassembled
allowed for considerable alteration of interior space; this
accommodated individual bedrooms for children when the
house was first built. These were later converted to larger
living spaces when the children had homes of their own. All
changes were in accordance with Wright's original plans.
The Hanna house is called Honeycomb House because the
Usonian structure's plan is fashioned from a hexagonal unit
system, a module that replaced the octagon as Wright's favorite form from this time on. The unit is one foot one inch;
each redwood board and sunk batten observes this spacing,
while each hexagon in the floor plan has a side two units
long. Honeycomb House completes the hillside to which it
clings, its floor and courtyard levels adjusting to the con-
tours of the hill; it is capped by a copper roof. It was
Wright's first work in the San Francisco region.

236 Mrs. **Abby Beecher Roberts** Residence, "Deertrack" (1936) Marquette, Michigan

A few miles west of Marquette, a long hill slopes southeastward through evergreen forests. Commanding this view is Deertrack, home of Abby Beecher Roberts. This engaging lady once cast Wright's horoscope around the then-accepted 1869 birthdate. Finding it not to fit the man as she knew him, she discovered that the fit was perfect for 1867, his actual year of birth. Her home has been expanded.

237 **S. C. Johnson** and Son **Administration Building** (1936) and
238 **Research Tower** (1944) for H. F. Johnson, president,
Johnson Wax Company
Racine, Wisconsin

Both the Administration Building (also called the Johnson
Wax Building) and the later Research Tower (rising at left
in the photograph) are of brick and glass. The main office
work space is articulated by dendriform columns capable of
supporting six times the weight imposed upon them, a fact
Wright had to demonstrate in order to obtain a building
permit. The glass is not in panes, but in tubing, and several
layers of different sizes are used to admit light but no view.
Industrial air pollution caused the tubes in recent years to
collect dirt; new synthetic resins now permit a permanent
seal to be achieved. Wright designed all the original furniture
for the building, including the three-legged secretary chairs,
which tip over if one does not sit with correct posture. The
tower is totally enclosed and does not allow for horizontal
expansion of work space. Free tours are conducted during
regular business hours. Herbert F. Johnson, grandson of
S. C. Johnson, also commissioned Wingspread (239).

239 Herbert F. Johnson Residence, "Wingspread" (1937)
Wind Point, Wisconsin

Herbert F. Johnson commissioned the Johnson Wax Building (237) as well as Wingspread; the latter is now headquarters of The Johnson Foundation. Wingspread is the last of the Prairie houses. Its pinwheel plan is zoned—that is, sleeping quarters are in the wing shown below, kitchen in the opposite, and so forth. This pinwheel, as Wright employs it, a simple variant of his favorite cruciform plan, extends from a central, three-story-high octagon. Pink Kasota sandside walls of the swimming pool, shown on next page, were undercut so that they seem to disappear, leaving only water and reflection. Wright considered this his most expensive and best-built house to date, and he noted that many had thought the site undistinguished until he placed the house on it. West wing carports (not shown here) have been converted into office space.

Herbert F. Johnson Residence and Swimming Pool

240 Ben **Rebhuhn** Residence (1937)
Great Neck Estates, New York

This house follows a cruciform plan and has a two-story-high living room. Cypress board and batten plus brick inside and out are the primary materials of construction. Stylistically, it appears to be a Usonian reworking of the Vosburgh house (197).

Scottsdale, Arizona

Taliesin West, Wright's winter home on Maricopa Mesa for
the Taliesin Fellowship, offered a new challenge in materials. The architect's primary solution was what he called
"desert rubblestone wall" construction. There are many
ways of achieving this, but all involve randomly placing
large stones into forms, then pouring concrete around the
stones while leaving most of the face next to the form exposed. In the Bott house (404) wet sand was forced between form and stone surface before the concrete was
poured. In the Austin house (345) crumpled newspaper,
instead of sand, was used to keep the stone faces from being
covered with concrete. At Taliesin West, the grouting was
allowed to seep around the edges of the stone face, then sur-
plus was chipped away to reveal the stone surface. Often,
washing with acid was employed to bring out color in the
stone.

In the dry heat of the Arizona desert, Wright found that
stretched linen canvas provided an ideal shield against flash
thunderstorms and the sun's glare and that it also adjusted
most effectively to rapid and wide temperature changes.
This material is shown close-up in photograph of detail.

Taliesin West now houses the Fellowship the greater part
of the year, and Taliesin Fellows conduct tours throughout
the day. (Photograph 242 by Bradley Ray Storrer.)

Taliesin West

Taliesin West, detail

Taliesin West, Sign

246 Frank Lloyd Wright, **Midway Barns** (1938) with
247 Dairy and Machine Sheds (1947)
Spring Green, Wisconsin

Under Wright's guidance, every Taliesin Fellow started his apprenticeship by working in and with the earth. Under the care of the apprentices, the rich Wisconsin soil provided much fresh food to the dinner tables shared by the entire Taliesin community. The first barns, located midway between Hillside and Taliesin, and the later dairy and machine sheds served the needs of an expanding architectural community in midwestern Wisconsin.

248 Otto Mallery of Tod Company, **Suntop Homes** (1938)
Ardmore, Pennsylvania

Based upon a Broadacre City model, these units have been
known as Suntop Homes, Cloverleaf, Quadruple Housing,
and The Ardmore Experiment. The original Suntop Homes
project was for the United States Government on a tract
near Pittsfield, Massachusetts. A change in housing administration and complaints from local architects that they,
not an "outsider," should do the project prevented its construction. There were to have been four of these units in
Ardmore, built in a row but each angled differently on the
sites. Only one was built. The building is divided into quarters, each of two stories plus basement and sunroof, and
houses four families. The exterior is of brick and horizontal
lapped wood siding; this siding is imitated in the wall now
surrounding the structure.

249 Charles L. **Manson** Residence (1938)
Wausau, Wisconsin

Hexagonal forms are employed in this brick, with horizontal
wood sheathing, structure. Its placement on the site takes
maximum advantage of a long northeast downhill view.

250 Rose **Pauson** Residence (1939)
Phoenix, Arizona
Mostly demolished

Only ruins remain after a 1942 fire. The desert rubblestone wall construction is fully revealed in the ruins, though the horizontal character of the structure is largely lost in the absence of the once-beautiful wood terraces and balconies.

Wright conceived the master plan for a whole college in 1938, although the realization of individual projects spanned the next decade and a half. Since Broadacre City never came to fruition, Florida Southern College offers the viewer a rare opportunity to see a unified plan of Wrightian thought on a city-planning scale. All the Florida Southern College structures employ textile block. Different plan modules are used; the Pfeiffer Chapel (251) is based on a diamond or double triangle, while the Roux Library (252)—not the new one on the northwest corner of the campus, but the one connected by Esplanades—is a large circle with diamonds. The areas between the three seminar buildings are now glassed in for additional office space. The Administration Building (255) is actually two structures with a garden courtyard between them. Esplanades link all of Wright's work on the Florida Southern College campus, and buildings not so linked are by other architects. Usually these esplanades stand free of other structures, but at the Science and Cosmography (256) and Industrial Arts (254) buildings they are an extension of the outer wall. The Minor Chapel (258) is so oriented on its site that the colored glass windows behind the altar are most effectively lit by the setting sun. Visitors to the campus are asked to report to the Administration Building before leaving their cars in campus parking lots.

Library

Pfeiffer Chapel

Seminar Buildings

Industrial Arts Building

Administration Building

Science and Cosmography Building with Esplanades

Minor Chapel (Danforth Chapel)

259 Sidney **Bazett** Residence (1939)
Hillsborough, California

This second house by Wright in the San Francisco region clings to its hillside plot by angling around hexagonal modules into a Y plan. Brick and horizontal sunk redwood batten construction were used.

260 Andrew F. H. **Armstrong** Residence (1939)
Ogden Dunes, Indiana
Angles of 30, 60, and 90 degrees interlock rectangular
spaces in this house of brick and horizontal board and sunk
batten. The top level is sleeping quarters, with a third
bedroom added (on the right in the photograph), and the
upper story of the two-story-high living room. The middle
level is the living room and work space, and the lowest level
is carport and entry. The basic axis is north-south, with
two-story-high windows looking northeast from the living
room over the Indiana dunes. Alterations to enlarge living
room and work space, designed in 1964 by John H. Howe
along with the bedroom addition, have been in progress for
several years.

261, 262 C. Leigh **Stevens Residence, Two Cottages,**
263, 264 **Guesthouse,** and **Stables with Kennels,**
"Auld Brass Plantation" (1939)
Yemassee, South Carolina

The main house is characterized by slanting exterior battered walls of clear native cypress lumber in natural finish
that are laid diagonally and held by brass screws. The original roof was of copper. The interior of the house contains
massive brick fireplaces. The grounds also hold a connecting complex by Wright of guesthouse, stables with kennels,
as well as two cottages for servants, all conforming to the
design of the main dwelling. The plan employs hexagonal
modules, including such built-in furniture as beds and chairs.
A second house on the property, adjacent to the main residence, is not by Wright.

Stevens Residence

Stevens Cottages

Stevens Guesthouse

Stevens Stables with Kennels

266 **Lloyd Lewis Residence** (1939) and **Farm Unit** (1943)
Libertyville, Illinois
This cypress and brick structure's living room and balcony
are on the upper story above ground-level entrances and the
bedroom wing. The farm unit is a poultry shed. Both structures are surrounded by dense forest, with light admitted
across the Des Plaines River. Mr. Lewis was editor of the
Chicago Daily News.

267 Stanley **Rosenbaum** Residence (1939) and
267A **Addition** (1948)
Florence, Alabama

Wright's only work in Alabama is an L-plan Usonian house
enlarged to a T plan by Wright in 1948. It has been kept in
excellent condition and was completely renovated in 1970.
The addition created a Japanese garden outside the new
living and master bedroom quarters.

268 Loren **Pope** (Pope-Leighey) Residence (1939)
Mount Vernon, Virginia

Horizontal sunk cypress batten dry-wall construction
around a brick core identify this as a Usonian house. It
was moved in 1964 from Falls Church to its present site
at Woodlawn Plantation, where it is open to visitors during
the summer months. New gravity heat slab was laid, and
the dry wall and masonry core set thereon. The new, lovely,
wooded hillside site altered one aesthetic factor essential
to the house's original site: the approach is now downhill,
and the flat roof is exposed to view, as it was not in Falls
Church.

269   Goetsch-Winckler Residence (1939)
Okemos, Michigan

In this Usonian unit built for Alma Goetsch and Katherine Winckler, brick finds its way beyond the core into the extremities. The dry wall is a typical Usonian horizontal sunk redwood batten sandwich. The house was originally part of a project for teachers at what is now Michigan State University; only one other unit from the master plan was built, the Rubin house (343) in Canton, Ohio.

270 Joseph **Euchtman** Residence (1939)
Baltimore, Maryland

This Usonian house carefully shuts out of view its close neighbor to the north and takes maximum advantage of its wedge-shaped lot, which most architects would have shunned. Its view southwest and southeast is across broad boulevarded spaces, yet it offers occupants complete privacy.

271 Bernard **Schwartz** Residence (1939)
Two Rivers, Wisconsin

The September 26, 1938, issue of *Life* magazine published
Wright's idea for a house "For a Family of $5000-$6000
Income," and the following year it was built on the right
bank of East Twin River at Still Bend in Two Rivers, Wisconsin. The house is of brick and horizontal cypress board
and sunk batten. Its two stories suggest a designation never
accorded it by the architect himself, the "two-story Usonian"
structure. The plan is a T, on a three-foot six-inch module.
It is so angled on its plot as to gain a full view east and south
along East Twin River without obstruction from neighboring
buildings.

272 George D. **Sturges** Residence (1939)
Brentwood Heights, California

Most of this house is cantilevered out from its hillside perch.
The brick and painted wood siding (the original was stained)
present an appearance of a house without windows; actually
the entire east wall, including living room and bedrooms,
opens to a balcony (on the left in the photograph) overlooking the street below.

273 John C. **Pew** Residence (1939)
Shorewood Hills, Wisconsin
The hillside site slopes gently from Mendota Drive, then
drops sharply to Lake Mendota. With its base on the slope
and one wing over the precipice, this limestone and cypress
structure is able to open its first floor to lake and woods
and preserve privacy for its second-story sleeping quarters.

274 Gregor **Affleck** Residence (1940)
Bloomfield Hills, Michigan

Here the sun room and sleeping quarters rest on the ground
while the living-dining space is cantilevered with the balcony
a half-story lower. The cypress siding has weathered to a
nice gray. An L, or F, plan, the house is taken from the
Broadacre City model of a "home for sloping ground."
Wright designed a second home for Mr. Affleck, whom he
knew as a boy when both lived in Spring Green, which was
not built.

275, 276 Arch **Oboler Gatehouse** (1940), **Retreat** (1941), and
275A,B **Additions** (1944, 1946)
Malibu, California

With additions designed in 1944 and 1946 by Wright, this
living complex is still "in construction." The main structure
was to be known as "Eaglefeather." Desert rubblestone wall
construction is used throughout, with horizontal wood siding. Situated high in the Santa Monica Mountains above
Malibu, the retreat commands a stunning view across mountain wilderness.

Arch Oboler Retreat

277 Theodore **Baird** Residence (1940)
Amherst, Massachusetts

Wright's only work in Massachusetts is a Usonian type of
brick and horizontal cypress board and sunk batten. The
plan is an I configuration, expanded at one end and at
the center for the living room (left and center in the
photograph).

278 James B. **Christie** Residence (1940)
Bernardsville, New Jersey

An L plan with living room dominating the end of one leg,
this project was not supervised in construction by Wright.
It is located in thick woods on gently sloping grounds.

279 Clarence **Sondern** (Sondern-Adler) Residence (1940)
Kansas City, Missouri

The original structure for Sondern was Usonian. Eight years later Wright added a large living room a quarter-story below the Usonian structure for Arnold Adler (307). The composite T plan encloses a terrace just above the steep drop to Roanoke Parkway. The residence is only a mile away from the Kansas City Community Christian Church (280).

280 Kansas City Community Christian Church (1940)
Kansas City, Missouri

This structure was not Taliesin-supervised during construction, and it was much altered from Wright's original plan. A diamond, or double triangle, module was employed. The church is open daily.

281 Carlton David **Wall** Residence, "Snowflake" (1941)
Plymouth, Michigan

Employing hexagonal forms, this brick and cypress structure curls around its rolling hill site, creating an enclosed
patio. The living room opens to terrace space looking west
and north (shown in photograph). An aerial view reveals
the snowflake geometry of the central living space. Immediately adjacent is the Goddard house (364).

282 Stuart **Richardson** Residence (1941)
Glen Ridge, New Jersey

If the Richardson house used less brick and more wood, it would be easy to call it a Usonian type. It is most notable as an early example of Wright's use of triangular forms, in the plan of the living room, derived from a hexagonal module.

283 Herbert **Jacobs Second Residence** (1943)
Middleton, Wisconsin

This is the second Wright house designed and built for the Jacobs family. It is the first solar hemicycle, of two stories, with its back set into the earth. Its glassed private facade opens onto a sunken terrace.

285 Lowell **Walter Residence** (1945) and **River Pavilion** (1948)
Quasqueton, Iowa

Half of the buildings from Wright's imagination that still
stand in 1973 were created by 1938, though half of his
thousand projects would not be on the drawing boards until the end of World War II. The war years halted most construction. Only three of Wright's 1941 designs were built,
and none from 1942. From his 1943 efforts only the Jacobs
second residence (283) saw relatively quick construction,
while the Guggenheim design (400) had to wait nearly a decade before the foundation was laid. In 1945 construction
activity resumed.

At Cedar Rock on the left bank of the Wapsipinicon River
is the Walter house and river pavilion. The pavilion is of
brick, but the main house derives from the "glass house"
for the *Ladies Home Journal*. It has a reinforced concrete
roof, with steel, glass, walnut, and brick elsewhere. Wright
called it his "Opus 495," and supervision during construction was by John deKoven Hill, one of the more notable
Taliesin Fellowship graduates.

Walter River Pavilion

286 Private Residence (1945)
Pecos, New Mexico

This is a summer house of desert rubblestone wall construction with roofing and siding of rough cedar shakes.

287 **Melvyn Maxwell Smith** Residence (1946)
Bloomfield Hills, Michigan

A Usonian structure of L plan, the Smith house was enlarged by the Taliesin Associated Architects in 1969-1970. Brick and cypress board and sunk batten are the basic materials used. Construction supervision was by John deKoven Hill.

288 Douglas **Grant** Residence (1946)
Cedar Rapids, Iowa

This rectangular, three-story house is of limestone (quarried by the Grants from the surrounding property), steel, concrete roofs and floors, and a copper fascia. The reinforced-concrete roof is 127 feet long; the roof forms were supported by 150 poplar trees. Excavation began in September 1949, and the house was occupied fifteen months later. Entry to the structure, of four-foot module design, is at the top floor (on the left in the photograph), from which one descends to the living room (at right).

289   Alvin **Miller** Residence (1946)
Charles City, Iowa

This single-story, clerestory lighted stone and cypress house
extends in its terraces and outdoor fireplace to the right
bank of the Red Cedar River.

290 Chauncey **Griggs** Residence (1946)
Tacoma, Washington

Located at the foot of a hill on Chambers Creek, this house features a two-story facade on the inside of its L plan. Soaring postwar construction costs caused delays in construction. The concrete-slab floor was laid long before the concrete-block core was raised, a good stone being unavailable. Siding and roofing are of cedar planks, arranged diagonally on most surfaces, though horizontally on some. Logs had originally been considered, and this finished product retains the rustic simplicity of a log cabin, without sacrificing the amenities that usually disappear in such a structure. Construction was supervised by Alan Liddle, a Washington architect.

291 Unitarian Church (1947)
Shorewood Hills, Wisconsin

The rising, green copper roof of this edifice symbolizes
hands held together in prayer. Limestone and oak are the
prime construction materials; the limestone was hauled
some thirty miles to the site by congregation members.
The auditorium holds 250 people, or 400 if the adjacent
hearth room is added. An additional wing, not visible in
the photograph, is by the Taliesin Associated Architects.
The building is open daily.

292 A. H. **Bulbulian** Residence (1947)
Rochester, Minnesota
One simple 120-degree angle serves both to fit this cement
brick and cypress structure to the brow of the hill and to
orient it to take fullest advantage of the morning sun at the
breakfast table and afternoon sun in the living room. It is a
very short distance from the Keys residence (321). (Photograph courtesy of Dr. A. H. Bulbulian.)

293 Amy **Alpaugh** Residence (1947)
Northport, Michigan

Brick, oak, and ash are the prime materials of this residence.
The living room (at left in the photograph) turns southwest
toward Lake Michigan and the den east to Grand Traverse
Bay. The original T plan has been altered by addition of a
greenhouse designed by Glen T. Arat Associates.

294   David I. **Weisblat** Residence (1948)
Galesburg, Michigan

The Galesburg Country Homes subdivision plan was drawn
up in 1947. Three structures employ Wright textile block
and wood. The method of construction dates to the four
California block houses (214-217). The Weisblat house was
the first of four structures that were eventually built. Its
living room roof is cantilevered from the fireplace masonry
core, so that the windows, comprising fully half the room's
wall space, carry no load and need no intermediary supports. John H. Howe of the Taliesin Associated Architects
was responsible for an addition to the basic T plan angled
at 120 degrees (not shown in the photograph), dated 1960.
Howe also supervised construction of all four Galesburg
Country Homes.

Galesburg Country Homes

295 Eric **Pratt** Residence (1948)
Galesburg, Michigan

A long I plan with central living room, this house faces
southwest down a long, slow slope. The westernmost unit
of the Galesburg Country Homes, it is primarily of Wright
textile-block construction.

Galesburg Country Homes

296 Samuel **Eppstein** Residence (1948)
Galesburg, Michigan

This structure in the Galesburg Country Homes master plan
is another I plan, oriented southwest-northeast with living
room at the northern extremity and garage beneath (in the
background of the photograph). In this particular unit, pre-
cision of the block construction is notable.

Galesburg Country Homes
297 Curtis **Meyer** Residence (1948)
Galesburg, Michigan

A solar hemicycle facing east down a gentle slope, the
Meyer house uses circles and circular segments throughout.
The central two-story drum sits in the crest of the hill,
enclosing stairs between the lower-floor living room and
the upper-level carport and bedrooms. The bedrooms look
over an inside balcony to the living room below (right in
the photograph), giving that room a two-story-high ceiling.
Concrete block is the main construction material.

Parkwyn Village is near the western edge of Kalamazoo, on a bluff over a small lake. Several houses were designed in the master plan; only four were built. The Levin house has an interesting treatment of its living room facade; the windows are stepped out in several bays, a design feature continued in a trellis (visible in the photograph). This room faces southwest. Wright textile block and cypress are the materials employed. A wing (not visible in the photograph) was added in 1960 by John H. Howe of the Taliesin Associated Architects. Howe also supervised construction of all the Wright-designed houses in Parkwyn Village.

Parkwyn Village
299 Ward **McCartney** Residence and
299A,B,C **Additions** (1949)
Kalamazoo, Michigan

This Parkwyn Village house was built, with expansion expected, on a diamond (double equilateral triangule) module. Kitchen core and dining-living room area (on the right in the photograph) were built first, and the bedroom wing (on left) was added after only four months. Enclosure of the portal to the north and a carport came later, but all were designed by Wright as part of the original plan and done in Wright textile block and cypress.

Parkwyn Village
300 Eric V. Brown Residence (1949)
Kalamazoo, Michigan
Mahogany is employed with Wright textile block in the Eric
Brown house, whose uphill roofline is at ground level. The
living room and attached terrace (at left in the photograph)
look out over broad fields to the pond below Taliesin Drive.

Parkwyn Village

301 Robert D. **Winn** Residence (1950)
Kalamazoo, Michigan

The Winn residence, situated at the dead end of Taliesin
Drive, is the only two-story unit of Wright's design in
Parkwyn Village. Its rectangular living room looks through
the hemicircular, enclosed, skylighted balcony. Wright textile block and wood are used. To the immediate north is a
house with a Wright-designed block, but that structure was
not built to Wright's plan.

302 Herman T. **Mossberg** Residence (1948)
South Bend, Indiana

This is a two-story L plan in red brick and cypress with cedar shingles. The L encloses the patio on this corner lot. The living room is the largest segment of the plan (foreground in the photograph), while the L wing contains sleeping quarters on the second floor, above kitchen and work space. Construction was supervised by John H. Howe. (Photograph courtesy of Denis C. Schmiedeke.)

303 J. Willis **Hughes** Residence, "Fountainhead" (1948)
Jackson, Mississippi

This house, a 120-degree L, or T, plan, looks into a deep
glen. Concrete, horizontal board and batten interior paneling, and copper roof are the materials employed. This is the
only example of modern Wright architecture in Mississippi
and an excellent demonstration of organic principles in its
blending of house with site and client's needs.

304 Carroll **Alsop** Residence (1948)
Oskaloosa, Iowa

Only in the carport is the T plan suggested; interior space
seems to articulate an L. Brick is combined with cypress
and red asbestos-shingled roof. The plan is oriented to the
northeast, but the living room (on the right in the photograph) opens not only in that direction but also southeast.

305 Jack **Lamberson** Residence (1948)
Oskaloosa, Iowa

Perched on a gentle hilltop, this triangular-plan brick and
cypress house is but a few blocks from the Alsop residence
(304).

306 Mrs. Clinton **Walker** Residence (1948)
Carmel, California

This stone structure is the only dwelling on the beach side of Scenic Road on Monterey Bay. It is mostly below street level, seemingly a natural extension of the rocky promontory at this curve in the beach front. The porcelain enamel-shingled living room roof is necessarily cantilevered from the masonry so that no weight rests on the recessing levels of glass.

307 Arnold **Adler Addition** to **Sondern** Residence (1948)
Kansas City, Missouri

Wright's contribution here was a new living room, a quarter-story below the original early Usonian style structure. It appears in the foreground of the photograph.

308 **Albert Adelman** Residence (1948)
Fox Point, Wisconsin

In 1946 Wright designed a laundry building for Benjamin Adelman and Son to be erected in nearby Milwaukee. Though this was never built, two residences were constructed for the Adelman family—this structure, whose covered walkway and garage turn the I plan into an L, and a residence in Arizona (344). The living room separates sleeping quarters at one end (right in the photograph) and kitchen-dining area at the other. The house is oriented to face south-southeast, and its western extremities are protected by shade trees. It is of buff-colored (integral color) block, stepped out 3/4 inch every second course, cypress, and cedar shakes.

309 Maynard P. **Buehler** Residence (1948)
Orinda, California

The living room of this concrete-block and wood house
(shown in the photograph) is offset to the L plan at 120
degrees so as to face west. Angling of the planes of the glass
facade under the broad rising eaves opens the view north
to nature and south to the swimming pool. The long leg of
the L includes sleeping quarters, and the short, work space.
The bedrooms open out to the swimming pool. Other structures on the grounds employ board and sunk batten to
blend with the one Wright-designed structure.

310 V. C. **Morris Gift Shop** (1948)
San Francisco, California

Originally a gift shop, the Morris shop has been renovated.
It has since been used as an art gallery and dress shop. It is
open during regular business hours. Its brick facade both
protects internal contents and invites visitors to enter the
portal. Circular forms are employed inside.

311 C. R. **Weltzheimer** Residence (1948)
Oberlin, Ohio

This house is an L-plan structure of the Usonian type, except that more masonry and less Wrightian dry-wall construction than would be normal in that type were used. The house has recently been restored to its original condition after alteration by an earlier owner.

312 Erling P. **Brauner** Residence (1948)
Okemos, Michigan

The Brauner house was an attempt to redefine the Usonian house concept. Here, Wright textile block replaces brick and dry-wall construction. It is located across Arrow Head Road from the Edwards house (313) and only a short distance from the Goetsch-Winkler (269) and Schaberg (328) houses.

313 James **Edwards** Residence (1949)
Okemos, Michigan

A red brick and red Tidewater cypress house with red asphalt shingles and floors of red concrete containing radiant heating, the Edwards dwelling is built into a hillside with its rectangular spaces joined at 120-degree angles and a terrace the full length of the plan. The wing on the right in the photograph is a later addition made by the Taliesin Associated Architects in 1968. Refinishing of the exterior woodwork is a 1972 project of William T. Martin.

314 Henry J. **Neils** Residence (1949)
Minneapolis, Minnesota
Aluminum window framing—unusual for Wright— scrap
marble, cypress, and cedar shingles are combined in this
house on the east shore of Cedar Lake. It was designed on
a three-foot six-inch module and completed in April 1951.

315 Howard **Anthony** Residence (1949)
Benton Harbor, Michigan

Employing a diamond-shaped module, this dwelling sits
high above the right bank of the Saint Joseph River. Stone
is complemented by cypress and a roof of cedar shingles.

316   Sol Friedman Residence (1948)
Pleasantville, New York

Three Wright-designed homes were built close to each other
in this densely wooded, hilly countryside within commuting
distance north of New York City. The Sol Friedman house
on "Toyhill" was, in geometry, the most daring. It is a two-
story stone and concrete structure, interlocking two cylin-
ders, with a mushroom-shaped carport.

Usonia Homes
317 Edward **Serlin** Residence (1949)
Pleasantville, New York

The Serlin house, second of the Pleasantville projects, employs stone, as do its Usonian neighbors, but also uses some horizontal siding. Projected extensions at both east and west ends to complete Wright's design were never constructed.

Usonia Homes
318 Roland **Reisley** Residence (1951)
Pleasantville, New York

This last of the Pleasantville projects continues the use of
stone as the basic building material, with wood siding. It
wraps around the hillside with a 120-degree angle. It is a single-story structure, except in its masonry core, which also
has a balcony.

319 Kenneth **Laurent** Residence (1949) and
319A **Addition** (1956)
Rockford, Illinois

The living room space of the Laurent residence (shown in the photograph) opens northwest down a long slope leading to the left bank of Spring Creek. Circular segments dominate the plan, interlocking with rectangular space in this single-story solar hemicycle. Common brick complements cypress. Wright also designed the southwest bedroom addition (not visible in the photograph).

320 Wilbur C. **Pearce** Residence (1950)
Bradbury, California

Though in plan the Pearce house superficially resembles the
Laurent, site and materials dictated a different architectural
expression. The Pearce house commands a location on a
foothill of the San Gabriel Mountains in the Bradbury Hills.
Its living room opens south to the San Bernardino Valley
and north to the mountains and the Mount Wilson Observa-
tory. The circular segments were constructed with concrete
block. Roof and carport are cantilevered with steel. Concrete-slab floor with radiant heating, Honduras mahogany,
and glass complete the list of construction materials.
(Photograph courtesy of Mr. Pearce.)

321 Thomas E. **Keys** Residence (1950)
Rochester, Minnesota

Nineteen-fifty was a banner year for designing; twenty-one
projects were finally constructed. Nine were solutions of
use of concrete block, although the Keys residence was first
intended for stone. The house is trimmed with pine. It is
based on the berm-type housing for Detroit auto workers
of 1942, first shown as a $4000 project in the 1938 *Archi-
tectural Forum*. Additions made in 1971 by John H. Howe
enlarge the living room and convert the former carport to
a guestroom and bath.

David Wright Residence (1950) and **Guesthouse** (1954)
Phoenix, Arizona

Living spaces are raised above ground by a spiral rampway
and other circular units in this concrete-block structure for
Wright's fifth child by his first wife. The guesthouse is also
of block but rectilinear in its forms. A 1965 addition is
by Lloyd Wright, eldest brother of the client.

324 Richard **Davis** Residence, "Woodside" (1950)
Marion, Indiana

This painted concrete-block, cedar-shingled, and redwood-trimmed home derives from the Lake Tahoe project of 1922, a plan of several cottages and barges based on the concept of the Indian teepee. The living room rises the full height of the central "teepee," from which the 120-degree-angled wings extend.

325 J. A. **Sweeton** Residence (1950)
Cherry Hill, New Jersey

In the Sweeton dwelling a red concrete-slab floor with radiant heat is complemented by interior redwood plywood board and batten and a red roof. This roof, now covered with asbestos shingle, was originally laid out in board, overlapping so that two-foot strips ran the length of the structure, emphasizing the horizontal character of the design. Similar emphasis is given in the block, vertical grouting filling the joints to the block surface, horizontal grouting normally recessed. Both carport and fireplace are cantilevered. The module is a four-foot square, the plan a stubby T with an extension off the master bedroom (not visible in the photograph) for additional work space. Mrs. Sweeton designed and wove the original fabric for drapes and furniture.

326 Raymond **Carlson** Residence (1950)
Phoenix, Arizona

This house for the editor of *Arizona Highways* magazine is of post and panel construction, using wood posts and insulated cement asbestos panels. Angled southwest to northeast on its corner lot, it rises three stories. A prominent clerestory takes advantage of light from the hot desert sun. Landscaping now totally obscures the house from neighbors and passers-by. (This photograph was taken in the early 1950s by Bradley Ray Storrer.)

327 **John O. Carr** Residence (1950)
Glenview, Illinois

This house is located on level ground deep into wooded
country. Its roof along the entry sidewalk carefully steps
around a great oak whose branches shelter the entire
structure. It is a T plan in salmon-colored concrete block.
The living room roof, an asymmetrical gable, is angled
southwest to northeast to admit delightfully changing
patterns of light both morning and evening. Patterned concrete block is used at the west end of the living room to
divide living from kitchen areas; it rises to about eye level,
but not to the ceiling, enhancing the sense of interior
spaciousness.

328 Donald **Schaberg** Residence (1950)
Okemos, Michigan

Mr. Schaberg notes that his house was built with over
55,000 bricks inside and out. It is roofed with cedar shakes.
The original plan was an L; the bedroom wing (left in the
photograph) is southwest of the central kitchen and dining
section, and the northeast living room adjoins a carport that
juts northwest from the main entrance. An addition made
in the 1960s by John H. Howe, who supervised the original
construction, altered the plan to a U. With its own entrance
hallway leading from the main entryway down the northern
wall, the addition runs northwest from the bedroom wing.
The main view is over a broad, wooded valley.

329 Ina Moriss **Harper** Residence (1950)
Saint Joseph, Michigan

The living room of this L plan (at right in the photograph)
turns from the bedroom axis to gain a view of Lake Michigan, directly across Lake Shore Drive. Salmon-colored (sand-
mold) brick and cypress are employed throughout.

330 Robert **Berger** Residence (1950)
San Anselmo, California

Approaching from below, one could easily drive by this house without seeing it, so deftly does it rest on one level ridge of the steep slopes of these north bay hillsides. It is best viewed overall from the opposite side of the valley, but then one has to search to separate mountain from desert rubblestone wall and wood, constructed on a triangular module.

331 Arthur C. **Mathews** Residence (1950)
Atherton, California

Two wings at 60 degrees to each other jut out from the main core around a patio. Sleeping quarters are in one wing, and living room in the other.

332 William **Palmer** Residence (1950)
Ann Arbor, Michigan

Constructed of cypress, sand-mold brick, and a matching block fired the same as the brick, this house grows out of the crest of a hill, opening from its triangular plan to a curving plateau that welcomes the morning sun.

333 Isadore J. **Zimmerman** Residence (1950)
Manchester, New Hampshire

A long house with a clerestory lighting the central living
quarters, its primary construction material is brick. The true
spaciousness of this home is not apparent from the public
approach. Its view is to the southwest over a large, beauti-
fully landscaped yard.

334 Robert **Muirhead** Residence (1950)
Plato Center, Illinois

Common brick and cypress are the structural ingredients
of this very elongated plan on a four-foot module that runs
southwest to northeast over flat farmland. In the photograph the bedroom wing is to the left, living room in the
center, and utility space to the right.

335 Karl A. **Staley** Residence (1950)
North Madison, Ohio

This long I plan parallels the nearby Lake Erie shore, southwest to northeast, opening the living room to a northwest exposure. Aside from this one seemingly all-glass facade, the structure is of stone.

336 S. P. **Elam** Residence (1950)
Austin, Minnesota

A two-story stone and cypress structure, this house inter-
locks triangles with rectangles. A rear terrace and the garage
are additions not of Wright design.

337 Richard Smith Residence (1950)
Jefferson, Wisconsin

This house opens onto a yard just off the Meadow Springs
Golf Club. Limestone, plaster, cypress, and cedar shingles
are integrated in this structure.

338 John A. **Gillin** Residence (1950)
Dallas, Texas

One of Wright's most extensive single-story structures, the
Gillen house looks eastward over gently rolling lawns
through floor-to-ceiling glass. Living and dining spaces are
articulated more by the ceiling than by walls, as right angles
are avoided, even in the kitchenette facilities of the guest
rooms. Stone is the primary construction material, and
glass, rather than wood, might be called the secondary.
There are also plaster ceilings and soffits and a copper roof.

339 Seamour **Shavin** Residence (1950)
Chattanooga, Tennessee

Wright's only work in Tennessee is also one of the few of the master's compositions that sit on, rather than wrap around or fit into, the crest of the hill. The resulting view of the Tennessee River and surrounding mountains is admitted to the house along its entire northern exposure. This is heightened in the living room by the northward incline of the ceiling, drawing one's attention to the exterior view. Native Tennessee limestone is the prime construction material.

340 Russell W. M. **Kraus** Residence (1951)
Kirkwood, Missouri

This artist's house bends around the hill in which it nestles, using triangular modules. The terrace door windows, designed by Mr. Kraus, are of geometrically patterned stained glass in very delicate tints, mostly of blue and green. The hilltop is open, while the downhill view is into wooded land.

341 Charles F. **Glore** Residence (1951)
Lake Forest, Illinois

This brick, cypress, and salmon concrete two-story structure overlooks a ravine, guardian of the dwelling's privacy
to the south. It is an I plan, with the master bedroom balcony opening into the two-story living room; the flues
of the fireplaces in both the bed and living rooms share the
masonry core. The Glore place was recently renovated.

342 Patrick Kinney Residence (1951)
Lancaster, Wisconsin

Stone and wood are set on triangular modules, with living room (at left in photograph) facing north and west. Former Taliesin Fellow John Howe added a northeast wing, which is detached from the main structure, in 1964.

343 Nathan **Rubin** Residence (1951)
Canton, Ohio
This house is essentially a mirror image of the Panshin
house, designed for the Usonian homes group in Okemos,
Michigan (269) but never built there. Brick and horizontal
wood siding sheathe the building whose sleeping quarters
and carport wing form a 120-degree angle.

344 Benjamin Adelman Residence (1951)
Phoenix, Arizona

A Usonian automatic house, the Benjamin Adelman residence has a two-story living room and kitchen lighted by the glass openings in the block pattern. Although its concept date is earlier than that of the Pieper residence (349), it was built after that house. The living room wall mural, with gilt and silvered mirror pieces, is by Eugene Masselink, who did many such designs for the Taliesin Fellowship.

345 Gabrielle and Charlcey **Austin** Residence,
"Broad Margin" (1951)
Greenville, South Carolina

Desert rubblestone wall construction was used in this house,
the exposed stone surfaces having been covered with newspaper before the cement was poured. This is one of the few
Wright houses where the sheltering roof is the characteristic
first noticed upon approach; it seems to extend the hill out
over the house. The entry hall, nestled in the hillside, serves
as a spine to the play, living, culinary, and sleeping quarters,
which all extend downhill off of this hall.

346 A. K. **Chahroudi** Residence (1951)
Lake Mahopac, New York

Located on the western shore of Klein's Island—historically, Petra Island—in Lake Mahopac, this cottage is sheltered by dense foliage. Desert rubblestone wall construction, some horizontal wood sheathing, and triangular modules are combined in this residence.

347 W. L. **Fuller** Residence (1951)
Pass Christian, Mississippi
Demolished, 1969

This single-story house on the very edge of the Gulf of
Mexico was raised on a concrete-slab foundation. After
Hurricane Camille, which destroyed most of the surround-
ing beach area structures, only the slab remained.

348 Roy **Wetmore Auto Service Station Remodeling** (1951)
Ferndale, Michigan

Wright designed a complete service station and auto showroom for Wetmore, but they were never built. Later he designed the remodeling of the existing Wetmore facilities.
Though some remodeling was done, work never advanced
beyond the initial stages. Some evidence of this work—
wood trim—remains today.

349 Arthur **Pieper** Residence (1952)
Paradise Valley, Arizona

The Pieper house is possibly the first constructed example of a Usonian automatic house. Pieper, then a student at Taliesin West, was a son-in-law of Wright by marriage to his daughter Iovanna. He was later divorced. In building the house, Pieper made the molds for the three-inch-thick blocks, poured the concrete, knit the blocks together with reinforcing steel rods and grouting, and eventually raised the entire structure, with some help from Taliesin Fellow Charles Montooth (two of whose houses are on lots immediately south of the Pieper plot). This is the "automatic" aspect of construction; the client can make the project a do-it-yourself home kit. Though two three-inch-thick walls were considered, as in earlier Wright textile block designs (214-217), and alternately a Usonian type sandwich insulating interior wall, only one thickness of block was completed, and today trellises hold vines as an added shading to help cool the walls from the desert sun. Usonian automatic structures tend toward one thick block wall, rather than two thin walls, for economy of construction, but the principle remains that of textile-block building. The original T plan with living room at the head of the T (at the right in the photograph) was altered to a mirror-F plan by addition of a dining room (not shown in the photograph) by Arthur Lawton.

350 Ray **Brandes** Residence (1952)
Issaquah, Washington

Mr. Brandes was the builder of another, later Wright-designed house in the Seattle area (389). He notes the similarity of his own residence to the Goetsch-Winkler house (269).
Although it may be similar in its central living room space,
its site placement commands a more favorable relationship
to the sun for this northwestern climate. The concrete-block
retaining wall is not by Wright.

351 Quintin **Blair** Residence (1952)
Cody, Wyoming

The only work of Wright's design in Wyoming is this stone and wood house on the plains east of Yellowstone National Park. The rising living room ceiling opens to a view of the entire eastern horizon. The southern porch has been enclosed.

352 Archie Boyd **Teater** Residence (1952)
Bliss, Idaho
High on the bluffs above the right bank of the Snake River,
this house, the only work by Wright in Idaho, looks to the
north and west. It is built of stone and wood. The knee
brace to the terrace roof is a later addition, not by Wright.

353 R. W. **Lindholm Residence,** "Mäntylä" (1952)
Cloquet, Minnesota

Mäntylä is a T plan so situated as to open living and sleeping
quarters to the setting sun. Painted cement block is trimmed
with wood. The Lindholms also built the Broadacre City Service Station in downtown Cloquet (414).

354 Frank S. **Sander** Residence, "Springbough" (1952)
Stamford, Connecticut

Springbough juts out from a rocky promontory toward the heavily wooded surroundings. Its well-shaded living room and balcony extension face south. Horizontal wood siding, now painted, complements brick foundation and core.

355 Harold Price, Sr., **Price Company Tower** (1952)
Bartlesville, Oklahoma

Based on the 1929 Saint Marks Tower project for William
Norman Guthrie, the Price Tower stands like a tall tree in
the rolling hills of eastern Oklahoma. The building is constructed of reinforced concrete with cantilevered floors,
copper louvers and copper-faced parapets, and gold-tinted
glass exterior. It is planned around a 60-degree parallelo-
gram module 2' 6'' across, 1' 10 5/8'' on a side. Its nineteen
floors plus spire tower 221 feet above the prairie base. The
tower is open to visitors during regular business hours.

356 Anderton Court Shops (1952)
Beverly Hills, California
This group of shops in one building is located in the fashionable downtown section of Beverly Hills. Entrance to all shops is off a ramp that winds its way upwards, in parallelograms, around a central open wall. Wright showed a clear facade in his plans and was never offered the signs for approval.

357 Private Residence (1952)
McLean, Virginia
This is a hemicycle of block and wood.

358 Robert **Llewellyn Wright** Residence (1953)
Bethesda, Maryland
A two-story hemicycle for Wright's sixth child by his first
wife, this concrete-block structure is wood faced at the
second story, where a balcony continues the hemicircular
line. Lloyd Wright landscaped the grounds in 1960.

359 George Lewis Residence (1952)
Tallahassee, Florida

The lower story of this two-story hemicycle is of concrete block, the upper, wood sheathed. The living room rises two stories.

360 Andrew B. **Cooke** Residence (1953)
Virginia Beach, Virginia
The points from which the concentric circles of the inner
and outer walls of the main living area were drawn are evident in the wedge segments of the patio floor. The brick is
baked from a clay imported from West Virginia, whose
color blends with the sand of Crystal Lake, next to which
the house stands. It is capped by a copper roof.

361 Jorgine **Boomer** Residence (1953)
Phoenix, Arizona

This house for a single person, which Wright designated a
"mountain cottage," is compacted into two stories around
a central chimney flue. It is of desert rubblestone wall construction with some horizontal wood sheathing, notably
in the bedroom balcony. It looks north, away from the
desert sun.

362 John J. **Dobkins** Residence (1953)
Canton, Ohio
Here the dominant feature is the living room with its glass
facade, which denies the rectangle in plan and in surface.
It receives sunlight from sunrise to sunset. Brick and wood
trim are combined with a copper roof. The residence is
located near the Feiman (371) and Rubin (343) houses.

363   Harold Price, Jr., Residence, "Hillside" (1953)
Bartlesville, Oklahoma

Hillside is a large L plan, with a two-story living room and
master bedroom overlooking the L. A hipped roof blends
house and sky. There has been one addition, a playroom
by William Wesley Peters, vice-president of the Frank
Lloyd Wright Foundation. Harold Price, Jr., is the son of
Harold Price, Sr., who commissioned the Price Company
Tower (355).

364 Lewis H. **Goddard** Residence (1953)
Plymouth, Michigan

An extended carport (not shown in the photograph) makes
this brick and wood house into an L plan. It is turned east-
southeast to gather the morning sun into the living room.
It is adjacent to "Snowflake" (281).

365 Louis **Penfield** Residence (1953)
Willoughby Hills, Ohio

Mr. Penfield's first house by Wright is of concrete block and
wood. Sleeping quarters are over kitchen facilities, both adjacent to the two-story living room, which looks through a
wooded hillside to the Chagrin River in the valley below.
From springtime floods, Mr. Penfield gathers stone, which
will go into the building of Wright's second house design for
this client, to be located southeast of the present structure.

366 Abraham **Wilson** (Bachman-Wilson) Residence (1954)
Millstone, New Jersey

Perhaps the idea for this house dates back to the 1941 project for the Ellinwood family. Like the Penfield house, it is of concrete block and wood with a two-story living room and sleeping quarters over the kitchen. The house was added to in 1970, on the north (at the left and outside of the photograph).

367 Wisconsin River Development Corporation, **Riverview Terrace Restaurant**, "The Spring Green," for W. H. Keland, president (1953)
Spring Green, Wisconsin

Perched on a hillside opposite Taliesin and just above the left bank of the Wisconsin River, this structure is the only restaurant designed by Wright that still stands today. Steel trusses were obtained from the flight deck of the aircraft carrier Ranger. Limestone, stucco, and various woods, including red oak paneling, are used. Originally "The Spring Green" was offered to the town Wright so dearly loved as a gift, and construction was begun by the Taliesin Fellowship in 1957. Halted for a variety of reasons, notably Wright's death, the project was again taken up in the late sixties. In a modified form, it was completed by the Taliesin Associated Architects as the first building in the Wisconsin River Development Corporation's planned resort adjacent to Taliesin. The restaurant is open during luncheon and dinner hours.

368 Willard H. **Keland** Residence (1954)
Racine, Wisconsin

The various wings of this structure create an atrium over which the two-story bedroom wing presides. This inner courtyard is, however, as much the creation of John H. Howe as of Wright, for it is the product of this Taliesin Fellow's 1961-designed playroom, greenhouse, and patio fountain addition (all on side opposite that shown in the photograph). Brick inside and out is laid under a copper roof. Mr. Keland is president of the Wisconsin River Development Corporation, which commissioned the Riverview Terrace Restaurant (367). Mrs. Keland is the daughter of H. F. Johnson, who built the Johnson Administration Building and Research Tower (237, 238) and Wingspread (239).

369, 370   **New York Usonian Exhibition House** and **Pavilion** (1953)
New York, New York
Demolished

After opening in the Palazzo Strozzi, Florence, and touring
Europe, the exhibit "Sixty Years of Living Architecture"
came to New York City. It was housed in the Usonian Exhibition House, on the site of the current Guggenheim
Museum (400).

371   Ellis A. **Feiman** Residence (1954)
Canton, Ohio

This wood-trimmed, brick structure is based on the 1953
New York Usonian Exhibition House (369). Its terrace/
lanai is fully open to the sun, while the roof skylight over-
hangs just enough to shade the living room in the summer
yet admit light in the winter. The Feiman residence is, in
interior space, an L plan, but the carport alters this to a
pinwheel. It is located near both the Rubin (343) and
Dobkins (362) houses.

372 Maurice **Greenberg** Residence, "Stonebroke" (1954)
Dousman, Wisconsin
Still not completed, the Greenberg residence cantilevers
from the brow of its hill. Originally designed, like Taliesin,
in native stone, it was finally built in brick, concrete, and
wood.

373 Beth Sholom Synagogue (1954)
Elkins Park, Pennsylvania

This edifice of concrete, steel, aluminum, glass, fiberglass, and oiled walnut is suspended from a tripod frame that allows the full upper floor complete freedom from internal supports. A separate chapel is directly below. The synagogue was dedicated on September 20, 1959. Tours are conducted most days, and a booklet explaining the design of the building is also available.

374 E. Clarke **Arnold** Residence (1954)
Columbus, Wisconsin
The Arnold residence is built in native stone from the Sauk
City area of Wisconsin. Originally of two wings set at 120
degrees to each other on a diamond module, its plan is now
a Y by the 1959 addition of a wing designed by John H.
Howe.

375 John E. **Christian** Residence (1954)
West Lafayette, Indiana

This brick and wood single-story house sits on a small hill
near Purdue Stadium. The plan includes a walled garden on
the northeast, the only part of this four-foot-square module
structure to employ a circular segment, southeast living
room (right in the photograph) and central work space under a clerestory. This clerestory has a fascia of copper; the
lower fascia of wood is to be surfaced with a three-dimen-
sional design constructed of copper.

376 Louis B. **Fredrick** Residence (1954)
Barrington Hills, Illinois

The Fredrick house commands the top of one of the Barrington Hills, nestling just below its crest. The roofline, instead of reaching outward as it rises, recedes to admit light. Mrs. Fredrick notes that the contractor's placement of the foundation, only a few degrees from Wright's designation, caused the light to shine much more deeply into the living room than had been intended. Three bedrooms, living room, work space, guest-playroom, and two galleries are enclosed by buckskin range brick and Philippine mahogany.

377 I. N. **Hagan** Residence (1954)
Chalkhill, Pennsylvania

From just below the peak of Kentuk Knob, the Hagan
house appears to grow out of the hillside. At the opposite
extremity, it is a ship's prow sailing the Pennsylvania Highlands. From above, it is part of the hill; from below, a strik-
ing complement to it. It employs hexagonal modules, completely eliminating right angles from the plan. Construction
materials are primarily native sandstone quarried at the site
and Tidewater red cypress.

378 **Harold Price, Sr.,** Residence, "Grandma House" (1954)
Paradise Valley, Arizona

The central room, which divides the I plan into wings, is an atrium whose roof, raised on pylons, creates an open clerestory to admit fresh breezes. This same roof provides shade from the desert sun and shelter from flash thunderstorms, yet its open skylight admits sun to play on the water in the central fountain. Concrete block is used throughout. Mr. Price also commissioned the Price Company Tower (355).

379 Cedric G. **Boulter** Residence (1954)
Cincinnati, Ohio

The Boulter house is of concrete block and wood, the latter
stained Taliesin red. As is the common practice in Wright
houses, the module is marked out in the Taliesin red-colored
cement floor, squares equal to three concrete blocks on a
side. A balcony juts into the two-story-high living room
from second-story bedrooms, its west extension becoming
an exterior balcony. The terrace retaining wall is battered.
A technique used in nearly all masonry work on Wright
houses is apparent in the laying of the block; grouting in
vertical joints is flush with the surface, while in horizontal
joints it is normally recessed. This emphasizes the horizontal
nature of the structure.

380 Hoffman Auto Showroom (1954)
New York, New York

This interior remodeling of the ground-floor northeast corner of a New York City curtain wall skyscraper was done for Maximilian Hoffman (390). At the time, Hoffman was an importer of the British Jaguar; the showroom has since been used as a New York office of Mercedes-Benz. The ramp (to the left in the photograph) curves around the main circle of the display floor. Posts of the skyscraper are surfaced with mirrors, as are some walls.

381   Frank Lloyd Wright, **Hotel Plaza Apartment Remodeling**
(1954)
New York, New York
Demolished, 1968

Wright remodeled an apartment in the Hotel Plaza to use
for visits to New York City while the Guggenheim Museum
and other New York and Connecticut projects were under
construction. While apprentices at Taliesin were building
the necessary furniture, painted in black lacquer with red
edges, Wright was having long red velvet curtains hung the
full height of the high-ceilinged room. Rose-colored borders
framed Japanese gold paper panels that were placed on the
walls. Circular mirrors became part of the semicircular window arches. Crystal balls were attached to cord pendants,
which, when pulled, turned on the mirror lights. The
Wrights last stayed in this second-story apartment, known
to some as "Taliesin the Third," on January 27, 1959.

382 Los Angeles Exhibition Pavilion (1954)
Los Angeles, California
In 1951 the exhibit "Sixty Years of Living Architecture"
opened in the Palazzo Strozzi, Florence. From there it went
to Zurich, Paris, Munich, Rotterdam, Mexico City, New
York City (369, 370), and, finally, Los Angeles. Here, the
pavilion was built contiguous to the Barnsdall Hollyhock
House (208). During the refurbishing of Hollyhock House
in the 1970s, the pavilion has been largely demolished.

383 John L. **Rayward** (Rayward-Shepherd) Residence,
"Tirranna" (1955)
New Canaan, Connecticut

Tirranna—an Australian aboriginal word meaning "running
waters"—is an intricate intermingling of the ellipse and the
square in a four-foot module. A concrete block of Wright's
design combines with Philippine mahogany and glass to
create a house, swimming pool, and pond wedded to the
Noroton River and its surrounding hills. The swimming pool
splits in half the eighteen-foot drop from living room to
pond, where a dam creates a waterfall. A series of fish steps
at the far end of the dam provides for passage of fish
through the twenty acres of woodland property. Landscaped by Frank Okamura, landscape architect of the
Brooklyn Botanical Garden, and Charles Middeleer, the
grounds contain such a quantity and variety of flora as to
qualify as a major botanical garden. While the built-in and
free-standing furniture, fabric designs, and carpet layout are
of Wright's design, with the assistance of John deKoven Hill,
there is also a treehouse for children designed by Taliesin
Associated Architects' chief architect, William Wesley
Peters. Though originally designed for Mr. Rayward, H. R.
Shepherd brought the design to completion. (Photograph by
Carol Ruth Shepherd.)

384 William L. **Thaxton** Residence (1954)
Bunker Hill, Texas

Deep among the tall oaks west of Houston sits this battered,
concrete-block-walled, triangular-moduled house. The detailing in the fascia alone contains over nine hundred pieces
of trim. The 60-degree L plan encloses a swimming pool.
There is an addition, not by Wright, which is detached from
the main dwelling.

385 Randall **Fawcett** Residence (1955)
Los Banos, California

Battered concrete block and angles of 120 and 60 degrees
form the basis of this house. Its two wings each make a 60-
degree angle to the main space, which contains the entry
and a large living room space with walk-in fireplace. A mod-·
ern version of the shallow, circular flower planter so often
favored by Wright is shown on the right in the photograph.

386 Gerald B. **Tonkens** Residence (1954)
Amberley Village, Ohio

A major statement in the history of Usonian automatic
houses, this residence sits on six acres atop a knoll. Pierced
blocks admit light to the work space core as a clerestory.
This core contains heating and cooling units raised above
floor level and other utilities. One wall of the core is the
living room fireplace. The L plan of the interior space
makes its 90-degree turn around the work space; the living
room, extended by a lanai, is the short L leg; sleeping quarters and study are in the longer leg. In the exterior plan, a
second L develops by way of a cantilevered carport at 90
degrees to the bedroom wing. The house is constructed on
a two-foot-square module with the standard wall block surface two feet by one foot. Wood for both paneling and
furniture is Philippine mahogany. The care exercised in the
seventeen-months-long construction of this dwelling is evident. Eric Wright, a grandson of the architect, supervised
construction from engineering drawings by William Wesley
Peters. Other supervisors included Thomas Casey and John
deKoven Hill (fabrics and furniture). John H. Howe assisted
Wright with the original drawings. As is common in Usonian
blocks, the interior surface is coffered. Engineering of the
block and reinforced-steel ceiling was by Mendel Glickman—
the only non-Taliesin principal on the project—in collaboration with Peters and the architect. Hill and Cornelia Brierly
designed the landscaping.

387 Toufic H. **Kalil** Residence (1955)
Manchester, New Hampshire

This is a Usonian automatic house of L or, with carport, T plan. There are no large windows; light is admitted through the pierced block, and the house is turned southwest to northeast to shade the patio in the afternoon.

388 Dorothy H. **Turkel** Residence (1955)
Detroit, Michigan

The pierced, light-admitting blocks around the two-story
living room—which faces south and east—are much larger
than those of the Kalil house (387), thus maintaining a
proper sense of scale in this larger house. Usonian automatic construction was employed in this L-plan structure.

389 W. B. **Tracy** Residence (1955)
Normandy Park, Washington

This Usonian automatic house nestles into a rise just above the cliff on the east shore of Puget Sound. Though the blocks appear to be uniform, they are of several forms for inside and outside corner, roof, and walls.

390 Maximilian **Hoffman Residence** (1955)
Rye, New York

The large living room of the Hoffman dwelling (visible in
the photograph) looks north and east over a swimming pool
and lawn to Long Island Sound. Kitchen and bedrooms are
south of this room, the bedrooms opening onto the yard.
The leg of the L plan covers the entrance to the grounds on
the back side of the house and continues into the garage
and servant quarters. Stone, plaster, and cedar shakes are
trimmed with a copper fascia. In 1972 Mrs. Martin Fisher
contracted with the Taliesin Associated Architects for the
addition of a wing. (Photograph by Ezra Stoller © ESTO,
courtesy of Mrs. Martin Fisher.)

391 Private Residence (1955)
Stillwater, Minnesota
This residence is one of the last Usonian houses.

392 T. A. **Pappas** Residence (1955)
Saint Louis, Missouri

In the rolling hills west of metropolitan Saint Louis sits this salmon-tinted cement-block house. It is a Usonian automatic unit whose masonry structure could be built from blocks assembled by the client to save on labor costs.

393 Robert H. **Sunday** Residence (1955)
Marshalltown, Iowa

A brick structure with wood fascia and trim, this L plan
was transformed into a T by an addition made in 1970
from 1969 plans of John H. Howe. This is possibly the last
of the brick Usonian homes. It faces southwest down its
hillside site, and its living room views three compass directions.

394 Warren **Scott Remodeling** of the **Isabel Roberts** Residence
(1955)
River Forest, Illinois

The Scott remodeling of the Isabel Roberts house (150)
involved brick veneer resurfacing, with blonde Philippine
mahogany in the interior. The east rooms of the lower level
have also been converted to a study by the Scotts.

395 Dallas Theatre Center (1955)
Dallas, Texas

The Dallas Theatre Center—locally also called the Kalita
Humphreys Theater—is of concrete in cantilever construction, with a 127-ton, concrete stage loft. The circular stage
drum, extending well above the rest of the concrete mass,
is the focus of the design, which, aside from circles, employs
modules with 60- and 120-degree angles. The 40-foot circular stage, within the drum, itself contains a 32-foot turntable. The theater can seat 404 people in eleven rows. The
terrace above the foyer (at left in the photograph) has been
enclosed to provide studio space and the foyer extended,
giving a more monumental feeling to the once-light entrance
wing. Tours are conducted daily.

THE KALITA HUMPHREYS
THEATER

396 Karl **Kundert Medical Clinic** (1955)
San Luis Obispo, California

A brick structure, this clinic is of L plan with its terrace enclosed by both the L and the retaining wall above the adjacent creek bed. Offices and laboratory facilities are in opposite wings off the central reception room below the clerestory. This clerestory is made of pierced wood panels with glass inset; such panels were used often by Wright in wood structures to admit patterned light, for example, in the Wilson residence (366). A similar principle underlies the pierced blocks of block houses, such as the Tonkens and Kalil residences (386, 387).

397 Kenneth L. **Meyers Medical Clinic** (1956)
Dayton, Ohio
This clinic's reception room is at one end of the 120-degree-
angled structure (in the foreground of the photograph),
with doctors' rooms at the other.

398 Paul J. **Trier** Residence (1956)
Des Moines, Iowa

The living room (at right in the photograph) of this wood-trimmed brick structure faces south-southwest, opening onto a terrace. For additional space, the Taliesin Associated Architects added a north wing in 1967.

399 Annunciation **Greek Orthodox Church** (1956)
Wauwatosa, Wisconsin

The main hall for religious services is spanned by the blue
ceramic-tile roof, which is supported by the reinforced-
concrete drum of the structure. The basement is open
space, adaptable to the varied needs of the church community. The church is open to visitors.

400 Solomon R. **Guggenheim Museum** (1956)
New York, New York

The main gallery of the Guggenheim is a continuous spiraling inclined ramp in concrete. Wright intended this spiral incline to counteract the usual dominance of right-angled architecture over the flat plane of a picture. He also intended visitors to take the elevator to the top of the spiral, then walk down to the ground floor. Overcoming the restrictions of the New York City building code took more time than design and construction, but the original design of 1943, labeled a "ziggurat," is still evident in the final plan. The museum is open daily and Sunday for a small admission charge.

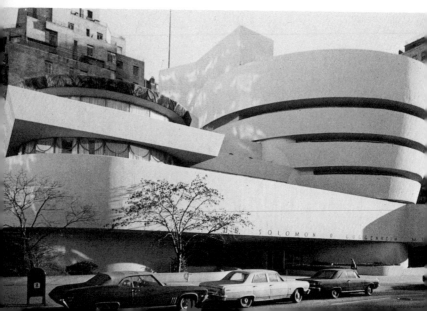

401 Wyoming Valley Grammar School (1956)
Wyoming Valley, Wisconsin

Not far south of Taliesin is this school, the only public elementary schoolhouse built from a Wright design. It is of concrete block and redwood with shingled roof. Employing 60- and 120-degree angles in its plan, it is actually a two-room school with central loggia. The large rooms are sky-lighted, and each has its own fireplace. The building is open when school is in session.

402 Private Residence (1956)
Wilmington, Delaware

Stone predominates inside and out in this structure. The hemicycle-plan living room facade opens onto a terrace.

403 **Allan Friedman** Residence (1956)
Bannockburn, Illinois

This is one of the few Y-plan houses by Wright. Utilizing 60- and 120-degree angles throughout, the wings house living room, sleeping quarters, and carport, intersecting at the entry and kitchen area. The built-in, and much of the freestanding, furniture is by Wright. The Friedmans received their final plan revisions just before Wright's death.

404 Frank **Bott** Residence (1956)
Kansas City, Missouri

The terne metal roof of the Bott residence seems to grow
out of the crest of the hill over which one approaches the
house. The living room and balcony cantilever far out over
the hill toward the left bank of the Missouri River, affording the Botts a lovely view of Kansas City and providing
complete privacy from neighbors that crowd the narrow
lot. Construction is desert rubblestone wall, employing one
mile of farmer's wall stone from nearby flinthills in Kansas
and Philippine mahogany on a four-foot module.

405 Clyde **Nooker Restoration** of the **Frank Lloyd Wright Studio** (1956)
Oak Park, Illinois

This 1956 remodeling of the Frank Lloyd Wright Studio (4) removed many of the alterations made after Wright moved to Taliesin and restored the building to essentially its 1895 appearance.

6-410 Marshall Erdman Company, **Prefab #1** (1956), including:

406 Eugene **VanTamelen** Residence
Madison, Wisconsin

407 Arnold **Jackson** Residence, "Skyview"
Madison, Wisconsin

408 Frank **Iber** Residence
Stevens Point, Wisconsin

409 Carl **Post** Residence
Barrington Hills, Illinois

410 William **Cass** Residence, "The Crimson Beech"
Richmond (Staten Island), New York

Of four prefabricated house designs by Wright for the Marshall Erdman Company, only two were ever constructed. This is the first. All five units built from this plan are virtually identical in their L plans but differ in detail. Each has a masonry core, with painted, horizontal board and batten siding on the bedroom wing. The living room is below the entryway at the inner intersection of the L, and kitchen-dining facilities are in the short leg, with attached garage or carport. All have a utilities space basement; the Jackson, Iber and Post houses complete this into a full basement. The Van Tamelen is of concrete block; the Jackson and Iber are of stone; and the Post and Cass employ brick.

VanTamelen Residence

Jackson Residence, "Skyview"

Iber Residence

Post Residence

Cass Residence, "The Crimson Beech"

411 Joseph **Mollica** Residence (1956)
Bayside, Wisconsin

This stone dwelling was constructed from a plan that is a mirror image of the Erdman units (406-410).

412, 413 Marshall Erdman Company, **Prefab #2** (1957)

412 Walter **Rudin** Residence
Madison, Wisconsin

This second of the four prefab designs for Marshall Erdman is the "one-room house." It is essentially a square plan. The large two-story living room (on the right in the photograph) is overlooked by a balcony outside the second-story sleeping quarters. The two units built are both of concrete block and painted, horizontal board and batten. The Rudin house is the original model and is situated on a flat site.

Marshall Erdman Company, Prefab #2

413 James B. **McBean** Residence
Rochester, Minnesota

The McBean residence is set into a hillside site and so angled
as to take maximum advantage of the sun both morning
and afternoon.

414 R. W. **Lindholm Service Station** (1956)
Cloquet, Minnesota

This is a cement-block structure, painted, with terne metal
roof and cantilevered canopy. The design derives from the
Broadacre City Standardized Overhead Service Station of
1932, except that ground-based fuel pumps are used instead
of the overhead fuel lines as envisioned by Wright. This is
the only service station constructed from Wright's designs.
Its service waiting room (in center of photograph) is over
the attendants' area, while mechanics' working areas are on
ground level.

415 Marin County Civic Center, **Post Office** (1957)
San Raphael, California

Wright's only constructed work for the United States Government is this building in the Marin County Civic Center. A nearly circular structure of concrete block and forms, this post office sits at the foot of the hill below the Marin County Administration Building (416). Nearby is a Taliesin-designed theater. Former Taliesin Fellow and San Francisco architect Aaron Green supervised all these government projects. The post office is open during regular office hours.

416 **Marin County** Civic Center, **Administration Building** and
417 **Hall of Justice** (1957)
San Raphael, California

Few were the buildings designed by Wright for governmental agencies, and fewer still were those that were built, namely only those in Marin County. The Marin County Civic Center includes a main Administration Building and contiguous Hall of Justice of similar concrete forms and terne metal roof. Reaching out from the domed library center, behind the eye-commanding pylon (functionally a radio antenna), each of these wings seeks a distant hill, complementing the spaces between them. The terne metal roof covers three single-story arcades. The buildings are open to visitors during regular business hours.

418 Wichita State University, **Juvenile Cultural Study Center** (1957)
Wichita, Kansas

Cast concrete, metals, and much glass constitute the two rectangular units either side of a patio that together comprise the first (Building A) of two works designed by Wright for this project. Both units are two stories high, with classrooms and office space, and courtyards symmetrically placed about the patio axis. The buildings, also known as the Harry F. Corbin Education Center, after the president of Wichita State University at the time of construction, are open to visitors during regular university session hours.

419 C. E. **Gordon** Residence (1957)
Aurora, Oregon
Wright's only work in Oregon is this concrete-block structure of T plan. The two-story living room (in the foreground of the photograph) runs north to the south bank
of the Willamette River, opening to both east and west
views. Bedrooms, with balconies, are in the head of the T,
over kitchen and work spaces.

420 **Duey Wright** Residence (1957)
Wausau, Wisconsin

Concrete block is here used to create the circular section of a living room that commands a westward view from high above the left bank of the Wisconsin River. Approximately an L plan, the design is said to imitate a musical note. The kitchen is adjacent to the living room, while sleeping quarters are in the long wing with a carport at its end. Duey Wright is not related to the architect.

421 Robert G. **Walton** Residence (1957)
Modesto, California

Situated near a south bank of the Stanislaus River, this concrete-block house with wood fascia and trim is of T plan. The south bedroom and east living room wings open to easterly views across the broad river basin from the low hillside site, opposite the entry shown in the photograph.

422 **Sterling Kinney** Residence (1957)
Amarillo, Texas

Battered red brick walls at all but the living room facades
(as shown in the photograph) characterize this house set on
the cap rock of the west Texas panhandle. A T plan, its
kitchen separates the living room and sleeping quarters,
opening both to the bedroom porch and the main living
space. A separate porch forms an L around the west and
north facades of the sunken living room, shown in the photograph above the goldfish pond.

423 Private Residence (1957)
Cincinnati, Ohio
This is an L-plan, brick structure.

424 Herman T. **Fasbender Medical Clinic**, Mississippi Valley
Clinic (1957)
Hastings, Minnesota

Formerly a medical clinic and now business offices, this
brick structure is given added character by the draping of
its terne metal roof.

425 **Lockridge Medical Clinic**, for Drs. Lockridge, McIntyre, and Whalen (1958)
Whitefish, Montana

A rectangular building, this former clinic is of brick, horizontal painted wood sheathing around the skylight, and concrete fascia. It has been converted into a bank and is open during regular business hours.

426 Carl **Schultz** Residence (1957)
Saint Joseph, Michigan
Pavement brick from the streets of nearby Benton Harbor
combines with mahogany trim in this house. Its living room
terrace (at left in the photograph) cantilevers out over a
ravine off the left bank of the Saint Joseph River.

427 Paul **Olfelt** Residence (1958)
Saint Louis Park, Minnesota
Triangular forms mold sleeping quarters into a hillside,
open the living room to a view downhill, and fit the whole
into the only level part of the terrain.

428 George **Ablin** Residence (1958)
Bakersfield, California

Salmon concrete block, cedar shingles, and wood trim are
combined in this house on a knoll next to the Bakersfield
Country Club. The living room opens to the southeast, its
view protected from nearby development.

429 Don M. **Stromquist** Residence (1958)
Bountiful, Utah

Wright's only work in Utah is a concrete-block structure
built on a triangular module. No other dwellings exist within a half-mile in any direction, and the structure, situated
halfway down the canyon wall, looks south to wooded wilderness. The master bedroom features a balcony that
reaches out over the canyon valley, and the living room, a
terrace, both triangular. (Photograph courtesy of Ray R.
Schofield.)

430 Seth **Petersen** Residence (1958)
Lake Delton, Wisconsin

Native stone and wood are used in this "one-room cottage" on the ledge above the south shore of Mirror Lake. The fireplace is central to the square plan, its masonry dividing the south half of the interior space in two. Acquired in the 1960s by the State of Wisconsin, it is on a fenced-in western limit of Mirror Lake State Park.

431 Pilgrim **Congregational Church** (1958)
Redding, California

Of desert rubblestone wall construction, this building was not Taliesin-supervised during construction and remains unfinished today. The main roof is suspended from concrete bents. The building is usually open during weekdays.

432 Arizona State University, Grady **Gammage Memorial Auditorium** (1959)
Tempe, Arizona

The last nonresidential design by Wright to be constructed is this auditorium that seats 3000 persons continental style (that is, with wide spacing between rows and no center aisle). There are 50 concrete columns cast on the site, and each rises 55 feet to support the outer roof, whose deck is gypsum and thin-shell concrete with a roofing of composition and sprayed-on asphalt. The exterior walls are brick and marblecrete (a marblelike composition material) in desert-rose finish; interior brick and sand finish plaster with acoustical tile. Walnut trim and reinforced-concrete floors complete the list of major construction materials. The grand tier is suspended forward of the rear auditorium wall on a 145-foot-long steel beam—a unique solution to the acoustical problems of a seating space between orchestra and balcony. No smoking is permitted in lobby or auditorium—there were intentionally no provisions made for ash trays. Tours are conducted daily. (Photograph right courtesy of Arizona State University.)

Arizona University, Grady Gammage Memorial Auditorium

433 Norman **Lykes** Residence (1959)
Phoenix, Arizona

This is the last residential design by Wright to be built.
Taliesin Fellow John Rattenbury did the detail work and
furniture and supervised construction, which took place
during 1966-1968. The living room is of circular plan, and
all other parts of the total plan are circular segments. Des-
sert-rose concrete block and Philippine mahogany are the
materials employed. The second-floor study above the
living room drum is an alteration to the plan made by
Rattenbury.

ILLUSTRATION CREDITS

The following photographs were reprinted from *Frank Lloyd Wright to 1910* by Grant Carpenter Manson, © 1958 by Litton Educational Publishing, Inc., by permission of Van Nostrand Reinhold Company.

The following photographs were reprinted from the collection of Henry-Russell Hitchcock.

Line drawings of the following buildings were done by Mark Reichert.

PLANS

The plans presented in this volume represent the various periods of Wright's creative activity in residential design. Many demonstrate the basic plans employed by Wright; cruciform L, and others are shown. Some show the basic modules and geometric forms with which Wright worked: the hexagon, octagon, triangle. Plans for the main floor only are shown, as examples of their types. (Plans for the Winslow, Willits, Robie, Mrs. Millard, Kaufmann, First Jacobs, Herbert F. Johnson, McCartney, and Laurent residences are from the collection of Henry-Russell Hitchcock.

Winslow Residence

This residence was Wright's first independent commission after leaving the firm of Adler & Sullivan. The plan is rectangular. The upper floor is sleeping quarters.

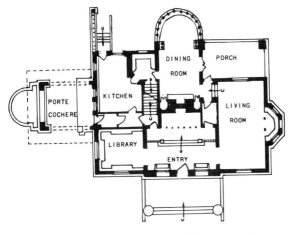

FIRST (MAIN) FLOOR PLAN

Husser Residence

While looking back to an early form, the octagon, this house already suggests Prairie characteristics. The main floor is the second of three. The lower level was a "basement" raised to ground level. This ground-level basement was later to become a characteristic of the Prairie house, although here it may have been designed to prevent flooding of the lakeside structure. The house is essentially an I plan. The upper (third) floor was sleeping quarters.

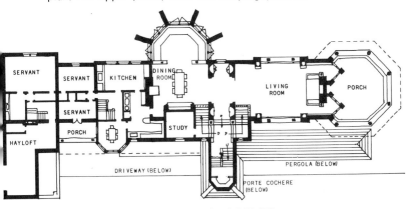

SECOND (MAIN) FLOOR PLAN

Willits Residence

This is a major early Prairie house of cruciform plan. Its upper floor is sleeping quarters.

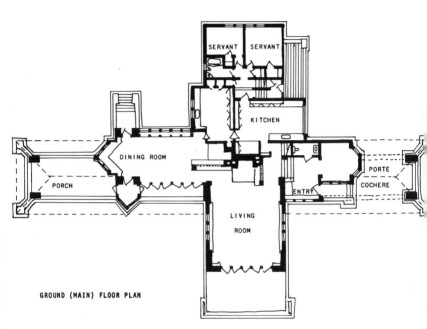

SERVANT   SERVANT

KITCHEN

DINING ROOM

PORCH

PORTE
COCHERE

ENTRY

LIVING

ROOM

GROUND (MAIN) FLOOR PLAN

Robie Residence

To many, this building is Wright's major statement in the Prairie idiom. The ground floor contains a billiards room below the living room and children's area below the dining room. The third floor is sleeping quarters. All three stories take no more height than most two-story houses of the same era.

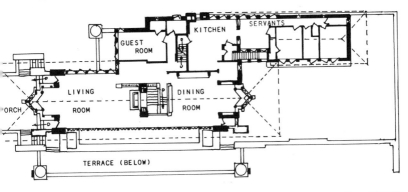

SECOND **(MAIN) FLOOR PLAN**

Mrs. Millard Residence

One of the California block houses, this residence looks into a glen below its entrance (main) level. The lower level has the dining room below the min-level living room and also includes kitchen and storage spaces. The upper level has sleeping quarters and balcony, looking over the living room.

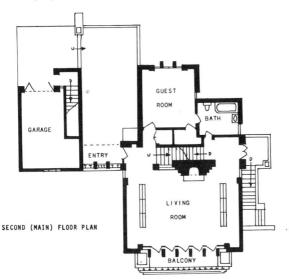

SECOND (MAIN) FLOOR PLAN

Kaufmann Residence, Fallingwater

This house over a waterfall rises three stories, including living quarters and adjacent terraces, above the main level. Its living room is roughly square but so open to its terraces that it hardly seems enclosed. Despite its three stories, the house appears horizontal.

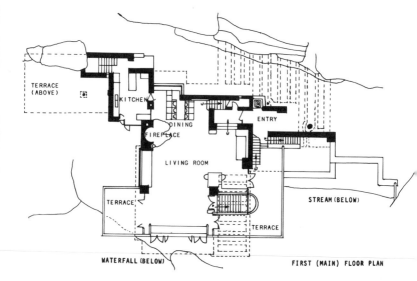

TERRACE (ABOVE)

KITCHEN

DINING

FIREPLACE

ENTRY

LIVING ROOM

TERRACE

STREAM (BELOW)

TERRACE

WATERFALL (BELOW)

FIRST (MAIN) FLOOR PLAN

First Jacobs Residence

The first of hundreds of Usonian house designs to be built, the Jacobs house is of L plan on a rectangular module. It is set on concrete slab, through which heating pipes, conducting gravity heat, run. It contains only a utilities basement.

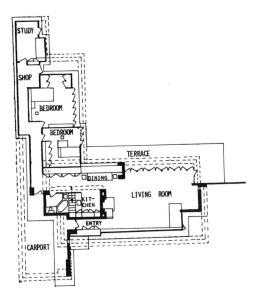

Hanna Honeycomb House

The Hanna residence is built on a hexagonal module and curves around its hillside site.

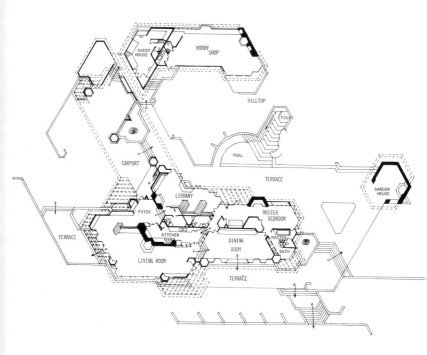

Herbert F. Johnson Residence, Wingspread

The wings of this dwelling spread to the four compass directions from a central octagon. The result is the largest, and last, expression of the Prairie house in a plan that may be called modified cruciform but that is actually a pinwheel. It is also a fine example of the "zoned house," a dwelling with different activities relegated to specific areas—noisy activities separated from quiet, children from guests, servants from the master of the house.

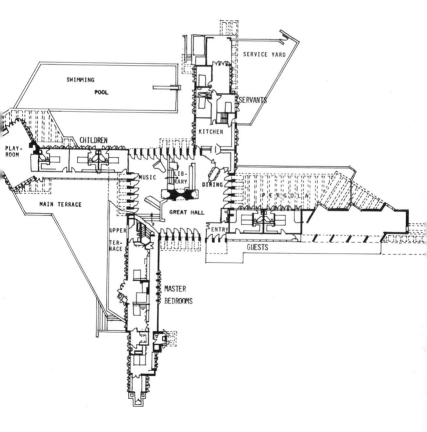

SWIMMING POOL

SERVICE YARD

SERVANTS

KITCHEN

CHILDREN

PLAY-ROOM

MAIN TERRACE

MUSIC

LIB-RARY

DINING

PERGOLA

GREAT HALL

UPPER TER-RACE

ENTRY

GUESTS

MASTER BEDROOMS

McCartney Residence

The basic module of this Wright textile-block house is a
diamond, but that diamond results in many patterns. Half a
diamond is a equilateral triangle, and half of an equilateral
triangle is a right triangle; this latter configuration is clearly
apparent in the roofline. A later addition saw a new carport
beyond the work space entrance and the old carport made
into a bedroom.

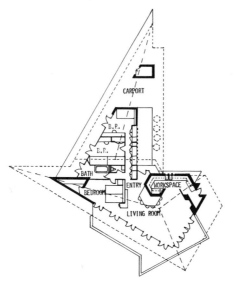

Laurent Residence

Wright's first major expression in circular segments was the
second Jacobs residence, which had a single center for all
radii of the basic structure. In the Laurent dwelling, there
are two centers for circles that intersect. A later bedroom
addition is beyond the entry, next to the carport.

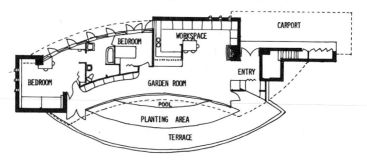

MAPS

In the seven maps here presented, one may trace the development of Wright's work over time and space. The first map shows the geographical distribution of all of Wright's opus. The other maps divide the constructed works into six time periods, with a dot for each extant constructed project or work and an x for each work of that period since demolished. Where the dots or x's are too numerous to distinguish in a given area, a figure indicates the number of works in that area.

1887-1898 Early Work: Eclectic and Original

1899-1909 Coming of The Prairie House

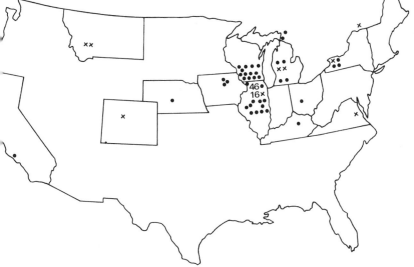

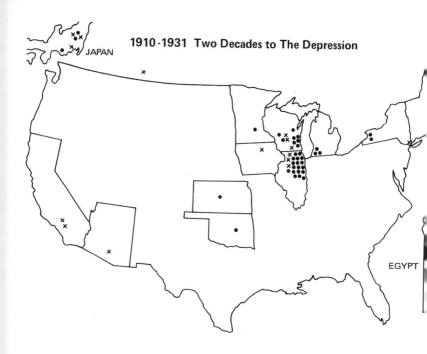

1910-1931 Two Decades to The Depression

JAPAN

EGYPT

1932-1942 Usonia I

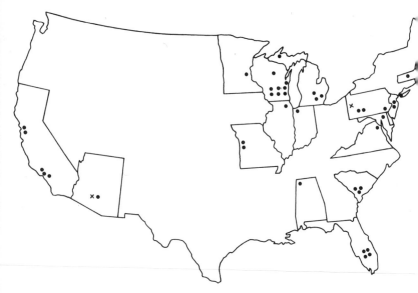

1943-1953 Of Hemicycles and . . .

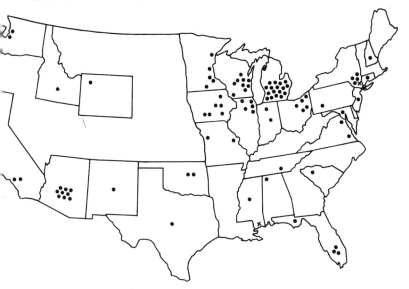

1954-1959 . . . Prefabs

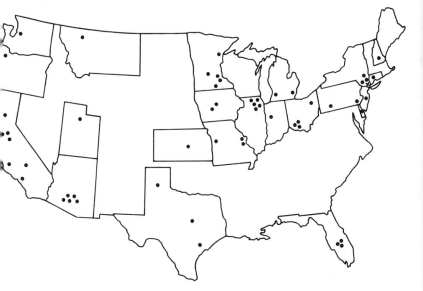

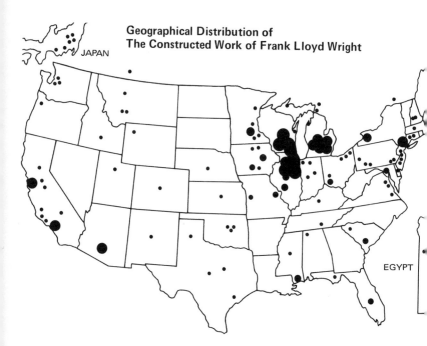

Geographical Distribution of
The Constructed Work of Frank Lloyd Wright

JAPAN

EGYPT

GEOGRAPHICAL INDEX BY ZIP CODE

Numbers refer to the catalog entry number.

Note: This geographical index of extant buildings is not meant to encourage visits to private homes. The privacy that Wright designed into his clients' residences must be respected. Buildings that are open to visitors are so noted in the text.

MA Massachusetts

01002 **Amherst**
         38 Shays St.   **Baird**, 277

NH New Hampshire

03104 **Manchester**
         117 Heather St.   **Kalil**, 387
         223 Heather St.   **Zimmerman**, 333

CT Connecticut

06840 **New Canaan**
         432 Frog Town Road   **Rayward**, 383
06903 **Stamford**
         121 Woodchuck Rd.   **Sander**, 354

NJ New Jersey

07028 **Glen Ridge**
         63 Chestnut Hill Pl.   **Richardson**, 282
07924 **Bernardsville**
         Jockey Hollow Rd.   **Christie**, 278
08034 **Cherry Hill**
         375 Kings Hwy.   **Sweeton**, 325
08849 **Millstone**
         Main St.   **Wilson**, 366

NY New York

10022 **New York City**
         430 Park Ave.   **Hoffman Auto Showroom**,
                                    380

10028 **New York City**
         Metropolitan Museum   **Little Residence II** (living
         of Art   room), 173
         1071 Fifth Ave.   **Guggenheim Museum**, 400

10306 **Richmond**
         48 Manor Ct.   **Cass**, 410

10541 **Lake Mahopac**
         Petra Island   **Chahroudi**, 346

10570 **Pleasantville**
         Usonia Rd.   **Reisley**, 318
         Laurel Hill Dr.   **Serlin**, 317
         Orchard Brook Dr.   **Sol Friedman**, 316

10580 **Rye**
         North Manursing Island   **Hoffman Residence**, 390

11021 **Great Neck Estates**
         9A Myrtle Ave.   **Rebhuhn**, 240

14047 **Darby**
         Lakeshore (Piarist Fathers) **Darwin D. Martin
                                    Residence, "Graycliff"** and
                                    "Graycliff" Garage, 225,
                                    226

New York (*continued*)

14214	**Buffalo**	
	125 Jewett Pkwy.	**Darwin D. Martin**
		Residence, 100
	118 Summit Ave.	**Barton**, 103
14216	**Buffalo**	
	57 Tillinghast Pl.	**Davidson**, 149
14222	**Buffalo**	
	76 Soldiers Pl.	**Heath**, 105
14610	**Rochester**	
	16 East Blvd.	**Boynton**, 147

PA Pennsylvania

15421	**Chalkhill**	
	Ohiopyle Rd.	**Hagan**, 377
15464	**Mill Run**	
	Bear Run	**Kaufmann Residence**
		"Fallingwater,"
		Guesthouse, and
		Guesthouse Alterations,
		230-232
19003	**Ardmore**	
	152-158 Sutton Rd.	**Suntop Homes**, 248
19117	**Elkins Park**	
	Old York Rd. at Foxcroft	**Beth Sholom Synagogue**,
		373

DE Delaware

| 19809 | **Wilmington** | |
| | | Private Residence, 402 |

MD Maryland

20034	**Bethesda**	
	7927 Deepwell Dr.	**Llewellyn Wright**, 358
21215	**Baltimore**	
	6807 Cross Country Blvd.	**Euchtman**, 270

VA Virginia

22101	**McLean**	
		Private Residence, 357
22121	**Mount Vernon**	
	Woodlawn Plantation	**Pope**, 268
23455	**Virginia Beach**	
		Cooke, 360

SC South Carolina

| 29609 | **Greenville** | |
| | 9 West Avondale Dr. | **Austin**, 345 |

South Carolina (*continued*)

29945   **Yemassee**
        Auld Brass Plantation   **Stevens Residence, Two Cottages, Guesthouse**, and **Stables with Kennels,** 261-264

FL Florida

32303   **Tallahassee**
        3117 Okeeheepkee Rd.   **George Lewis,** 359

33802   **Lakeland**
        South Johnson Ave. at   **Florida Southern College,** Lake Hollingsworth Dr.   251-258

AL Alabama

35630   **Florence**
        117 Riverview Dr.   **Rosenbaum,** 267 **(Addition,** 267A)

TN Tennessee

37404   **Chattanooga**
        334 North Crest Rd.   **Shavin,** 339

MS Mississippi

39216   **Jackson**
        306 Glenway Dr.   **Hughes,** 303

39564   **Ocean Springs**
        6 Holcomb Blvd.   **Louis Sullivan Summer Residence** and **Stables,** 5, 6

        East Beach (next to   **Charnley Summer** 6 Holcomb)   **Residence** and **Guesthouse,** 7, 8

KY Kentucky

40601   **Frankfort**
        509 Shelby St.   **Ziegler,** 164

OH Ohio

44057   **North Madison**
        6363 West Lake Rd.   **Staley,** 335

44074   **Oberlin**
        127 Woodhaven Dr.   **Weltzheimer,** 311

44094   **Willoughby Hills**
        2203 River Rd.   **Penfield,** 365

44709   **Canton**
        452 Santa Clara Dr. N.W.   **Feiman,** 371
        518 44th St. N.W.   **Rubin,** 343

44714   **Canton**
        5120 Plain Center Ave. N.E. **Dobkins,** 362

45220   **Cincinnati**
        1 Rawson Woods Circle   **Boulter,** 379

Ohio (*continued*)

45237 **Amberley Village**
6980 Knoll Rd.   Tonkens, 386

45243 **Indian Hill**

Private Residence, 423

45429 **Dayton**
5441 Far Hills Ave.   Meyers Medical Clinic,
397

45505 **Springfield**
1340 East High St.   Westcott, 99

IN **Indiana**

46368 **Ogden Dunes**
Cedar Trail at The Ledge   Armstrong, 260

46601 **South Bend**
715 West Washington St.   DeRhodes, 125

46614 **South Bend**
1404 Ridgedale Rd.   Mossberg, 302

46952 **Marion**
1119 Overlook Rd.   Davis, 324

47906 **West Lafayette**
1301 Woodland Ave.   Christian, 375

MI **Michigan**

48013 **Bloomfield Hills**
5045 Pon Valley Rd.   Melvyn Maxwell Smith,
287
1925 North Woodward   Affleck, 274
Ave.

48104 **Ann Arbor**
227 Orchard Hills Dr.   Palmer, 332

48170 **Plymouth**
12221 Beck Rd.   Goddard, 364
12305 Beck Rd.   Wall, 281

48221 **Detroit**
2760 West Seven Mile Rd.   Turkel, 388

48864 **Okemos**
2410 Hulett Rd.   Goetsch-Winckler, 269
2504 Arrow Head Rd.   Edwards, 313
2527 Arrow Head Rd.   Brauner, 312
1155 Wrightwind Dr.   Schaberg, 328

49001 **Kalamazoo**
2662 Taliesin Dr.   McCartney, 299
2806 Taliesin Dr.   Eric V. Brown, 300
2816 Taliesin Dr.   Levin, 298
2822 Taliesin Dr.   Winn, 301

49022 **Benton Harbor**
1150 Miami Rd.   Anthony, 315

Michigan (*continued*)

49053	**Galesburg**	
	11036 Hawthorne Dr.	**Pratt**, 295
	11098 Hawthorne Dr.	**Eppstein**, 296
	11108 Hawthorne Dr.	**Meyer**, 297
	11185 Hawthorne Dr.	**Weisblat**, 294
49085	**Saint Joseph**	
	207 Sunnybank	**Harper**, 329
	2704 Highland Ct.	**Schultz**, 426
49117	**Grand Beach**	
	Crescent Rd.	**Vosburgh**, 197
	13303 Lakeview	**W. S. Carr**, 199
	13189 Lakeview	**Joseph J. Bagley**, 198
49416	**Whitehall**	
	5260 South Shore Dr.	**George Gerts**, 77
	5324 & 5370 South Shore Drive	**Mrs. Thomas H. Gale Summer Residence** and **Residence Duplicate I**, 88, 89
49503	**Grand Rapids**	
	450 Madison Ave. S.E.	**May**, 148
	505 College Ave. S.E.	**Amberg**, 166
49670	**Northport**	
	North Peterson Park Rd.	**Alpaugh**, 293
49754	**Marquette Island**	
	Les Cheneaux Club	**Heurtley Summer Residence Remodeling**, 75
49855	**Marquette**	
	Deertrack, County 492	**Abby Beecher Roberts**, 236

IA Iowa

50158	**Marshalltown**	
	Woodfield Rd.	**Sunday**, 393
50323	**Des Moines**	
	6880 North West Beaver Dr.	**Trier**, 398
50401	**Mason City**	
	West State St. at South Federal	**City National Bank Building** and **Hotel**, 155, 156
	West State St. at South Enterprise	
	311 First St. S.E.	**Stockman**, 139
50616	**Charles City**	
	1107 Court St.	**Miller**, 289
52326	**Quasqueton**	
	Cedar Rock on Wapsipinicon River	**Walter Residence** and **River Pavilion**, 284, 285
52403	**Cedar Rapids**	
	3400 Abel Dr. S.E.	**Grant**, 288
52577	**Oskaloosa**	
	1907 A Ave. East	**Alsop**, 304
	117 North Park Ave.	**Lamberson**, 305

53115	**Lake Delevan**	
	3459 South Shore Dr.	**A. P. Johnson**, 87
	3409 South Shore Dr.	**Wallis Summer Residence**, 79
	3335 South Shore Dr.	**Fred B. Jones Residence, Gate Lodge, Barn with Stables,** and **Boathouse,** 83-86
	3211 South Shore Dr.	**Charles S. Ross**, 82
	3209 South Shore Dr.	**George W. Spencer**, 81
53118	**Dousman**	
	Highway 67	**Greenberg**, 372
53208	**Milwaukee**	
	1102-1112 North 27th St.	**Munkwitz Duplex Apartments**, 200
53211	**Milwaukee**	
	2420 North Terrace Ave.	**Bogk**, 196
53215	**Milwaukee**	
	1835 South Layton Blvd.	**Richards Bungalow**, 203
	2714 West Burnham Blvd.	**Richards Small House**, 202
	2720-2732 West Burnham Blvd.	**Richards Duplex Apartments**, 201
53217	**Fox Point**	
	7111 North Barnett	**Albert Adelman**, 308
53217	**Bayside**	
	1001 West Jonathan	**Mollica**, 411
53225	**Wauwatosa**	
	North 92nd at West Congress St.	**Greek Orthodox Church**, 399
53402	**Wind Point**	
	33 East 4 Mile	**Herbert F. Johnson**, 239
53403	**Racine**	
	1525 Howe St.	**S. C. Johnson Administration Building** and **Research Tower**, 237, 238
	1319 South Main St.	**Hardy**, 115
53405	**Racine**	
	1425 Valley View Dr.	**Keland**, 368
53549	**Jefferson**	
	332 East Linden Dr.	**Richard Smith**, 337
53562	**Middleton**	
	3037 Old Sauk Rd.	**Jacobs Second Residence**, 283
53581	**Richland Center**	
	316 South Church St.	**German Warehouse**, 183
53588	**Wyoming Valley**	
	Route 23	**Wyoming Valley Grammar School**, 401

Minnesota (*continued*)

55416 **Minneapolis**
       2801 Burnham Blvd.   **Neils**, 314

55416 **Saint Louis Park**

                                   Olfelt, 427

55720 **Cloquet**
       Route 33 at Stanley Ave.   **Lindholm Residence**, 353
       Route 45 at Route 33   **Lindholm Service Station,**
                                   414

55901 **Rochester**
       22 Skyline Dr. S. W.   **Bulbulian**, 292
       36 Skyline Dr. S. W.   **Keys**, 321
       1532 Woodland Dr. S. W.   **McBean**, 413

55912 **Austin**
       309 21st St. S. W.   **Elam**, 336

MT   Montana

59829 **Darby**
       Bunkhouse Rd.   **Como Orchard Summer**
                                   Colony, 144

59937 **Whitefish**
       341 Central Ave.   **Lockridge Medical Clinic,**
                                   425

IL   Illinois

60010 **Barrington Hills**
       265 Donlea Rd.   **Post**, 409
       County Line Rd.   **Fredrick**, 376

60015 **Bannockburn**
       200 Thornapple   **Allan Friedman**, 403

60022 **Glencoe**
       790 Sheridan Rd.   **Brigham**, 184
       850 Sheridan Rd.   **Glasner**, 109
       1023 Meadow Rd.   **Kissam**, 192
       1027 Meadow Rd.   **William F. Ross**, 191
       1030 Meadow Rd.   **Root**, 189
       1031 Meadow Rd.   **Kier**, 190
       272 Sylvan Rd.   **Perry**, 188
       Sylvan Rd.   **Ravine Bluffs Development**
                                   Sculptures and **Bridge,**
                                   185, 186
       265 Sylvan Rd.   **Booth Residence**, 187

60025 **Glenview**

                                   John O. Carr, 327

60035 **Highland Park**
       1445 Sheridan Rd.   **Willits Residence** and
                                   Gardener's Cottage with
                                   Stables, 54, 55
       1689 Lake Ave.   **Millard**, 126
       1923 Lake Ave.   **Mary M. W. Adams**, 108

60043 **Kenilworth**
       205 Essex Rd.   **Baldwin**, 107

Illinois (*continued*)

60045	**Lake Forest** 170 North Mayflower	**Glore**, 341
60048	**Libertyville** 153 Little Saint Mary's Rd.	**Lloyd Lewis Residence** and **Farm Unit**, 265, 266
60091	**Wilmette** 507 Lake Ave.	**Baker**, 151
60126	**Elmhurst** 301 South Kenilworth Ave.	**Henderson**, 57
60134	**Geneva** 1511 Batavia Rd. 318 South Fifth	**Fabyan**, 129 **Hoyt**, 120
60170	**Plato Center** Rohrsen Rd.	**Muirhead**, 334
60302	**Oak Park** 404 Home Ave. Lake St. at Kenilworth Ave. Lake St. at Oak Park 210 Forest Ave. 238 Forest Ave. 6 Elizabeth Ct.	**George W. Smith**, 45 **Unity Church**, 96 **Scoville Park Fountain**, 94 **Thomas**, 67 **Beachy**, 117 **Mrs. Thomas H. Gale** **Residence**, 98
	313 Forest Ave. 318 Forest Ave. 333 Forest Ave. 400 Forest Ave. 408 Forest Ave. 428 Forest Ave. 951 Chicago Ave.	**Hills**, 51 **Heurtley Residence**, 74 **Moore Residence** and **Stable**, 34, 35 **Copeland Residence** **Alterations**, 158 **Copeland Garage**, 159 **Frank Lloyd Wright** **Residence** and **Playroom** **Addition**, 2, 3 **Frank Lloyd Wright Studio**, 4 (**Nooker Restoration**, 405)
	1019 Chicago Ave. 1027 Chicago Ave. 1031 Chicago Ave. 1030 Superior St. 334 North Kenilworth Ave. 611 North Kenilworth Ave. 223 North Euclid Ave. 317 North Euclid Ave. 321 North Euclid Ave. 710 Augusta Ave. 520 North East Ave. 534 North East Ave. 636 North East Ave. 515 Fair Oaks Ave. 540 Fair Oaks Ave.	**Thomas H. Gale**, 16 **Parker**, 17 **Walter M. Gale**, 20 **Wooley**, 23 **Young Alterations**, 36 **Balch**, 168 **George Furbeck**, 43 **Charles E. Roberts Stable** **Remodeling**, 41 **Charles E. Roberts** **Residence Remodeling**, 40 **Harry S. Adams**, 179 **Cheney**, 104 **Goodrich**, 42 **W. E. Martin Residence**, 61 **Rollin Furbeck**, 44 **Fricke Residence** and **Emma Martin Alterations** and **Garage**, 58-60

Illinois (*continued*)

60305	**River Forest**	
	Auvergne Pl. at Lake Ave.	**Waller Gates**, 65
	515 Auvergne Pl.	**Winslow Residence** and
		Stable, 24, 25
	530 Edgewood Pl.	**Williams**, 33
	603 Edgewood Pl.	**Isabel Roberts**, 150 (**Scott**
		Remodeling, 394)
	562 Keystone Ave.	**Ingalls**, 161
	559 Ashland Ave.	**Davenport**, 68
	615 Lathrop Ave.	**River Forest Tennis**
		Club, 119
60420	**Dwight**	
	122 West Main St.	**Frank L. Smith Bank**, 111
60422	**Flossmoor**	
	1136 Brassie Ave.	**Nicholas**, 118
60432	**Evanston**	
	2420 Harrison St.	**Charles E. Brown**, 110
60506	**Aurora**	
	1300 Garfield Ave.	**Greene**, 176
60510	**Batavia**	
	605 North Batavia Ave.	**Gridley Residence**, 121
60521	**Hinsdale**	
	121 County Line Rd.	**Frederick Bagley**, 28
60525	**LaGrange**	
	345 South Seventh Ave.	**Hunt Residence I**, 138
	108 South Eighth Ave.	**Goan**, 29
	109 South Eighth Ave.	**Emmond**, 15
60546	**Riverside**	
	300 Scottswood Rd.	**Coonley Residence**, 135
	290 Scottswood Rd.	**Coonley Gardener's**
		Cottage, 136
	336 Coonley Rd.	**Coonley Coach House**, 137
	350 Fairbanks Rd.	**Coonley Playhouse**, 174
	150 Nuttell Rd.	**Tomek**, 128
60604	**Chicago**	
	209 South LaSalle St.	**Rookery Building**
		Remodeling, 113
60610	**Chicago**	
	1365 Astor	**Charnley Residence**, 9
60612	**Chicago**	
	3005-3017 West Carroll Ave.	**E-Z Polish Factory**, 114
	2840-2858 West Walnut St.	**Waller Apartments**, 31
	253-257 North Francisco Ave.	**Francisco Terrace Apartments**, 30
60615	**Chicago**	
	1322 East 49th St.	**Blossom Garage**, 133
	4858 Kenwood Ave.	**Blossom Residence**, 14
	4852 Kenwood Ave.	**McArthur Residence, Residence Remodeling**, and **Stable**, 11-13
	5132 Woodlawn Ave.	**Heller Residence**, 38

Illinois (*continued*)

60616	**Chicago** 3213-3219 Calumet	**Roloson Apartments,** 26
60620	**Chicago** 9326 South Pleasant Ave.	**William Adams,** 48
60626	**Chicago** 7415 Sheridan Rd.	**Bach,** 193
60628	**Chicago** 12147 Harvard Ave.	**Foster Residence** and **Stable,** 49, 50
60637	**Chicago** 5757 Woodlawn Ave.	**Robie,** 127
60643	**Chicago** 9914 Longwood Dr.	**Evans,** 140
60644	**Chicago** 42 North Central Ave.	**Walser,** 91
60653	**Chicago** 700 East Oakwood Blvd.	**Abraham Lincoln Center,** 95
60901	**Kankakee** 687 South Harrison Ave. 701 South Harrison Ave.	**Hickox,** 56 **Bradley Residence** and **Stable,** 52, 53
61008	**Belvedere** Harrison at Webster	**Pettit Mortuary Chapel,** 116
61111	**Rockford** Spring Brook Rd.	**Laurent,** 319
61606	**Peoria** 1505 West Moss	**Little Residence I** and **Stable,** 70, 71 **(Clarke Additions,** 152)
62522	**Decatur** 2 Millikin Pl. 1 Millikin Pl.	**Irving,** 165 **Mueller,** 167
62703	**Springfield** 301-327 East Lawrence Ave.	**Dana Residence** and **Lawrence Memorial Library,** 72, 73

MO   Missouri

63122	**Kirkwood** 120 North Ballas Rd.	**Kraus,** 340
63141	**Saint Louis** 865 South Masonridge Rd.	**Pappas,** 392
64111	**Kansas City** 3600 Bellview Ave.	**Sondern,** 279 **(Adler Addition,** 307)
64112	**Kansas City** 4601 Main St.	**Kansas City Community Christian Church,** 280

Missouri (*continued*)

64116   **Kansas City**
      3640 North Briarcliff Rd.   **Bott**, 404

KS Kansas

67208   **Wichita**
      255 North Roosevelt Blvd.   **Allen**, 205
      Brolund Dr. at 21st St.   **Juvenile Cultural Study Center**, 418

NE Nebraska

69001   **McCook**
      602 Norris Ave.   **Sutton**, 106

OK Oklahoma

74003   **Bartlesville**

                            Harold Price, Jr., 363
      N.E. 6th St. at Dewey Ave.   **Price Company Tower**, 355

74105   **Tulsa**
      3704 South Birmingham Ave.   **Richard Lloyd Jones**, 227

TX Texas

75219   **Dallas**
      3636 Turtle Creek Blvd.   **Dallas Theatre Center**, 395

75220   **Dallas**
      9400 Rockbrook Dr.   **Gillin**, 338

77024   **Bunker Hill**
      12020 Tall Oaks   **Thaxton**, 384

79606   **Amarillo**
      Tascosa Rd.   **Sterling Kinney**, 422

WY Wyoming

82414   **Cody**
      Greybull Hwy.   **Blair**, 351

ID Idaho

83314   **Bliss**
      Old Hagerman Hwy.   **Teater**, 352

UT Utah

84010   **Bountiful**
      1151 East North Canyon Rd.   **Stromquist**, 429

AZ Arizona

85013   **Phoenix**
      1123 West Palo Verde Dr.   **Carlson**. 326

Arizona (*continued*)

85016   **Phoenix**
      East Sahuaro Dr. at   **Arizona Biltmore Hotel**
      Camino Acequia   **and Cottages,** 221, 222
      5710 North 30th St.   **Benjamin Adelman,** 344
      5808 North 30th St.   **Boomer,** 361
      (5800) Orange Rd.   **Pauson,** 250

85018   **Phoenix**
      6836 North 36th St.   **Lykes,** 433
      5202 East Exeter Rd.   **David Wright Residence**
            and **Guesthouse,** 322, 323

85252   **Scottsdale**
      (11000) Shea Rd.   **Taliesin West,** 241-245

85253   **Paradise Valley**
      7211 North Tatum   **Harold Price, Sr.,** 378
      6422 Cheney   **Pieper,** 349

85281   **Tempe**
      Apache Blvd. at Mill Ave.   **Gammage Memorial**
            Auditorium, 432

NM   New Mexico

87552   **Pecos**

            Private Residence, 286

CA   California

90027   **Los Angeles**
      4800 Hollywood Blvd.   **Barnsdall Hollyhock House,**
            208
      4800 Hollywood Blvd.   **Barnsdall Studio Residence**
            A, 210
      4800 Hollywood Blvd.   **Los Angeles Exhibition**
            Pavilion, 382
      2607 Glendower Ave.   **Ennis,** 217

90028   **Los Angeles**
      1962 Glencoe Way   **Samuel Freeman,** 216

90049   **Brentwood Heights**
      449 Skyewiay Rd.   **Sturges,** 272

90069   **Hollywood**
      8161 Hollywood Blvd.   **Storer,** 215

90210   **Beverly Hills**
      332 North Rodeo Dr.   **Anderton,** 356

90265   **Malibu**
      32436 West Mulholland   **Oboler Gatehouse, Retreat,**
      Hwy.   and **Additions,** 275, 276

91010   **Bradbury**
      5 Bradbury Hills Rd.   **Pearce,** 320

91103   **Pasadena**
      645 Prospect Crescent   **Mrs. Millard,** 214

93103   **Montecito**
      196 Hot Springs Rd.   **Stewart,** 160

California (*continued*)

93306	**Bakersfield** 4260 Country Club Dr.	**Ablin,** 428
93401	**San Luis Obispo** 1106 Pacific St.	**Kundert Medical Clinic,** 396
93635	**Los Banos** (21200) Center Ave.	**Fawcett,** 385
93921	**Carmel** Scenic Road at Martin St.	**Walker,** 306
94010	**Hillsborough** 101 Reservoir Rd.	**Bazett,** 259
94025	**Atherton** 83 Wisteria Way	**Mathews,** 331
94108	**San Francisco** 140 Maiden La.	**Morris Gift Shop,** 310
94305	**Stanford** 737 Frenchman's Rd.	**Hanna,** 235
94563	**Orinda** 6 Great Oak Circle	**Buehler,** 309
94903	**San Raphael** North San Pedro Rd. at U.S. 101	**Marin County Post Office,** **Administration Building,** and **Hall of Justice,** 415-417
94960	**San Anselmo** 259 Redwood Rd.	**Berger,** 330
95350	**Modesto** 417 Hogue Rd.	**Walton,** 421
96001	**Redding** 2850 Foothill Blvd.	**Congregational Church,** 431

OR   Oregon

97002	**Aurora** South Bank, Willamette River	**Gordon,** 419

WA   Washington

98027	**Issaquah** 212th Ave. at 24th St.	**Brandes,** 350
98166	**Normandy Park** 18971 Edgecliff Dr. S.W.	**Tracy,** 389
98467	**Tacoma** 7800 John Dower S.W.	**Griggs,** 290

Canada, Ontario

	Desbarats Sapper Island	**Pitkin,** 76

England

> **London** S.W.7
> Victoria and Albert Museum **Kaufmann Office**, 233
> Exhibition Rd.

Japan

> **Tokyo**
> 31-4, Nishi Ikebukuro **Jiyu Gakuen Girls' School,**
> 2-chome, 213
> Toshima-ku
> 1-30, Komazawa 1-chome, **Hayashi**, 206
> Setagaya-ku
>
> **Meiji Mura**
> near Inuyama City, **Imperial Hotel** (lobby
> Aichi Prefecture reconstruction), 194
>
> **Ashiya**
> 173 Yamate-cho, **Yamamura**, 212
> Ashiya-shi, Hyogo-ken

ALPHABETICAL INDEX

Works are indexed by clients and by the boldfaced part of the building titles in the catalog entries. Names of other artists working with Wright and alternate project titles are also included. Numbers refer to the catalog entry number. When a name appears in boldface, followed by catalog entry number, without further classification, it refers to a residence.

Cute Is a Four-Letter Word

Clara Conrad had every intention of hang-gliding her way through eighth grade into glorious new fields of popularity. She was sure she could swing it with the help of her friend Angel, who knew the route and how to maneuver.

First on Clara's "must list" was polishing up her basic good looks. Next, with hard work and a few inside tips on technique from Angel, she'd move into a coveted position on the Pom Pon squad. And finally, dream of dreams, she'd attract the attention of Skip Svoboda, basketball star of Harrison Junior High. How much farther could a girl go?

Clara has her setbacks in the form of Halcyon, an overbearing girl from out East; a closer involvement with a rat science experiment than she'd counted on; and gossip-laden skirmishes with other girls on the squad. But though she has to change direction, Clara isn't about to trim her wings.

In *Cute Is a Four-Letter Word*, Stella Pevsner brings humor and insight to the story of a girl's reaching out toward the world, and discovering that being "somebody" is a surface thing compared with being "somebody who cares."

Cute Is a
Four-Letter Word

Other Clarion Books by Stella Pevsner

And You Give Me a Pain, Elaine
Keep Stompin' Till the Music Stops
A Smart Kid Like You
Call Me Heller, That's My Name

Cute Is a
Four-Letter Word

STELLA PEVSNER

❈ ❈ ❈

 Houghton Mifflin/Clarion Books/New York

Cover illustration by Ruth Sanderson

Houghton Mifflin/Clarion Books
52 Vanderbilt Ave., New York, NY 10017

Library of Congress Cataloging in Publication Data

Pevsner, Stella.   Cute is a four-letter word.

Summary: A young girl discovers that being popular
and dating the most sought-after boy in the eighth grade
isn't as fulfilling as she thought it would be.
[1. School stories] I. Title.   PZ7.P44815Cu
[Fic]   79-23626 ISBN 0-395-29106-2

For Jim Giblin
and Marjorie Naughton

Cute Is a
Four-Letter Word

ONE

This was going to be The Year of the Clara.

I know the words don't have much by way of a musical ring, but what can I say? My name is Clara and this was going to be my year.

I came to that great decision one day last August, about a week before school was due to begin. Of course, to grown-ups, who break out a new calendar, along with bottles of this and that, the new year begins . . . well, you know when.

It's not International Law or anything when the new year has to occur. Various nationalities and religions set up their own dates for new beginnings, and I'm thinking right now especially of the Chinese, who have their own time and even their own names, like Year of the Horse, Year of the Monkey and so on.

To kids, for sure, the new year really begins in the fall when school starts. So that's why I decided the time was right to begin again. Clara Conrad was

1

going to shine forth as herself for a change, instead of as the girl who.

I guess the *girl who* needs some clarification.

For starters, I'm the girl whose mother is a grade school principal. So what's the big deal? I'll give an example. You have a substitute teacher, a pushover, who can't handle the class. Some funny stuff goes on. And when the day of reckoning arrives, who gets the zero-in look with the I-expected-more-of-you-people speech? Right. The daughter of the principal of another school. Or say, just for argument, said daughter tries to ease things for the substitute. You know what happens. Glares, sneers, Miss Goody-Goody remarks.

Granted, the substitute situation is a sometime thing, but every day a principal's kid has to decide whether to go along with the crowd, hang back, or be neutral.

That's one thing. Another is that I'm the *girl who* has an older sister with a fantastic talent. Laurel is eighteen, and when she plays the piano you could swear someone had slipped a Horowitz on the turntable. Not that I, personally, can snap out the name of the exact performer. I'm just giving an example.

Laurel, who drifted through her school years in a dreamlike state, became like a person possessed when seated at the piano. Over and over, chords, scales, sections of a work. When I was younger, it used to make me want to bang my head against a wall.

Angel (she's my best friend) asked me just last year how I could stand it, and I asked, "What?" because by then Laurel's playing had become a house sound like a refrigerator humming or a furnace kicking on. But having a someday-famous pianist going at it all the time had a somewhat unnerving effect on kids who stopped by.

Actually, not many kids did stop by. Not only because of the aforementioned reasons, but also because I was the *girl who* had the unenviable job as practically full-time after-school baby-sitter to one Jay Frank Fogarty.

I inherited Jay Frank, the kid next door, when he graduated from nursery school into kindergarten and have been stuck with him ever since. His mother, Sheri, who is looked down on by some of the neighbors because of her candid way of expressing herself, works at a data processing place and gets home around six. She's divorced. So Clara Conrad, sitter-next-door, has been rushing home from school for the past four years, cutting herself off from extracurriculars, losing out on fun times with the crowd, and missing out on the boy-girl events, rare though they were, that took place after school hours.

But this year, The Year of the Clara, was going to be different.

3

First, regarding Laurel, the constant sound-of-music syndrome was over because my sister had gone off to New York City where she was enrolled in the Juilliard School of Music. That place, in case you don't know, is the golden-oldie of the classical music scene. It's an *event* to be accepted at Juilliard.

Second, the idea of my being a principal's daughter had finally lost ground as a hot news item.

As for Jay Frank, he was like a Siamese twin who had finally, through the miracle of science, been cut loose from me. Actually, it was neither science nor miracle but rather a natural growth process. Sheri (she's always let me call her that) had decided that her son, now going into fourth grade, was finally capable of unlocking a door, getting his own after-school snack, and amusing himself until she got there. So that left me home free. Home, free to do as I liked. And I was going to make the most of it. Put myself first, for a change.

"Clara, Clara!" I actually said the words aloud, alone in the house that afternoon. "This is your year! You will make yourself so memorable that even the most jaded of teachers (and I could name a few) will sigh as you stride across the stage for your diploma and say, 'We shall never see the likes of her again, not in our lifetime.'"

"You will make your home such a hot-shot place for social carryings-on that people will fight for standing room on the Clara Conrad scene. And you will meet HIM. The one. The boy who will win your heart and the right to have his name printed in waterproof marker on your gym shoes." It was all going to happen!

Barefooted, I raced into the living room, leaped on and off the sofa, spun around, and with arms outstretched fluttered out to the hall. Then leaning forward, using hands as well as feet, I mounted the stairs. At the top, one arm raised, I made a proclamation: "Citizens, you have just seen the Year of the Frog, the Year of the Butterfly, the Year of the Monkey. You are now about to witness . . . the Year of the Clara!"

And that was the afternoon of the evening I first heard about Halcyon.

TWO

I was crouched over the newspaper on the living room floor, checking out the movie ads. Mom was sitting on the piano bench, idly leafing through some sheets of music. I hoped she wasn't thinking of picking up her playing where she'd left off years ago.

"Clara," she said sort of hesitantly, "there's something I want to talk to you about."

I put my finger on the point I'd reached in the listings but didn't look around. The thought came to me, Oh, boy, she's going to ask me to take lessons again, disregarding the fact that even Laurel agreed years ago that I was a lost cause as far as music was concerned.

"Mom," I said, "I can read music, I know what it's about, but I can't play it, I don't want to play it." I ran my finger down to the next listing.

"Oh, stop. This has nothing to do with piano lessons. I want to talk to you about a letter that came today."

I turned around. "Is something wrong with Laurel?"

6

"Nothing at all. But there may be some changes in her plans, and you and I are directly involved. If you'll just put that paper away and give me your attention, I'd appreciate it."

There were only a couple of more movies, and even at a glance I could see the big R ratings, like most of them these days. I flicked the paper aside and flopped into a chair. "What's up?"

Mom seemed about to say something about my flip attitude (I know that look in her eye), but she let it go.

"Annie Schuyler wrote. You remember her, don't you? My old sorority sister from back East?"

"Sure. She brought me my little jeweled cat statue that time. Is she still in the decorating business?"

"She is, but that's not what she's writing about. She has an only niece, of whom she's very fond, and that niece has a daughter. A daughter your age."

I couldn't see what all this had to do with us or with Laurel, but it was clear that Mom was building up to something. I sat there waiting.

"Annie's niece and her husband have an art gallery, and for a while it did very well, but now with the economic crush it's on relatively shaky ground. They're having to cut back on their life style, and one of the things they feel they can no longer afford is to send their daughter to an expensive boarding school."

I can't explain how at that moment I knew it, but I

7

did. This boarding school girl was the threat, the thing the letter was all about. Still, I sat there waiting. Waiting to hear what was coming next.

Mom, for once, looked a little bit at a loss, as she picked up a blue envelope lying just above the piano keys. Mom usually is in pretty good command. She has to be, dealing with kids and teachers and parents the way she does. She's old, in her late forties, and looks old, with that braided-bun hair-do and her stout figure. But nothing seems to shock her or rattle her, and I guess she's tops when it comes to dealing with tricky situations. So now, seeing her look of indecision, I got kind of nervous.

"Mom," I said, "what is it? What's the letter about?"

She looked at me directly. "Clara, we've always lived comfortably, thank goodness, and I've never had to touch the insurance your father set aside for the education of you girls. But he couldn't have known at the time he died how expenses would rise through the years."

"Do we . . . do we have to sell the house?" I knew a girl whose folks had done that. The thought was terrifying. Our house was a white elephant in a way, and maybe too big for the two of us, but it was the only home I'd ever known.

"Oh, the house." Mom gave a little fan of the letter. "We're better off hanging onto this, with the tax situation as it is. No, it's Laurel. Her expenses.

8

The bills are just horrendous. Oh, Clara, don't get alarmed," she said, as I leaned forward. "We'll manage, somehow we'll manage. It's just that now something has happened that can at least lighten the load of her expenses."

If that was the case, why this heavy conversation? Again, some signal came through to me. There was a catch. There was a catch that somehow involved me. And that girl. That girl my age. I just couldn't make the connection between her not being able to afford boarding school and our being able to afford sending my sister to Juilliard. "Can I read the letter?"

"May I," Mom said automatically. I swear, she'd correct my grammar if I were on my death-bed. "Yes, you may," she said, taking the pages from the envelope, "or I could just tell you. Annie tends to ramble."

"Then tell me. It can't be all that bad," I said, trying to lighten things up.

Mom's look shifted toward the window where, from beyond Jay Frank's house, there was open prairie. She looked back at me. "The girl I mentioned, the girl your age . . ."

Here it comes, I thought. The kicker. I tried to hold the smile.

". . . her name is Halcyon. She's attended boarding schools for years. She's accustomed to that type of school life. But, as I mentioned, her parents

9

can't manage it this year. However, they've refused financial help from the aunt, my friend Annie."

So what was the big deal? "Don't they have schools she could go to in New York City? Isn't that where they live?"

"Yes, in an apartment near Lincoln Center. But Halcyon . . ."—Mom gave a slight twist of the lips—"Halcyon is making a tremendous fuss about going to a city school there for eighth grade. She says she'd be an outsider, and oh, I don't know what all, but whatever it is, her parents can't seem to handle it."

"Huh!"

"I know, it sounds peculiar, but I gather the girl has built up some kind of ego thing about boarding school that's kept her from making friends with the two or three public school girls in her building, and she says she'd rather do anything than try to break in with them, as she puts it."

Tough toenails, I thought, but I didn't say anything.

"I guess you know what I'm getting at," Mom said.

"No, I don't." I honestly didn't right then. What did the problem of some snob kid in New York have to do with Mom and me?"

"Well, here it is. Annie came up with a suggestion, and surprisingly enough, Halcyon agreed and so did her parents." Mom paused. "You see, if Halcyon came out to live with us she'd still be going to school out of state and could save face, strange as it seems. And, there wouldn't be the financial burden on her family."

I was so dazed by this development that I just let Mom's next words—". . . and Laurel could stay in the apartment with Halcyon's parents."—fly right over my head. Mom smiled. "It would be a kind of domestic student exchange program."

"*Here?*" I kind of croaked. "That girl wants to come live here? With us, in our house?"

"Well, it's big enough, goodness knows. And actually, the experience of attending a suburban school in the Midwest might be good for Halcyon."

"For her!" I leaped out of the chair. "And what about me? How's this supposed to affect my life?"

"Well, Clara . . ." Mom looked a bit disconcerted. "I should think it would be an interesting experience for you. Having a girl your own age . . ."

"A creepy kid who thinks she's too good for public school!"

"Now, just a minute. I didn't say anything . . ."

"You said she can't or won't or whatever make friends . . ."

"I know that may be hard to understand. But Clara, you've gone through all the grades with more or less the same classmates . . ."

"Don't think all of them like me!"

11

"Come now . . ."

"Well, I'm not exactly Miss Popularity. I mean, kids like me all right and I get along pretty well, but I've had things go wrong along the way. I didn't just ease into where I am now." I knew I was babbling and more or less contradicting myself. What I meant and couldn't come out and say was that I'd had to work and work hard to prove I was a regular kid even if my mom was a principal and half my life was tied to babysitting. "They ought to just *make* her go to school there and take her knocks," I said, switching back to the real issue. "That's what I'd do, if I were the parents." I flopped back onto the chair.

Mom half smiled as she riffled the pages of the letter. "Basically, you're right, Clara. But it's not fair for you and me, out here, to make judgements. All we need be concerned about is the question of whether or not to accept the offer. That's what it amounts to."

"Does it amount to a lot of money?"

Mom hesitated. "Enough. Not an overwhelming amount, but I would say enough to make a difference."

I felt really rotten, and cornered. Rotten because I hated to agree, and cornered because I knew it was the only decent thing to do.

I lowered my head. "When would she come out?"

"School starts . . ." Mom's sentence ended in a sigh. The staff, if you can believe it, dreads opening

12

more than students, who tend to like the first couple of days.

"Very soon." I supplied her answer. "So all this is kind of sudden, isn't it?"

"Apparently the battle in Halcyon's family has been going on all summer, and everyone's been upset," Mom said. "Just recently, Laurel went to Halcyon's house on a visit with Annie, and somehow, the idea surfaced. Everyone out there thinks it's perfect."

"How about Laurel?"

Mom shrugged and smiled. "Oh, you know your sister. Give her a good piano and she's content as a clam, just anywhere."

Lucky Laurel. In a way I envied her for being so dedicated to one goal. On the other hand, I wouldn't want to have everything so clearcut. I wanted to experience a lot of things. I'd really meant it when I'd flung out my arms and raced around saying, "Here I am, world. Are you ready for me?"

"What are your feelings, Clara?"

I came back with a clearing of throat. "It's okay with me, I guess, if you guys . . . you grown-ups . . . work it out." Maybe it wouldn't work out. "As I said, it seems awfully sudden, but . . ."

"I'll call Annie, I think. And get a few more facts. And then call Laurel."

"Are you going to call the parents, too?"

"No, I should think they would call me."

That's what I was thinking. "Do you have a picture of that girl?" I couldn't bring myself to say her name.

"Of Halcyon? No. Why?"

"Just curious." She was probably a real gross-ball. I faked a yawn, stood up, stretched, and mumbled something about going up to listen to some rock.

Mom took hold of my hand as I started to pass by, and pressed it against her cheek. "Clara," she said as I paused, "I know we haven't spent a lot of time together lately. I—well, I was looking forward . . ." She didn't seem to know how to put it so I helped her out.

". . . to a quiet year?" (I really didn't mean that as a slam against Laurel and her playing.)

Mom laughed. "Let's say I was looking forward to our having quiet times this last year of yours in grade school. Before . . ."

I guess she meant before I got involved in the hyped-up activities of high school. Little did she know I wasn't waiting. I was going to begin NOW.

"Oh, well." I gave her a light kiss on the cheek and tore upstairs.

But in my room, I stood, wondering. Was it really going to begin . . . my Year of the Clara . . . when I fully intended to fly free? Or would this Halcyon blast in like rough weather and send me into a tailspin?

Well, I wouldn't let her. I was going to be in charge. I was, I was.

I walked to the mirror and looked at my reflection. "You are, Clara," I told it. It didn't look altogether convinced.

THREE

The next day my best friend, Angel Barclay, came over and Fergy McNutt trailed behind, looking agreeable as usual. Fergy is a fairly tall, thin kid with stringy hair and glasses and not much going for him in the looks department. That doesn't seem to make any difference to Fergy, and neither does the fact that behind his back, or even to his face, kids call him Nuttsy.

"What brings the two of you over here together?" I asked, putting it bluntly. I'd known both of them for years, but usually they didn't travel as a pair.

"We have a little proposition to put to you," Angel said, glancing around the backyard. "Do you mind if I sun myself while we talk? There isn't too much time left to set my tan."

She dragged our aluminum and plastic chaise from under the tree, flipped the pad over to the cleaner underside and, checking the sky, got out of her jeans and scoop-necked top. Her tan, going in all directions from the green bikini she had on underneath, looked pretty well set to me. And her shape was pretty well established, too.

Angel lay on her stomach and watched as Fergy and I dragged up webbed chairs to the edge of the shade and sat like spectators at a varsity show.

"Well?" I said, feeling kind of silly without knowing why. "What's the proposition?"

"Tell her, Fergy," Angel said, propping herself up on her arms and pulling at her bangs. Angel's bangs are separated at the center and pulled out to little blond wings at the side. They're like a trademark.

"Rats," Fergy said. "We want to raise rats." He tilted his white canvas hat forward to shade his eyes. "Preferably in your cellar."

I sat there for I don't know how many seconds.

"Well?" Angel finally said. "Do you have any objections?"

"Did you say . . . rats in our cellar?" I looked at Fergy, who was stretched as far as he could while still staying attached to the chair seat. "Why our cellar? And why raise rats at all?"

"Your cellar because our house doesn't have any, and Angel's is all fixed up as a family room." Fergy paused to let that register. "As for the rats, they're going to be our experiment for the science fair in January. We can get them from a lab, guaranteed free of disease."

"Oh, that's wonderful," I said. "I wouldn't want any diseased rats running around the house."

17

"They won't be running anywhere," Angel said serenely. "We'll keep them in cages. Won't we, Fergy?"

"I can get the cages, too," Fergy said. "The only problem is space, and that's how come we thought of your cellar, Clara. You don't use it for anything that I can recall."

Angel lowered her head to the chaise and let her arms dangle over the sides. She picked at a blade of grass. "Your mother surely wouldn't object. I mean, it *is* an educational project."

"You guys! *I'd* object! I don't want those creepy little things in my house. Not for a science project or anything else."

"People can get quite attached to rats," Fergy said in his mild, agreeable voice. "Even people who as a general rule don't care for mice."

"Not me. I'd never get attached. And besides, what if you two got sick or busy or something and couldn't get over to take care of them? Huh? How about that?"

"Clara," Angel said, She gazed at me with those Botticelli blue eyes. The very eyes that had knocked over hearts like a row of dominoes, beginning with kindergarten, and which last year had claimed the undying affection of Skip Svoboda, basketball hero of Harrison Junior High. "Do you honestly believe that either Fergy or I would shirk our duties for any reason whatsoever?"

I couldn't honestly believe they would. Fergy had never missed a deadline as editor of the school paper, had never had to ask for extra time when a paper was due, and had never received anything but rave reviews at parent-teacher conferences. As for Angel, her fly-away heavenly looks were deceptive. She was a down-to-earth meat and potatoes person when it came to the banquet of life.

I have to tell you something about Angel Barclay. She is as close to a programmed person as I ever hope to meet. To show you how planned she is, I can reveal this fact: Her name was picked out before she was even born, and her looks met the specifications. "What if you'd been a boy?" I asked her once.

"*What ifs* are a waste of time," she answered.

Fergy hoisted himself up. "If you don't mind, Clara, I'd like to check out the cellar for dampness. It's a long time since I've been down there. Also, I'd better check the ventilation."

"Check the cobwebs, while you're at it," I called after him. "And the grime."

"You're being surprisingly negative about this," Angel said. She gave a little shriek as she brushed an ant from her wrist.

"I just don't understand your sudden interest in science," I said. "Fergy, yes. He's the type all right. But you?"

"I've been revising my Plan. And science, I discovered, is an area I've overlooked." Angel flipped to

19

her back and spoke into the sky. "I'm giving up Pom Pon Squad, Clara. One year is enough. It doesn't get you anything."

"It got you Skip Svoboda."

"I've put a question mark after Skip."

"A *what?* You *mean?*" Stunned, I stared at Angel.

"Don't get me wrong. Skip's fine, for what he is. But . . ."

"Are you actually trying to tell me you don't like Skip any more?" The very suggestion nearly wiped me out.

"I like him. But there's really no place for him in my Plan. It seems this whole past year was kind of a waste. A floating thing. I need to get back to solid ground and fasten some moorings. That's why Fergy's science thing with the rats attracts me."

From Skip Svoboda to rats. Only Angel could ever consider a switch like that. Here *I* was, thinking of how I wanted to fly free this year . . . hang-glide my way through eighth . . . and here *she* was, just the opposite. "Angel," I said, "I find you hard to believe. Tossing all the good things aside, just like that. Everything I've envied." Just in time I added, "Like Pom Pon."

Angel squinted one eye against the glare of the sun and fixed the other on me. "You want to make Pom Pon?"

Did I want to make Pom Pon? Does a rock band

want to hit the charts? Does a model want to make the cover of V*ogue?* "I wouldn't mind," I said.

"Then how about making a deal? If you turn over the cellar to us and our experiment, I'll turn over my position on the Pom Pon Squad to you."

My heart fluttered like a pennant. Need I tell you that getting into Pom Pon is every junior high girl's idea of paradise? The costumes, the excitement, the glory!

While I wasn't quite ready to accept the fact that even Angel could cast aside someone like Skip, the Pom Pon nix was possible. Angel had been into a lot of things, like chess, figure skating, weaving, Berlitz Russian. But as soon as she got good at them, she'd go on to something else. She'd been captain of the squad last year, so in her mind that could have been it for Pom Pon.

"You really mean it?" I said, staring. "You'd really turn over your place on Pom Pon to me?"

Angel gave a shrug that said *Sure, why not?*

"But I've never even tried out."

"Clara, how could you? All these years tied up with little Pesty next door. You're free now. Free to turn cartwheels."

"Yeh. But Angel, once the word gets out that there's a place vacant you know what'll happen. There'll be such a mad rush of bodies I won't stand a chance."

21

"Leave that to me. I'll get you on. We'll have a few coaching sessions. I'll teach you all the tryout tricks, and I'll get you that position before the rest of the girls wake up and smell the Ovaltine."

With anyone else that would have been so much hogwash. But Angel means what she says. She's so organized that when she goes into action things fall into place for her. No question about it.

She has a Life Plan, a Weekly Plan, and a Today's Plan. She has a notebook with spaces marked off for each division.

I operate on a far simpler plan: Get through today. With the sub-head, Do Not Procrastinate. I'm terrible the way I put things off. Maybe if I made lists like Angel, I'd go ahead and get things done. But I put off making lists.

Angel let me look at her Life Plan once. It had things in it like:

Age 14–18 *High School*

Besides required courses, each year take a subject in a different field to test aptitude and interest.

Each year, different type of after-school and summer job.

Class President—junior year.

Visit colleges between junior and senior year.
Make selection.

Senior year. Accept favorite college.

Age 18–22   Attend college.

Age 22   Graduate with honors.

Age 22–23   Year abroad, filling in cultural gaps.

Age 23–27   Get well established in career. Develop meaningful hobbies in preparation for enriched middle years.

Age 27   Marry (?)

Age 29   Have child (????)

"Why did you put the question mark after marriage?" I asked her. "Don't you think there'll be any single guys around by then?"

"The way things are going, there may not be *marriage*," Angel said. "No, really, you never know, so I don't like to plan ahead too far."

That was the day, I think, that I couldn't decide whether to walk to town and buy a birthday card for my aunt or just hang around the house and write a letter.

Fergy came back, slapping his canvas hat against his leg to knock off the cobwebs. "Place looks perfect," he said. "Just needs a little cleaning up. Okay if we come over Saturday?"

"Hey . . . I didn't say! Besides . . . my mother."

Fergy patted my shoulder. "You'll handle that okay. You leaving, Angel?"

She checked her watch. "I'm ready."

As she started putting her clothes back on, I thought of something. "Saturday? Saturday isn't so good. That's the day I'm getting a new sister."

You could hear the snap on Angel's jeans clink shut. "You're *what?*"

"On Saturday. I tried to call and tell you but you're always off somewhere."

Angel glanced toward the house. "New sister? What do you mean?"

"A live-in sister is what I mean I'm getting. Some kid from New York City. It's kind of a trade. Laurel's going to live with *her* parents."

"Isn't this kind of sudden?" Angel asked. "How old is she, anyway?"

"Our age. And sure, it's sudden. I'm not too thrilled about it, but what can I do?"

"What's her name?" Angel went on.

"*Hal*cyon." I made it sound nasal.

"Mmmm. Interesting."

"It's dorky," I said.

"Actually, it's Greek." Fergy furrowed his brow. "There was a goddess Halcyone, I believe, who pitched herself into the drink because . . . uh . . . because. I don't remember exactly. But it was probably over some guy. Goddesses were always doing themselves in over unrequited love."

"I wouldn't," Angel said.

24

"You're not a goddess, Angel," Fergy said. "Try to keep that in mind."

Before they got any further along on the kidding-insult routine, I broke in, "Halcyon's a boarding-school kid. And like me, she may not be hot on the idea of rats in the cellar. It's going to be hard enough for her to get used to living out here in the boonies. So don't take the rat deal as a sure thing, you guys."

Angel looked at me. "Pom Pon" was all she said.

I pictured those crimson sweaters and the white pleated skirts. And I could feel the tingle rising from my sneakers and jetting straight to my scalp as the applause bounced from the bleachers. I couldn't let all that slip by.

"If you could just put it off until next week?" I walked them toward the front yard. "On account of Halcyon?"

"Okay. Next week," Fergy said.

Angel gave a twist to her wings. "On account of Halcyon. I wonder, Clara, if you know what you're getting into with this girl."

I was wondering all right.

Angel and Fergy left and I returned to the back yard. I began thinking about how little control I had over my life. How could I have known a week ago that that kid from New York was going to come live with us? How could I have known this morning that we were going to have rat boarders in the basement?

25

And could I have guessed, even an hour ago, that a terrific Pom Pon plum was about to fall into my frail little hands?

One thing was clear. The Year of the Clara was going to be one big bundle of surprises. So . . . I'd go with the flow and make the most of everything.

I started turning cartwheels, and you know what? I was dynamite. "Watch out, world!" I said, reaching toward the sky.

It was a good thing I looked up at that moment. A bird was flying low and dropped a little excess baggage that just missed my head.

In every way, my life was dropping little surprises.

FOUR

After the cartwheels, and especially after the rat talk I felt like showering, but I'd promised Mom faithfully that I'd clean out Laurel's room *today*. ("Clara, just get at it.") After lugging those boxes around I'd probably feel like another shower.

"Put everything away in categories," Mom had ordered. "Clothes, books, and so on. Label the boxes and then put them in the back of her closet."

"Why does it have to be today?" I asked in my usual put-off fashion.

"Because."

Long ago, I'd learned there was no use arguing when Mom used that particular tone.

I started with Laurel's closet. She had taken along some summer clothes and most of her fall things. I packed what was left into separate boxes, labeled *Summer*, *Fall*, and *Winter*. We'd send the winter things later.

My sister hadn't dreamed, when she left, that someone else would be using her room, or I'll bet

27

she'd have gotten rid of lots of stuff. But maybe not. There were no juicy notes or hate lists. Just programs from recitals, concert programs, music notebooks. I put it all into a box and labeled it *Nostalgia*. If anyone ever went through my stuff—and I cringed at the thought—they'd probably label it *Garbage*. But to each his own, I say.

I was about to tackle things from the tops of dresser, desk, and bedside table when I heard the Day Camp bus grind to a halt on the corner, followed by the yells of the escapees. As usual, a couple of minutes later, the front doorbell rang.

"Hey, come on in, Jay Frank," I yelled down the stairs. Since we don't have air conditioning, we do have direct contact with the outdoors, which can be fairly convenient at times.

I collapsed on the top step, and as soon as I heard the screen door slam, called out, "I'm up here."

Jay Frank came to the foot of the stairs, and I have to say that as grimy and sweaty as I looked and felt, I was Miss Plastic-Wrapped Perfection compared to Jay Frank. At best, he's kind of a sorry-looking excuse of a kid, with that skinny little nine-year-old body and a face that can only bring to mind the word "pathetic." Today, he looked like the last straggler from an obstacle course.

"Hey, Jay Frank, want to come upstairs and help?" He wouldn't be much help, but I had to keep on with the cleaning.

"Help with what?"

"Oh, well." I started down because habit is stronger than resolution, and I had long been in the habit of mother-henning Jay Frank.

"Rough day, huh?" I said, when I got the close-up shot of his thin face, awash with streaks of dirty sweat. The hair in front of his ears and along his neck was clinging in damp little clumps.

"I have a headache and the bus driver made the kids shut the windows when they started to spit out and then they sang *Ninety-Nine Cans of Beer on the Wall* real loud and they got down to seventeen before I got off."

If Jay Frank had told all that to his mother, Sheri would have said something like, "That's life, kid." It's not that she's insensitive. She just believes in toughening up her son's hide to ward off the slings and arrows of life, as they say.

"Come on out to the kitchen," I told him. "Hawaiian Punch fights headaches three ways."

We sat opposite each other at the kitchen table and split a can and discussed his day, which had contained everything guaranteed to de-energize kids so they'd pass out the minute they got home, because that's what the parents were paying for.

"I haven't had such a fun day, either," I told Jay Frank, after he'd recited his sorry tale.

"Whatcha been doing?"

I told him about all the work that had been piled onto me because of the Halcyon creature. Then I got around to telling him about the rats.

"I'll help," he offered, perking up. His face was a sight to behold, what with the dried sweat, the dirt, and now smears of pink around his lips. "I'll come over every day after school and . . ."

"Hey." I just had to interrupt him. "There's a new game plan, remember? I'm not going to be your sitter any more. That means . . ."

His face seemed to shrivel a little. "I know." He turned away on the chair, and I could hear the teentsy sound of shoe laces against the linoleum. Or did I just imagine it? At least one of his sneakers was always untied.

"I have to go home," he said to empty space. He picked up his glass and took it to the sink and washed it. That was another thing Sheri rammed home. *Pick up after yourself, kid*. He still had to lean forward slightly to reach the faucet and I thought, he's too little. It isn't right for him to be on his own. Not yet.

"Hang around a while," I said. "Keep me company while I finish Laurel's room. You don't have to help."

He touched the bump of his new house key under his T-shirt. "I guess I'll just go home and lie down a while."

"Hey, Jay Frank!" I said, faking excitement. "You did it after all my years of harping. Said *lie* instead of *lay!*"

"Chickens lay, people lie," he said, with a thin smile, repeating the phrase I'd told him over and over.

Not content with that progress, I pushed on. "And are you *lying* down or *laying* down?" Living with a principal leaves its mark.

"I'm not doing either," Jay Frank said with a steady look. "What I'm doing is leaving. Good-bye."

"See you," I said to the back of him as he let himself out. The screen door clicked shut, and I was left standing there.

I felt like a rat. A rat deserting a sinking ship. Jay Frank wasn't sinking, but all the same he didn't need that shove from me.

Because Mom is a firm believer in pleasant dinner conversation, I put my two pressing topics on hold until after we'd finished eating.

"Oh, by the way . . ." I started off as we were clearing the table. I stopped as Mom gave me a slightly alarmed look.

" 'Oh, by the way' is a phrase that makes parents wary," she said after a moment.

"Why is that?"

"Because it's often followed with words like, "I'm

31

to be a Stop Sign in the traffic play tomorrow and I need a costume."

"Mom! That happened way back in the third grade. Lately, I've felt more like *Yield* on the Highway of Life."

I thought I was doing pretty well saying that right off the top of my head, but Mom looked more taken aback than impressed.

"Would you care to explain that remark, Clara?"

Again, a snap answer. "Everyone always wants me to give way for their own convenience."

That hit the mark. *Halcyon*. I didn't have to say the word. Mom had no moss on her. "But it's not all that bad," I continued, "because I finally have a chance to do something *I* want to do." Meaningful pause. "I'm going out for Pom Pon this year."

"Pom Pon, Clara?" Mom looked truly surprised. "What suddenly brought that on? And is it something you want to do? Seriously, now?"

"Mom! Any girl in Harrison Junior High would shave her head bald to get on Pom Pon."

"I had no idea."

"That's because you're in K-6 where games are just games. Pom Pon's the real stuff, Mom."

"And the competition is keen, you say?"

"Deadly. But Angel's promised to help me. She's going to coach me to take *her* place." I stuck the plates into the dishwasher. "There's just one little thing . . . a kind of favor . . ."

"Yes?"

I almost hyperventilated with a single breath. "Angel and Fergy, in return, would like to set up a bunch of rat cages. With rats. In our . . . cellar?"

Mom stared. And stared. And stared.

"Don't you . . . don't you get it?" I was becoming a little disconcerted. "They use rats for experiments—scientists—and this is a school science fair project and . . ."

"Are you saying . . ." Now Mom's face was kind of puffed with unbelievability. "Saying that your friends plan to dissect animals here . . . in our house?"

"Dissect! Mom, what do you think they are, a couple of zombies on the loose? They just want to keep rats."

"For what purpose, precisely?"

I hadn't thought to ask, precisely, and that was really too bad. "Like I told you, for a science fair project," I said, as though she was at fault for not paying attention. "One of those little things they do . . . you know . . . for science fairs," I repeated lamely.

"Why our cellar?" I wasn't crazy about the tone Mom's voice had taken.

"Because they don't have any other place."

"Clara, did you tell them they could use our cellar, without even . . ."

"I said I'd have to talk it over with you, but I didn't

33

see how you could mind, because it's educational."

"It's also smelly and a nuisance. And a responsibility."

"You know Angel and Fergy," I protested. "They're as responsible as anyone can get."

"Experiments. I don't like the sound of that word at all," Mom said.

I could see her point. And I could also see that crimson Pom Pon sweater and pleated skirt on someone like Doris Sycow, instead of me. "Behavior!" The word just leaped into my mind. "Animal behavior. That's what they're studying, or will, if you'll just . . ."

"Oh?"

"And you've got to admit that's very important for man . . . I mean . . . humankind. Why people—psychologists—learn all kinds of things from studying the habits of animals. Even if they are only rats."

"I see. When did this whole subject come up?"

"Just today. I told Angel and Fergy I couldn't make any promises until I'd checked it out with you." I sounded so self-righteous I couldn't believe it. What *had* I said, as a matter of fact? "But I told them you probably wouldn't mind." I remembered that much. "I also said they shouldn't count on anything until next week, after Halcyon gets here." I sniffed, just a little, to show how well I was bearing up under this handicap.

Mom poured dishwasher stuff into the compartment and set the dial. "Speaking of Halcyon, is her room ready?"

"Ummm." I'd never quite got back to it after Jay Frank left. "Partly. It's partly ready. I'll be sure to have it done before she gets here Saturday."

"Clara. Go up and finish it. Now."

I sighed. "All right. But could I call Angel first?"

"If it's vital."

"I've got to let her know, Mom. About the rats . . . the behavior experiment with the rats. Is it okay, Mom?"

Silence.

I looked around from the phone. Mom was standing like a giant post, eyes closed, a resigned look on her face. She was making a *Yield* sign with her fingers.

FIVE

Mom and I stood by the window in the airport waiting area where Halcyon was supposed to disembark, watching planes taxi in and out.

"How are we supposed to recognize her?" I asked. "Did her folks send a mug shot?" If so, I hadn't seen it. I was feeling pretty nervous about meeting this kid face to face.

"No," Mom said. "But I doubt there would be two girls your age traveling on this precise plane alone. And she'll be on the lookout for us. I think that's her plane now."

It seemed like forever as we watched the jet maneuver into position. Finally people started trickling down the carpeted corridor and into our area. Suddenly Mom said, "There she is!"

And there she was. There could be no doubt of it.

The girl I saw was about my height, but heavier. She had long, dark hair smoothed back by a headband and wore tight pants and a fluttery Madras top. All this was topped by a peevish look.

Her name (we'd looked it up) was Greek all right,

36

and it meant calm and tranquil. Halcyon looked ready to explode. From her expression you'd think she'd expected a path to be cleared for her. Instead she was stuck in the mob, loaded down as she was with an overnight bag, purse, camera, and tennis racquet.

Mom started forward, like a tugboat through the crowd, and I bobbed along in her wake. Mom reached Halcyon, held out a hand in welcome, and after a bit of shifting, a hand reached out.

"And this is my daughter, Clara," Mom said as I shuffled up.

"Hi." I held out my hand and got the strap of a canvas bag hooked onto it. I almost pitched forward from the weight. "Is this everything?" I asked, really believing it was possible.

Halcyon gave me a withering look. "My baggage is *checked*," she said. "I just hope they didn't lose anything."

"We'll get it," Mom said, unperturbed. "How was the flight, Halcyon?"

"Terrible. You can just bet I'm going to have my father complain to the airline about the hassle they gave me about my things. Oh! My prints!" She dropped everything but her purse and camera and dashed over to a stewardess just emerging from the tunnel. The stewardess, looking none too pleased, went back toward the plane, with Halcyon following.

I lowered the bag to the floor and looked at Mom. "Calm. Tranquil," I murmured.

Halcyon came back carrying a cardboard carton with a handle attached. The stewardess walked over to the desk, said something to the man there, and they gave us the kind of looks that let us know we were not all-time favorites. Halcyon started picking up her stuff.

"I'll carry the tennis racquet," Mom said, which was a smart move.

"I'll take something else for balance," I said, and reached out for the camera case.

Halcyon jerked back. "Oh, no. No one carries this but me. It's a Leica, and my father would go into cardiac arrest if anything happened to it. You can take this." She handed me a tote bag that practically pulled my arm out of the socket.

When we reached the luggage claim, Halcyon dragged out three bags, one of them super-size.

Blinking, Mom said, "I'll try to find someone to help."

She came back with a guy in uniform. "I'll get the car," she said. "You girls wait out at the curb with all this."

We waited a long time, Halcyon and I, in the heat of that Saturday noon, with the roar of the jets and the fumes soaking into every pore.

"I just can't believe this scene," Halcyon said, pacing like an executive. "Here I am, nauseated, and now this delay."

"I guess if they'd known, they'd have built the garage closer."

"In New York you don't have this kind of inconvenience. I need a coke. Where's the refreshment stand?"

" 'Way back inside. There isn't time."

Halcyon hoisted the biggest bag on end, sat on it, crossed her arms, and tapped her foot. I had the feeling that I could fade into the exhaust fumes and disintegrate and Halcyon would neither notice nor be able to give a description of me to the police.

"I'll have that tote bag over there," she said suddenly. "It's got my hair things in it."

I'll have. I really liked that. And yet I took the bag over to her.

Halcyon handed me a dryer, a curler, and then the bag, itself, after she'd pulled out a brush. She flicked off the tortoise headband and began brushing her hair. It was too long for this day and age, in my opinion, but it was the best looking thing about her. Her features were the kind that would look okay on someone older but had no particular school girl charm. "I'm going to have to wash this hair again today, you can just bet," she said, "because if there's one thing I can't stand . . ."

"Here comes Mom." I crammed the stuff back

39

into the bag and held it out for Halcyon to drop in the brush. She took her time.

After much rearranging, we finally got most of the baggage into the trunk, but the big bag had to ride on the back seat with guess who crammed in beside it.

Halcyon, obviously an old pro at buttering up older people, suddenly went into an act. "It's so super magnificent of you, Mrs. Conrad, to take me in like this," she said.

Mom, trying to cut over to the outer lane, away from taxis and cars with opened trunks, could only murmur some polite nothing.

"I mean," Halcyon went on, "I'm touched. I really am, that you'd put yourself out for a strange girl like me."

Strange doesn't cut it, I thought. Try obnoxious. Offensive.

"My parents are grateful, and so am I," she said. "The Midwest is something I've always been curious about, and here I am, right in the heart of it, thanks to you."

"The Midwest can get a little dull at times," Mom said. "Except for the weather, of course. It changes all the time."

"I love change!" Halcyon said, missing the point. "I love changing schools."

"Oh, really?" Mom surged ahead in the cleared lane. "Why is that, Halcyon?"

"It's more interesting, don't you think? Meeting new people all the time? Of course, I view things through the eye of a photographer."

"Is photography your hobby?" Mom asked.

"Hobby! It's my profession. Or at least it will be."

"That's interesting."

"My parents have a gallery, and one of these days I'm going to have a one-man show there."

Her use of the expression *one-man* grated on me.

"Did you take lots of photography courses?" Mom asked. "At the schools you've attended?"

"Schools! They didn't teach photography any place I've been. I've had a classical education."

"Well, that's wonderful," Mom said. "And so you've developed this . . . uh . . . profession all on your own?"

"You bet. And it hasn't been easy. I've had to fight, fight, fight for space to work in, and I got no encouragement from the faculty, not even the art department, when it came to showing my work. They're just so narrow."

"Harrison Junior High isn't classical," I said, just to get in on the conversation, "It doesn't even have much class, does it, Mom?"

"It's a very nice school," Mom said, with a warning glance in the rear-view mirror. "Well-rounded. In fact, it's rated as one of the best suburban schools in the state."

"That's why I agreed to come out here," Halcyon

41

said, looking straight forward. "I thought it was about time to broaden my scope. See what life is like for the average kid in the Midwest."

You fake, I thought. You came out here for no such reason. You're here because your folks couldn't afford to send you to private school and you couldn't come down to the level of the kids in your building. I could just see Halcyon lording it over them whenever she had the chance. But to come out here and live with strangers, just to save face! Boy, I'd never do such a thing. Of course, I was just an *average Midwest kid*.

I saw a difficult year stretching ahead. True, I had great plans, and true, Angel was going to help them come about. But *The Year of the Clara* didn't seem like such an arm-flinging thing any more. It might even call for a pair of boxing gloves.

SIX

As we left the tollway and drove the three miles into town, Mom rambled on to Halcyon about how the outlying areas were building up with shopping centers and housing developments. But our village itself has stayed pretty much the same (she wasn't just kidding), even though a lot of the people who now lived there commuted into the city every day.

Our house is only four blocks from what you could laughingly call the heart of the town, but it's almost like country. Maybe it's because the land going off from ours is low-lying and marshy, so no one wants to build out there. In fact, there's a weed-ringed pond down a little distance from our house and Jay Frank's.

"That's where we live, just ahead," Mom said, turning the corner. "The big white house."

"Oh," Halcyon said. "Two stories."

At least she didn't say, "How unimpressive," or "It looks like it needs some work."

After Halcyon glanced around for a bellboy who

43

didn't materialize, we all struggled inside the house with the stuff. Halcyon and I did most of the struggling, because Mom, after carrying in two of the smaller bags, excused herself from the action. It was just natural with her. Mom's a mental mover, not a physical worker. At school she has trillions of kids at her beck and call to carry things around and run errands.

Halcyon, when she had to, could really move, and we had the stuff upstairs in no time. Before I knew what was happening, she was grabbing all of Laurel's boxes from the closet and dumping them into the hall. Then she eyed the furniture.

"You'll have to help me shift this bed to the other side," she said, in that bossy tone I'd already come to know. "And that chest goes over there."

"Actually, what's wrong with things the way they are now?"

"I want to be comfortable. *Okay?*"

Her *okay* translated to *what's wrong with YOU?*

It was obvious that, for some unknown reason, Halcyon had no intention of liking me. Feeling confused and guilty, I helped her rearrange the furniture.

Halcyon took a shower and shampooed her hair and was drying it when I went up to tell her lunch was ready.

"This will take a while," she said over the hum.

"My hair is just so thick and long. I have to spend hours on it."

"Then do you mind if we go ahead? Mom has some errands."

"Be my guest," Halcyon said.

Words failed me, as they seldom do.

We did eat, and Mom went off. I had stuck the potato salad (from the deli section of the supermarket) and jello (same source) away and was wrapping the cheese and ham when Halcyon strolled into the room.

"I'll have some of that," she said.

I put it back onto the platter and was about to get out the rest of the stuff when I got a better idea. "Help yourself," I said. "Just put it back when you're finished. In this heat . . ."

"I meant to ask you about that, upstairs," Halcyon said, piling about three slices each of meat and cheese on bread. "What's wrong with the air-conditioning?"

"Nothing's wrong. We don't have any."

She stop-motioned. "I never heard of such a thing!"

"You have now."

"But it's hot up there!"

"It cools off at night. Some."

Halcyon bit into her sandwich. "Do you have any Pepsi around this place?"

"Just diet 7-Up."

45

"All right. I'll have some."

I just loved that *I'll have some* expression of hers and sooner or later I'd tell her so.

Although watching people eat is not one of my favorite pastimes, I sat there while Halcyon attacked the sandwich. I'd like to think it was to keep her company and try to make her feel welcome, but to be honest, I guess I was out to prove what a pleasant person I am.

"What was it like at boarding school?" I asked, trying not to sound impressed, just interested. "Was it fun?"

Halcyon scooped some dripping mustard from the plate and smeared it back onto the sandwich. "Fun? To some kids, I guess you could call it that. The Looney Tunes crowd."

"What do you mean?"

"Oh, they carried on like crazy. Every week some new caper."

"Like what?"

Halcyon looked bored. "For one thing, they'd penny doors. You know what that is, don't you?" At my negative shake of the head, she said, "The doors to the dorm rooms opened out. Kids would wedge pennies on the outside, under the sills and the girls couldn't get out. They'd have screaming fits."

It sounded kind of like fun to me. "What else?"

"They put vaseline on the toilet seats. Stuff like that. The faculty never knew about those things,

46

but there was a big ruckus when a girl got caught putting a cigarette in the fingers of a statue, which just happened to be of the founder of the school."

I smiled, which was a bad move.

Halcyon finished off her drink and plopped down the glass. "Those guys kept the whole place in an uproar, so the serious ones, the ones with a *career* in mind, just couldn't get any place because of the commotion. And I was kept from moving around at night, the only free time I had to try to develop my film, because the staff wouldn't make any exceptions to the dorm rule." She got up and looked in the refrigerator. "Don't you have any more chilled 7-Up?"

"No. There's an eight-pack in that cupboard. You'll have to use ice."

Halcyon took a few ice cubes and dumped the rest in the sink to melt. She didn't put the cap back on the bottle.

I did it, and then said mildly, "We kind of save ice cubes because our refrigerator doesn't have an automatic ice-maker."

"Oh, don't be so bossy," Halcyon said. "Just because you live here."

Bossy? Me?

"Anyone home?" Jay Frank had his face against the screen door.

"Come on in," I called, burning at Halcyon's remark.

47

Jay Frank came in, looking shy, and I introduced him to Halcyon.

"Pull up a chair, stranger," Halcyon said. "Want me to make you a sandwich?"

"He's already eaten," I said.

"I've already eaten," Jay Frank told Halcyon.

"Then help me kill this bottle, no use letting it go to waste," she said, pouring the drink and taking out another tray of ice cubes.

"You're nice," Jay Frank said to Halcyon, after a glance at me.

"He usually drinks Hawaiian Punch," I said, giving him a look which he chose to ignore. "Did you want something special?" I asked. It was rude, I knew, and it wasn't fair to take out my general annoyance on Jay Frank, but the admiring look he was giving Halcyon really rankled. I mean, all the tender, loving care I'd showered on him all these years was going right down the chutes for a lousy glass of pop.

"I just wanted to meet your new sister," Jay Frank said.

Where had he heard that word? Had I actually used it in front of him?

"We're not sisters," Halcyon said, beating me to it. "Want to come up and help me put up my photos?"

Before I realized it, they were going upstairs and there I was left with the clean-up.

Okay, I thought, I'll do it this time, but there are

going to be some rules laid out around here. As I was finishing, Jay Frank appeared and asked for a hammer and small nails.

"What for?"

"Halcyon needs them."

I took them up myself. Halcyon had framed photographs laid out in formation on the bed.

"You're not going to hang all those, are you?" I asked.

"No, dear, I'm going to stand here and hold them against the wall for the next few months."

The look I gave Jay Frank stopped his giggles. "You've got what, about twenty photos there?" I said to Halcyon. "I doubt if Mom wants that many holes in the plaster."

She hesitated, hammer in hand, then shrugged. "Come to think of it, I'd rather highlight one or two. Maybe I'll attach a light to shine onto them."

You do that, I thought.

"These are kind of funny pictures," Jay Frank said, studying them one by one. "No people."

"I deal in reality," Halcyon said. "Buildings and garbage cans and alleys *are* what they *are*."

You fake! I wanted to shout. I'll bet you don't photograph people because you can't focus on them. You're so two-faced yourself. But all I said was, "See you guys later."

Halcyon didn't bother to answer as I left the room. But, then neither did Jay Frank. Creep! Traitor!

SEVEN

"**I** thought maybe you'd bring Halcyon along," Angel said over at her house Tuesday afternoon. "I'm dying to meet her." She gave me a look. "Or are you two still not hitting it off?"

"Listen, I try. But she acts as though I'm just someone she has to put up with. Me!" I flopped onto Angel's bed. "Besides, she's always going off, taking those dumb pictures. Know where she is today?"

Angel, standing at her desk, glancing at some papers, asked, "Where?"

"Chicago."

"Chicago!" Angel gave me a surprised look. "Alone?"

I nodded. "On the train. Off she went, big as you please, camera slung on her shoulder. I doubt Mom even knows. She's off at school, getting ready for tomorrow."

"She sounds so sure of herself. Halcyon, I mean." Angel's tone had a hint of awe in it. But then, after a glance at me, she quickly added, "Still, there are limits. Your mother is a very patient person and understanding, but yet . . ."

"She can strike like a killer whale," I finished, "when pushed too far."

"Speaking of your mother," Angel said, coming over to the bed with one of the papers, "did you square it away with her? About the rat experiment? Fergy's assembling the materials, and we'd like to get started next week."

"Yeh, sure, it's okay." I guessed it was. That conversation with Mom seemed so long ago.

"Well, good." Angel handed me the paper. "Here's our sketch for the rat run. The process is quite simple. We place a rat here . . ."—she pointed—". . . then raise a lever and see how long it takes him to race down to this point here to get the pellet of food."

"That's really fascinating," I said, bored out of my skull.

"Really. We'll do the run for several weeks, with variations. Some days we'll withhold food, and then the next day check to see if the rat has lost interest."

I had lost all kinds of interest myself. Handing back the sketch, I said, "Just be sure the cellar doesn't smell. That's the main thing."

"It won't. Oh, Clara, those rats are so cute. We were looking at some the other day and I could hardly keep my hands off them."

"Have you seen Skip lately?" Now what kind of weird word association made me say that?

"As a matter of fact, yes." Angel sighed. "He's become such a bore."

"*Skip?*" There was a little squeak in my voice.

"Sports, sports, sports. I tried to lead him off into other subjects, like an article I just read about cloning, but do you know what? He said circus things are for kids. Can you actually believe that boy? He doesn't even read *Newsweek*."

"Athletes don't have time for current events."

"Ha! If Skip's an example, they have plenty of time to spend in front of a mirror. His blow-dryer must get a real workout."

"Angel, you sound so mean. You used to like him a lot last year."

"He's changed. Skip's become the Big Star. I don't go for that image."

I'd go for it. Impulsively, I asked, "Have you thought any more about Pom Pon? About how to get me on the squad?"

"I've taken the first steps." Angel put the sketch back on her desk. "Had a little talk with Miss Curry about my dropping out, and then I mentioned your name, how talented you are, what an asset you'd be, et cetera. Now it's up to you to work like a demon and not make me out a liar."

I suddenly felt rigid. "Angel, you know I can do

cartwheels and splits . . . things like that . . . but when am I going to learn those special things you need to know for tryouts?"

"Right now. Let's go out in back."

Working in the yard, on grass, was not too good in a way, but at least when I fell I didn't break anything. As I'd said, I could do cartwheels . . . but six in a row? Angel just didn't let up for a minute.

"Now do two flips, a twirl, two more cartwheels, and then a split. And raise your arms and smile up at the crowd there at the last." She snapped her fingers. "Go!"

"Oh, hey, come on," I complained. "That's too much."

With hands on her hips, Angel said, "Nothing's too much when you've got a goal. Come on, get up and stop panting like a decrepit collie. You've got to prove you're better than any of the other tryouts. Not *as good as*. Better. And then . . ." She shrugged. "You're on. After all, fair is fair."

Although my face already felt on fire and sweat trickled down my cheeks and matted my hair, I did what Angel commanded. Over and over. The whole backyard began to tilt a little and sway as I went into a twirl, twist, and tumble routine.

"That's it for today," Angel finally said, with a glance at her watch. "You look good, Clara. Considering."

"Good!" I sprawled on the grass. "Angel, I'm a wreck. I'll never be able to keep up. Not in my condition."

"I told you! You've got to work! Get into shape. Then you'll smile and not even sweat. I know it isn't easy, Clara, but that's the way it has to be, if you want to earn the reward." She dropped down beside me. "You could compare it to the way Fergy and I have to shape those rats to make them go after *their* reward."

"I love your comparison." Sitting up, I mopped my face with the bottom of my T-shirt.

"You want to continue or not?" Angel's eyes, fixed on me, looked like scoops of sky. "You can make it, Clara. But it's up to you to decide if it's worth the effort."

I could see those bleachers full of admiring faces. Hear the band. See myself as the darling of the football-basketball team. I smiled. "Think I'll look good in the outfit?"

Angel smiled back. "Knockout. Pure knockout. They'll have to put blinders on the guys to keep their minds on the game."

Not *him*, I thought. Let him look for all he's worth. But would Skip even notice me? After Angel? That was a far-out idea, even for a daydream.

"Hello there, you look as though you had a bad day," was the way Halcyon greeted Mom

54

as she came dragging in around six that night.

"Bad doesn't begin to describe it," Mom said.

Halcyon leaped up from the kitchen table where she'd been fiddling around with her camera. "Here, let me take your briefcase." It was more of a satchel. "My, it's heavy."

"Loaded with work." Mom sat down. "It seems to get worse every year, or else I'm getting old."

"I guess you'll be retiring soon."

Mom looked up. "I'm not *that* old."

"Here's some iced tea," I said, handing Mom a glass. With Halcyon gone all day we still had plenty of ice cubes. "I put together some dinner, but it's not great."

"Thanks, honey. Anything will do."

"I'll just take this stuff upstairs and then set the table," Halcyon said. She was being unusually agreeable.

"No rush, unless you two are hungry. I'd like to put up my feet and relax for a few minutes." Picking up her glass, Mom headed for the lounger in the living room.

"I had a snack in the station, so don't rush on my account," Halcyon called.

"There's a letter from Laurel," I said, walking with Mom. It's on the piano."

I handed her the envelope, but instead of looking at it, Mom looked at me. "What did Halcyon mean, she had a snack in the station? What station?"

"I guess she meant in Chicago. She went in today to take photos."

Mom's breath hissed a little as she leaned forward with a jerk. "Halcyon!" As though on cue, Halcyon came into the room, carrying her camera. "Am I to understand," Mom said, "that you went into the city today? Alone?"

"That's right." Halcyon's tone was pleasant, without a trace of worry. In her case, I'd have been shaking in my shoes.

"Without even letting me know."

"The idea just came to me, and I took off." Halcyon ventured a smile. "Mrs. Conrad, you're probably just not used to girls who get ideas and act on them."

Mom was, I think, stunned into silence.

"There was no problem," Halcyon went on. "Chicago's simple to get around in. I took some shots in . . . what do you call it? The Loop? And then I hiked over to Lake Shore Drive and caught the sweep of buildings along the lake. But my best roll, I believe, will be the one from Belmont Harbor."

"You found your way up there?" Mom looked almost more astonished than angry. "To Belmont Harbor?"

"I caught a bus. And then coming back, I took a cab to the station. My mother says that as long as you have cab fare and a sense of direction you can get any place. And here I am."

After a pause, Mom said, "All right. It's done. But next time you get an idea, Halcyon, check with me before you act on it. If I'm at school, contact me, even if I'm in a meeting. Is that clear?"

"Okay." Halcyon gave me a glance I couldn't quite read. Then she turned and went upstairs.

Mom looked at me and I couldn't read her expression either. Abruptly, she leaned back, stretched out on the lounger and closed her eyes. She seemed almost to be fighting a smile, but maybe she was just gritting her teeth. Laurel's letter was lying in her lap, still unread.

I went back to the kitchen. Boy, if I'd tried a caper like taking off to Chicago . . . pow! But I guess if you have enough gall, like Halcyon, you can get by with anything in this world.

During the first part of the meal no one said very much. Halcyon was lying low, testing the atmosphere, and Mom looked as tired as before.

"Is the enrollment up again this year?" I asked, to break the silence.

"No, as a matter of fact, it's decreased. We've had to cut out one of the fourth grade classes in Randolph School so that makes the other two classes larger than we'd like. The teachers aren't very happy

57

about it. There are other problems, but I guess they'll get ironed out eventually. They always do."

"What's my school called again?" Halcyon asked.

"Harrison Junior High," I told her. "It's the biggest one around. And the best. We won in the finals last year. Basketball."

"Oh, sports." Halcyon said with a near sneer.

I gave her a put-down look and turned to Mom. "What's new with Laurel?"

"Working hard. Delighted with Juilliard. Oh, and she's had several meetings with your parents, Halcyon, and it's all set for her to move in this weekend. She's pleased with the arrangements, and I must say I'm happier knowing there is someone around to keep an eye on her."

To keep my sister from sounding like an infant, I added, "Laurel's so wrapped up in her music she doesn't know where she's at, most of the time."

"I admire her so much," Halcyon said. "She's like me, really dedicated to her work."

Again, what gall! As though there were any comparison! "My sister's going to be a real talent someday, isn't she, Mom?" Then, turning to Halcyon, I said, "Laurel was into music before I was even born." I was warming up. "In fact, when I came along, Mom and Dad let Laurel decide what to call me, and that's why I was named Clara. After the girl in the *Nutcracker* ballet."

"You were not! You weren't named after her!"

I stared at Halcyon, speechless.

"You were named after Clara Schumann, the pianist."

This was so incredible I was at a loss. I looked at Mom for support. She picked up the iced tea pitcher, filled my glass, and gave me a glance. "Halcyon may be right. It sounds possible. I don't remember."

"I know I'm right!" Halcyon said. "Laurel told me herself. I mentioned to her that *Clara* was an old-fashioned kind of name and she told me this Schumann person was her ideal at the time. How did you get your name, Mrs. Conrad? *Jessie?*"

"That story has been lost to the ages," Mom said. "And it's just as well."

Mom retired to the desk in her room after dinner, leaving Halcyon and me to clean up the kitchen.

Halcyon must have sensed, from my short answers, and the way I slammed things around, that I wasn't too thrilled with her conversation at dinner, but she didn't let on. "Tell me about the kids at school," she said, putting things away. "Are they cut-ups or serious?"

"Some of each."

"Do you have any best friends?"

I told her about Angel whom I'm sure I'd mentioned before, and this time really laid it on thick. She was the prettiest, the smartest, the most everything (true, of course) that ever came down the pike. "We've been friends since kindergarten," I finished, "and always will be."

"That's okay, if you like being that close to one person," Halcyon said. "I guess I'm too independent. Besides, I'd never let friends or the social scene get in the way of my work. My *photography*," she added, as though I didn't know.

"I think there's a camera club that meets after school," I said. "But as far as a darkroom . . ."

"Forget it! I'm planning on setting up my own. Here."

"Here? Where?"

As though she'd rehearsed it in her mind, Halcyon walked to the bathroom, just off the kitchen, and turned on the light. "This would do fine. I could cover up that window."

"Hey, you can't do that! This is Mom's. She moved her stuff down here and redecorated after Laurel and I more or less took over the bathroom upstairs. So don't think that now . . ."

"Oh, all right." Halcyon jabbed off the light. "But there must be another water source somewhere. This kitchen's too open. How about in the basement?"

"There's no water except in the laundry room. But you wouldn't like it in there. It's so dreary, with no windows or . . ."

"No windows?" Halcyon's eyes widened. "Dark? Faucets?"

60

She was too much! "No. There's a stream running through, and we pound the clothes on the rocks."

"Which way is it?" Halcyon was already flicking on the stairway switch and clomping downstairs.

"That room to your left," I said, following. Wow, she'd gross out when she saw that room.

But Halcyon was enchanted. Looking around, she said, "Do you think I could develop down here when it's not being used for laundry?" A little pulse fluttered at the base of her throat.

"Ask Mom." I left, and Halcyon followed. "I'm sure she won't care, so long as you clean up and don't mess up the laundry. She likes for kids to have hobbies."

Wrong word. "I told you before, it's more than a hobby with me," Halcyon snapped. She stopped abruptly at the foot of the stairs and surveyed the larger room. "This will be okay, too," she said. "I can string up some wires and clip the prints onto them to dry." She took a step up and paused. "In fact, I might just set up a work table in this area, for cutting and trimming and mounting."

"Be my guest," I said.

Upstairs, we watched TV for a while and ate a bunch of junk. Then, feeling guilty because of my diet lapse (Angel had told me what foods to eat and what to avoid for high energy), I decided to go to the backyard and work out in the moonlight. Halcyon was by now hogging the bathroom anyway, with her big shampoo routine.

My muscles ached, but I worked out the pain. The things Angel had taught me seemed easier this time around. The combination of her strict coaching and my determination would truly turn the tide. This would be The Year of the Clara for sure!

And then the thought hit so hard I fell right out of a cartwheel and landed on one knee. Where had my mind been at, earlier, when I'd blithely told Halcyon she could use the cellar? The cellar had been promised. Promised for the high art of rat-shaping.

I drew up my knees to my chin, kissed the bruised one, and pondered on the ironies of life. Here was one cellar, dark, dingy, and neglected for years. And now suddenly it had become the Most Wanted Place for two parties, both with purpose and determination.

Fair is fair. Angel's words filtered into my mind.

Absolutely. She'd asked first, I'd known her longer, she was already into a school project. There were all kinds of reasons why Angel and the rats should win over Halcyon and her photography.

I'd just have to break the *no developing* news to Halcyon. I'd rather be whipped. Tomorrow would be soon enough to tell her. Or the next day. Whichever came first.

EIGHT

"Are you about ready?" I asked Halcyon the next morning. "I'd like to get to school early."

"So, go," she said.

I shrugged and left. It was okay by me. I didn't need Halcyon hanging like an albatross around my neck. It was sort of unsettling, though, to think she didn't want to be associated with me, either. I mean, what had I done?

"Where's your girl friend?" Angel asked, as I joined her on the front steps of the school. "I was looking forward to meeting her at last."

"She's not my girl friend, and once you meet her you'll wish you hadn't."

Angel squeezed my arm. "Come on, Clara. She couldn't be that bad. Listen, I just saw Fergy and it's all set for this coming weekend. That's one good thing about starting school in the middle of the week. Saturday comes so soon."

"Angel. About the cellar. There's something I ought to . . ."

63

"You look different," she blurted. "Oh." The tiny frown smoothed. "You've fixed your hair a new way. It's darling. And your eyes . . ."

I shrugged. "I was just trying to copy the look of a magazine model. Is it too much?"

"Oh, no. I love it. Clara . . . ?" She gave a little laugh. "You don't have to blush. It's just me."

But it wasn't. Off in the distance, walking toward us was Skip Svoboda. "I'll meet you here after school," I said. The thought of seeing Skip up close, after I'd purposely planned for it, gave me stage fright. "Wait for me," I said over my shoulder.

"What were you going to say about the cellar?" Angel called.

"Tell you later." Later would be soon enough.

But after school, just as I met Angel, Halcyon came along. I introduced them, and we stood around for a while comparing classes. Naturally the subject of Skip didn't come up. I wondered if Angel had stayed to talk to him in the morning. I hadn't seen him again all day. The subject of the cellar didn't come up, either. I knew I should mention it while the two contenders were there together, but I just didn't. In some ways I'm quite the coward.

As Halcyon and I walked home, I asked her what she thought of Angel.

"Sweet kid."

"Sweet, yes, but not weak." Just a little advance warning there. I knew I should go on to warn Halcyon that she'd have to change her plans about using the cellar, but I didn't. I just hoped I wouldn't be around when she finally found out.

As a matter of fact, I wasn't. Around, I mean. I was over at Jay Frank's that Saturday, hearing how he had managed the last couple of days in the twilight time before Sheri got home. So far, so good. But Jay Frank must have been staying awake nights, thinking up possible crisis situations.

For example: "What if I'm making a milkshake and the blender breaks?" *"Clean up the mess, kid."*

"What should I do if someone calls and asks if I'm home alone?" *"Lie. Oh, Jay Frank, just tell them your mother can't come to the phone, she's busy. She is busy, you know, unless she goofs off at work."*

"What if I find a spider in the bathtub?" *"Make friends with it, or else turn on the shower,"* I sighed. "Could we just concentrate on the vital stuff? You're sure you know how to dial for fire, police, paramedics?" We'd only gone through the routine about ten thousand times.

"I know, I know. But if something happens, couldn't I just call you first?"

I felt like pounding my head against the wall. "How many times do I have to tell you I'll be staying after school most nights? That is, if I make Pom Pon."

"Maybe you won't." Jay Frank wrapped his thin arms around his chest.

"Oh, great. You're a real morale-builder. Why don't you just pay attention to what I'm telling you instead of putting me down?"

"I *am* paying attention," he said. "I know what to do. Only . . ."

"Only what?"

"I don't know what to do when nothing happens." He gave me a look from those hazelnut eyes. "I can't play games alone, and Sheri says I can't have friends over when she's not here."

I was getting irritated. "Read. Watch TV. Do your homework. Find a hobby. You can't hang onto other people all your life."

"All right," he said softly.

"I've got to go home now," I said, turning away to keep myself from weakening and reaching out to him. "Angel and Fergy are coming over to set up the rat run, and I should be there to back them up when Halcyon throws the big fit."

"Fit?"

"She's going to blow her stack. I should have told her, but I didn't quite get around to it. There may be blood spilled before the afternoon is over."

"Well, you know how to dial the paramedics."

Cute kid.

I could hear pounding from the lower depths as I let myself into the kitchen, so I clipped downstairs, wondering how long Angel and Fergy had been there and how come they hadn't fetched me from next door, since I'd left a note outside.

"Hi," Angel greeted me, winging back her bangs. "Halcyon let us in, so we thought we'd just get started. How does it look so far?"

"Great," I said, glancing at what looked like nothing much at all. "Hi there, Fergy."

He waved at me with the hammer and went back to pounding nails.

To Angel, against the noise, I said, "I didn't know Halcyon would be back from her errands so soon. Did she throw a big scene?" The pounding stopped and those last words came out as a shout. Halcyon also came out . . . of the laundry room. I felt like crawling.

"You're back," she said brightly. "Everyone's been getting organized while you were away. I've got more of the stuff I'll need and I'm setting up . . ."

"But . . ." I looked toward the laundry room, at the rat-run-to-be, at Angel, and then at Halcyon. No sign of fits or fireworks.

"Isn't it great that we'll all be working down here together?" Halcyon went on, with an admiring look at Angel. "It'll be like a cooperative lab."

"What do you mean?" I couldn't quite take it all in.

"We've got it all planned," Halcyon said, looking

67

smug and triumphant. "We'll work down here together. Angel and Fergy and I."

Angel and Fergy and I.

I should have felt relief. Instead, I felt like a
shut-out in my own home. After a weak smile, I
turned abruptly and hurried upstairs.

I thought Angel might come up, too. But she
didn't.

"I'm glad you guys got together on your plans," I
said, as I paused to catch my breath after my workout over at Angel's that night. "But I think I should
warn you . . ."

Angel nodded, "Halcyon's probably no fun to live
with. You would know that better than I would.
But . . ."

"Yes?"

"But she's trying to get along."

"Meaning that I'm not?"

"Oh, Clara, you're the easiest person to get along
with that I know. You've just got to be firm with that
girl and not let her walk all over you. She'll respect
you for it, believe me."

"As you said, you don't have to live with her."

Instead of answering, Angel started pulling off her
clothes to take a shower.

"I'll leave as soon as my muscles unknot," I said,
too pooped to move.

"That's okay." In bra and pants, Angel laid out

68

her clothes for the next day. On top of the heap she put pink underpants with *Sunday* embroidered on the side. She was wearing *Saturday*.

"What would happen if one of those wore out or got lost in the laundry?" I asked.

Angel smiled. "I have spares, of course."

"Of course." I got to my feet. "In your book there's no such thing as chance. I wish I could lock into that system."

"It's no fat deal. Just advance planning. That's the way things work. Just like my coaching and slipping you the tricks of the trade is going to land you on Pom Pon. You'll see."

I saw all right, and it was just as Angel said. In the third week of school, when tryouts for Pom Pon finally took place, I got up when it was my turn and gave, if I may say so, a stunning performance. Actually, I imagined myself as Angel, going through the routines the way she had demonstrated them to me, with flair and poise. It paid off. I felt keyed up as I went back to the group. Miss Curry was making lots of notes and some of the girls glared, so from that I knew I'd been good.

The next day, when the winners were posted, I tore down the hall and found Angel. "I made it! Hey, I made it!"

"Super! I'm so glad! Oh, Clara, you're going to be sensational!" She gave me a hug. "I just love your

69

enthusiasm. That special spark is the best thing you've got going for you, other than your looks, of course."

"My looks? Since when have I had looks?"

She laughed. "You always have had. You know that. But now you're on the way to becoming a knockout. Don't pretend you haven't noticed, when everyone else has."

"Like who?"

Angel flung out her arms. "Should I make a list?"

"Cut it out." I could feel myself blushing again. There was only one name I truly cared about, and for all I knew, he was still enthralled by Angel.

I hung around the house and called a few kids who had also made the squad. When Halcyon got home, I told her the news.

"I guess that's considered hot stuff in the boonies, huh?" she said, digging into the refrigerator as usual. "Want to split this last piece of pie?"

"No, thanks. I'm surprised someone in your crowd didn't see the notice and mention it to you."

Halcyon gave me a look. "Why would they care? That Pom Pon jazz went out with the fifties. I'm just glad there are a few kids around the school who know where they're at."

I was burning. "If you mean your new friends, they're nowhere. Just drudges. Out for grades, and that's it."

"Not true! They're very interested in my *work*."

70

With a shrug, I murmured, "To each his own."

Halcyon snatched up her plate, scraped and rinsed it, and went upstairs. She claimed assignments here in the Midwest were simple compared to what she was used to in boarding school, but I noticed she studied every night without fail.

I thought Mom, at least, would swell with motherly pride over the Pom Pon news when we were alone after dinner, but she took it as a matter of course. "Wasn't that the general idea, to get on the squad?" she asked. She took hold of my arm. "Good heavens, look at the size of that bruise!"

I jerked away. "Mom, you don't seem to realize . . . the competition!"

"I guess not." She smiled. "But give me a break, will you? This is all so new to me."

And you look so tired, I thought. I hugged her. "It's just that this is the beginning . . ."

"Of what?"

"Of everything!"

"Oh, Clara. I am happy for you. Really. Congratulations." She kissed me. Then, with a sigh, she pulled away. "On to paper work. The everlasting paper work."

"I've got homework, too." I pushed a gray hairpin back into one of Mom's braids and gave it a pat. "See you."

But upstairs, instead of studying my lessons I studied myself in the full-length mirror. Looks. Did

I have looks? Angel should know, although her own meant little to her.

But looks didn't necessarily lead to popularity. If I was going to make this my all-out year I'd have to tag every base.

Angel had her *future* list. I'd have my *present*.

Grabbing a sheet of paper, I headed it POPULARITY MUSTS. That stopped me for a while, but finally I came up with the following:

POPULARITY MUSTS

1. Be as cute looking as possible
2. Get on Pom Pon (done)
3. Hang out with the right crowd
4. Go out with the cutest guy possible (!!!!!!)
5. Get invited to parties
6. Keep in fashion (Needs work)
7. Keep up grades   (" ")
8. Be friendly with *everyone*

There came a sudden pounding of hoofs and Halcyon dashed into my room.

"What do you want?" Why couldn't she learn to knock before barging in?

"Here are some proofs, close-up shots of one of the rats downstairs. This one's Little Blue."

"Who?"

"You know. I told you they put dye marks on the

rats' foreheads to tell them apart. Isn't he a sweetie?"

Halcyon stuck one of the ugliest photos I'd ever seen in front of me. "Don't touch it," she said, "it's still damp. I just thought you'd like a preview."

"It's revolting," I said, walking over to my closet.

"Huh! Well, you can just bet . . ."

I checked through a few shirts and then, wondering at the silence, turned around. Halcyon was reading my list. "I can't believe this," she said.

"Give me that!" I raced over and snatched the paper from her hand. "You've no right . . . !"

With a smile that was almost a smirk she left the room.

I slammed the door after her and then yanked open a desk drawer and shoved my list under a pile of old spiral notebooks. I felt as though Halcyon had seen me naked or something. It was worse, in a way. She had seen my bare thoughts.

Gritting my teeth, I vowed not to let it worry me. I didn't care what Halcyon thought. She'd had a low opinion of me from the moment we met, for no reason, and she'd made no effort to try to understand me.

I got out my books and turned to the English lit assignment.

The truth was, I didn't understand Halcyon, either. And a further truth was that I didn't intend to try.

NINE

It entered my mind that Halcyon might tell her special group about my popularity plan, but in the next couple of days the drudges I happened to meet didn't react in any way. So I guess Halcyon either forgot about the list or considered it beneath mention. At least I could be glad she didn't stoop to gossip.

But other kids, because of Pom Pon, did begin to notice me. As if by magic, I had suddenly become *someone* at Harrison Junior High. Girls I didn't even know all that well started saying, "Hi, Clara!" in the halls, and some of the guys began hanging around. True, most of the things they said were put-down kidding remarks—that's par for the course in eighth grade. The really big thing, though, was that the other girls on the First Squad started being friendly.

Liz Halston, for example, who had never talked to me before unless I was with Angel, rushed up one day in the hall and smiled as though I was her closest friend. "The group's getting together at my house Friday night," she said. "Bring along practice clothes because we want to get that pregame routine down pat. Oh, and bring money, too," she said, giving a little wave as she pulled away to go down a side corridor.

"Money?"

"For send-outs," she called. "Chow-chow."

"Oh. Sure!"

As Liz faded away so did my smile. Money. How much? And was this a routine thing?

I didn't have much money at my fingertips. Mom gave me an allowance for helping around the house, but it didn't go very far. She'd always made me deposit the Jay Frank baby-sitting money in my savings account. I'd probably have to ask her to increase my allowance or else try to talk her into letting me withdraw some money. Neither idea appealed.

I was still standing in the hall, mulling over the situation when a hand slipped along the back of my neck, like a strangler casing the territory. I jumped a mile.

"Hey, relax," a voice said.

I twisted around and almost passed out on the spot because there I was, face to face with Skip . . . Skip Svoboda! "Oh, hi," I said. I wondered if he could feel the goose bumps.

"Hi, yourself." Whenever I'd seen Skip up this close before, Angel had been beside him. Had he grown even handsomer during the summer, or was it just a new hair styling plus rugged maturity? I felt weak.

His eyes, the color of blue jeans, looked down into mine. (Skip, naturally, is tall.) "Hear you made Pom Pon," he said, with a smile that was teasing and a voice husky with undertones.

"Yeh. Who told you? Angel?" Why did I have to say that?

He gave a little negative shrug. "The guys keep track." For another moment his look locked with mine. Then, abruptly, he was off.

I sagged against the wall. What did it mean? *Everything?* Had—but this was unbelievable—had Angel honestly meant that she was through with Skip? And was she in fact turning him over to me? But that, of course, was impossible. Skip Svoboda was his own man. He could have any girl in Harrison Junior High as a steady.

Naturally, I didn't even mention Skip at the party Friday night, but I certainly tuned in when the girls started talking about the team members. It didn't seem to matter if a guy was a no-show in the looks department or if he had the personality of a fig. If he played on the first team, he was up for grabs.

Liz Halston's house is in a really plush neighborhood. We had the whole recreation room downstairs to work in, once we'd pushed the Ping-Pong table to the side. There was even a soda fountain built into the bar, but there was nothing in it.

76

Liz passed out a few soft drinks and then said she was ready to take orders for pizza. "Just don't forget, you guys," she told us, "you've got to throw in for a tip, too. I mean, the kid is delivering and we live out a-ways."

"We ought to meet at houses closer into town from now on," Beth Anne Meyers said. "I'd offer my place, but we don't have a big enough room to practice in. How about you, Erica?"

"Okay. We have a big basement."

"Mindy?"

"Yeh. How about you, Clara?"

"I . . . uh. We just have a cellar. It wouldn't be any good. Besides, Angel and Fergy are using it for a science project."

"Isn't that girl—Halcyon—using it, too?" Mindy asked. "I heard her carrying on about her photography in the cafeteria the other day." Mindy made a face. "She brags a lot, doesn't she?"

Liz walked over. "How come she's living with you, anyway, Clara?"

Before I could answer, Leanne butted in. "Don't you know? She got kicked out of some swank boarding school because of wild pranks. The school insisted she apologize, but her folks wouldn't let her and yanked her out instead. I think it's awful, Clara, that you got stuck with her just because she's a friend of the family."

I shrugged. "We go our own ways." I'd had no

idea Halcyon had been telling a story like that, but as little as I liked her, I wasn't going to blow her act. She hadn't blabbed about my popularity list, so in turn I'd keep quiet about her family's money problems. As Angel had pointed out, fair is fair.

"Really," Liz said, sweeping her hair to the side, "who cares about that girl and her snob school anyway? Let's practice while we wait for the pizza. Some of us really need to sharpen up." She didn't look at me.

We made a little progress, but I could see it wasn't going to be easy. Every night after school we worked out. Even after a month my muscles still ached the next morning.

Sometimes when Miss Curry made us go over and over a routine, or when some of us had to sit on the sidelines, bored out of our skulls while one or two worked to get the moves, I'd wonder why I'd ever let myself in for this punishment. The promise was there . . . the big show-off time at the games . . . but sometimes it seemed the promise would never take place. Work and wait. Work and wait. And there was always criticism. If not from Miss Curry, from the girls themselves, who had fallen into complaints and insults. I felt let-down.

In the meantime, now that I wasn't home after school, wouldn't you know that all kinds of things were going on there? Not great things, to my way of thinking, but there was a kind of loop-the-loop excitement in the air.

One night in October when I got home early I went down to the cellar to check out the action. The run was set up and there were cages lining one wall. Angel greeted me with "Purple did it in point six three seconds! Some kind of record!"

"Thrilling."

"Isn't it!" She brushed back her hair and turned to Fergy. "Would he do it again, do you think, for Clara?"

"I don't know." Fergy resettled the canvas hat on his head. He looked like a proud parent, torn between a natural desire to show off his prodigy and a concern for its health.

"Don't put a strain on Little Purple's heart. Not on my account," I said. "I have to live with myself, remember."

"You're putting us on," Angel, who is nobody's fool, observed. "But that's all right. I'd rather you did that than have you pretend something you don't feel."

"Yeh," Fergy said. "The real feeling comes from working with these animals every day and getting top performance out of them. We're about ready to go into phase two."

"What's that?" I asked.

"They're onto the reward system, which is sprinting down the runway for food," Fergy said. "Now they've gotta learn to reach out for it."

"Reach out where?"

"See this little lever?" Fergy moved to the end of the run with me following. "I just finished setting it up. At first, when the subject comes near to it, he gets a food pellet."

Angel, hovering close by, added, "We have no idea how long it will take to sink into their skulls . . . the idea of reward, I mean. But once it does, we move on to the next phase. They have to put a paw on the *lever* to release the food!"

"I want to be here for that one," I said. "Sounds like a real biggie."

Fergy pulled at the sides of his hat. "We'll let you know, if you shape up your attitude."

"Shape up your rats and let me worry about my attitude. I suppose you'll notify the wire services, the networks, maybe even NASA when Little Blue or Little Purple or whoever first puts his tiny paw on the lever?"

"Not quite. We go another step farther." Fergy cleared his throat. "After the subject learns to put a paw on the lever, he has to *press* it!"

Dead silence. Then, "That's it? He learns to press the lever?"

They nodded. Angel looked radiant.

"What would happen," I asked, "if your so-called

subjects pressed the lever and surprise, surprise—no pellet?"

Fergy looked solemn. "If that happened often enough, they'd lose interest."

Like I'm doing right now, I thought. At that moment my attention was drawn to a line strung across the room with another batch of disgusting rat photos attached. "Can't Halcyon find something else to photograph?" I asked. "Not that I want to put down your little friends, but there is, after all, a whole world of other things out there."

"Maybe you could suggest that to her," Angel said to Fergy. "I have the feeling she's making our rats nervous with that flash. Little Red was edgy yesterday, didn't you think? What was his time, again?"

I left them muttering over their charts and headed upstairs. I tossed my sweater onto a kitchen chair and looked in the refrigerator for a quick snack. There'd been a couple of peaches yesterday, but they were gone. We'd made a poor economic exchange between Laurel, the food-untouchable, and Halcyon, the human disposal. I lifted the milk carton but it lapped with the weight of about an inch. That glutton! We'd had a full quart this morning. I slammed the door shut.

I was thinking of running out to the store or making Halcyon go when someone rang the back doorbell. Jay Frank scuttled inside. He stopped when he sighted me. "Hey, Clara, how come you're home?"

81

"They canceled practice because of a teachers' meeting. How are you, kid?"

"Fine." He was hugging a book to his chest.

"You lose your key?"

"Nope." He fished it out on its chain.

"How are you getting along?" He looked okay. Thin as always, but he didn't have the forlorn look I'd sort of expected, and tried to avoid seeing.

"I have a new friend," he said. "Besides Angel and Fergy and Halcyon."

His saying those names cut through to me a little. I focused on the other. "Who's your new friend? Does he live near here?"

"So far I can't figure out where he lives." Jay Frank slid sideways onto a chair, still clutching the book. His sneaker laces, in spite of all my training, still dangled, untied.

"Why won't he tell you where he lives?"

Jay Frank looked at me as though I'd lost my marbles. "Because raccoons can't talk."

Oh, no! Not another member of the animal kingdom. "You have a raccoon for a friend, huh?"

"Yes, and I'm learning all about him." Jay Frank laid the book on the table. "Fergy loaned this to me. So now I know it's either a hollow log or a culvert."

"What is?"

"Where he lives! What do you think!"

I didn't care much for Jay Frank's tone, or for the

82

conversation in general. "So go crawl into a log or into a culvert," I muttered.

"I guess I could just follow Racky home some night after I feed him. After he gets tamer."

"Racky. Is that what you call him? That's really original."

"His real name is Rac. I just call him Racky for short."

I ripped a sheet of paper from the telephone pad and handed it to Jay Frank along with a ballpoint. "Write *Racky*. R-a-c-k-y."

He printed it, his fingertips whitening with the effort.

"Now write *Rac*. R-a-c."

He did.

"Okay, look at them. How can *Racky* be short for *Rac* when it has more letters?"

With lips pressed together, Jay Frank gave me an I-hate-you look. Then he threw the pen across the room, grabbed his book, and ran out the door.

I stood there looking at the pen, and then I went over and picked it up. Why had I deliberately done that to Jay Frank?

I didn't know why, and I didn't want to think about it. I took a couple of dollars out of the spare money jar and went out to buy some milk.

TEN

All during dinner Halcyon carried on a non-stop monologue about the Great Rat Experiment. "This is only a demonstration, what we're doing," she said. (Since when was it a "we"?) "Did you know, Mrs. Conrad, that even the lowest forms of life can be trained? Like inchworms . . ." She looped up a limp slice of fried onion. "Inchworms can be trained to avoid light."

Thrills, chills and excitement. "I'll clear up," I said, pushing away from the table. What with the rat and worm topics, I'd had it.

When Mom finished her coffee, she said, "Halcyon, how would you like to show me what you're doing downstairs?" I don't think she meant for her voice to sound like an indulgent parent's at Kindergarten Open House, but that's the way it came through to me. She paused. "Clara, I'm expecting a call from Mr. Stein, a teacher, so be sure to let me know."

I was doing the electric skillet when the phone

rang. I had to dry my hands before I could grab the receiver and say, "Mrs. Conrad's residence."

"My, how formal. Hi, there."

My heart zinged like a rubber ball on elastic. Then it pinged back into place. "Uh . . . hi."

"Skip Svoboda."

I *knew*. Who else had a voice like that? "Oh. Hi." (Don't sound too eager, Clara. But don't sound dull.) "How are you?"

"Great. The reason I'm calling . . ."

I clutched the counter and willed my voice to sound calm. "Yeh, why are you calling?" A little laugh there, keep it light.

"I'm calling because some of us guys were wondering, nothing special you know, but kind of wondering who was up for captain of Pom Pon this year."

"Oh?" What a big deal thing to call about. "I don't know. Miss Curry said there's no hurry. We should get to know the routines first and . . ."

"Yeh, I heard she's that way. You've gotta give her a nudge. Our team took care of election first week."

"I guess you're captain, huh?" Brilliant. Everyone knew Skip was captain. I hurried on with, "You're right, we should get at it, the games are about to start. Have you talked to Liz, too?"

"No way. You can handle it." His soft, easy tone made my heart go *ping* again. What was the meaning of this conversation? I felt flattered and confused.

"Well . . ." was all I could manage.

"Well, that's about it," Skip said. "Just thought I'd see if you could hurry things along."

"I'll try . . ." (But why?)

"You'd better," he said with a gentle laugh. Then, "You're real cute, Clara."

"Wh . . . what?"

Again the little laugh. Was I imagining, or was it affectionate? "I'd rather repeat it in person. See you. S'long."

Hanging up, I was practically at point pass-out, but the sound of Mom's footsteps snapped me back.

"Didn't the phone ring? Why didn't you call me?"

"It was for me." I stood there, palms on the counter.

"Clara? Is something wrong?"

"No." I turned. Thank goodness Halcyon had stayed downstairs. "That was Skip. Skip Svoboda." Just saying his name did something to me.

"Oh, yes." Mom made the familiar gesture of re-anchoring a hairpin in her braid. "Where have I heard that name?"

"Mom, he's only our star basketball player, and not bad on the football field either. He even had his picture in the paper once."

"Ummm." She was trying, but still came up a blank.

"Mom . . . don't you remember, Angel used to go out with him? I mean, they used to pair off at pep rallies and after-game parties and school things like that. She talked to you about him. I know she did."

"Now I remember." She started from the room and paused. "Did you say Angel *used* to go out with him?"

"Yeh." Why did I feel so funny? "I guess so."

Mom glanced at her watch. "I'm going to watch that *Medieval Castles* rerun on TV, but I'll probably hear the phone. Clara?"

I looked at her and she looked at me.

"Never mind." She shook away the thought. "Nothing."

I felt relieved that whatever it was, she hadn't said it. I didn't want anything to dim the glow. *You're real cute, Clara.* Skip had actually said that. I felt weak all over again.

There's something about being in a state of bliss that cocoons you from annoyances. That evening, unable to settle down to studying and too restless to stay in my room, I actually accepted Halcyon's invitation to come into her room and help her select rat photos for a future *definitive exhibition*, as only she would put it.

"Where are you going to show them?" I asked, taking in the glossies spread across her bed, dresser, and desk and being surprised that the basic repulsiveness of them didn't even get to me on this night.

"It depends." She picked up two photos that looked identical and chose one. "This is the better, don't you think?"

"For sure. What are you going to shoot next?"

"I may move on to humans. With them I could probably get more variety of expression."

A quick look showed that she was serious. I paused, then said, "Would you take my picture some time?"

"Why?"

I felt flustered. What *was* the deep, hidden reason? *Gary carried Mindy's picture in his wallet.* If Skip . . . oh, he wouldn't . . . but if . . .

Halcyon was studying my face as though I were some object. "I might use you for practice," she said after a bit, "but I can't promise you any prints."

"Why not?"

"It depends on how they turn out. I wouldn't want any inferior work floating to the surface after I become famous."

I heaved a sigh. "Forget it, Halcyon. Just forget it."

She gathered up her prints. "All right, I will. I'll be looking for people with character in their faces anyway. Like bums, streetwalkers . . ."

I should have been offended, I guess, but for some reason as I left Halcyon in her room, I felt sorry for her. She was so far out she wasn't even in the game.

The next morning I got up early to put in extra time on looking knock-out, but I didn't see Skip once.

He was so much on my mind, though, that I just had to mention his name when Angel and I were having lunch. She didn't react, so that gave me the courage to tell her he had called me last night.

"Oh, I'm glad." She actually did look pleased. "I hope you two can get together. That is, if you want to."

If I want to! Sometimes I couldn't believe Angel. "Isn't that up to him?" I said, with a shrug.

"Clara! You can have any guy you like. You should know that."

I didn't know it. But I did know one thing. I wanted Skip Svoboda and now, with Angel pulling herself out of the running . . . maybe I had a chance. But there was no way of knowing for sure. Not yet.

A low blow was handed out at Pom Pon practice after school.

"The orders got mixed up a little," Miss Curry said, "but the outfits have finally arrived. As with all things, the prices have gone up this year, but we're stuck with the same school budget. So you girls are going to have to make up the difference in cost."

There were a few faces that showed concern, but not to the degree I was feeling.

89

"The show pom pons, the vinyl ones, are covered by the budget, of course," Miss Curry went on. "But I'll have to ask you girls to pay for the practice ones yourself. They're made of paper, as you know, and get pretty beat up. But each pair you buy should last a few weeks, if you're careful."

"When should we bring the money?" Erica asked.

"Next practice, if possible. I'll give you the charge slips later. Now girls, I want you to line up for the march formation. Frankly, I'm not impressed with what you've been doing so far, and if you don't get it together mighty fast I might just pull you out of the parade next week."

There was a lot of grousing around because no one particularly liked marching. It was tough to do the steps and still stay in formation.

"I thought we were going to elect our captain today," Liz Halston said, pulling her famous injured expression. "You said we would."

"I said *soon*." Miss Curry started handing out the paper pom pons. "You won't need a captain if you don't get the march formation down pat today. Let's get started, and later, if there's time, you can try on the outfits."

"I wish she'd retire," Liz muttered. "All she cares about is *show*."

"And all you care about is being elected captain," Mindy said. "For all the good it will do you."

"What's that supposed to mean?"

"Girls!" Miss Curry came over with a handful of pom pons. "Could we please get going?"

The practice went fairly well, and later we did get to try on the crimson pullovers with their white accent bands and the short pleated skirts that showed white inside pleats when we twirled.

Me—Clara Conrad—decked out in the official Pom Pon outfit! I could hardly believe it was real. The snuggly, covered-up feeling of the top . . . then the short, fluttery skirt . . . and then the long, cool stretch of bare legs down to the socks and sneakers just about knocked me out. It made play costumes, Halloween get-ups, new holiday outfits just nothing by comparison.

Liz Halston's voice came through to me. "I really think, Miss Curry, we should have the election. We're late this year as it is, and you may know that the boys . . ."

Miss Curry looked up from her check list, ran a hand through her hair, and with a sigh said, "Oh, go ahead. Here's some paper, Liz. Tear it up ballot size and everyone write down the name of the girl you want for a leader."

"Should we vote for co–captain, too?" Leanne, the only other new girl besides me and the alternates, asked.

"No, the runner-up will be co–captain."

91

I stood with my ballot, not knowing what name to put down. Liz? She seemed the obvious choice, now that Angel had dropped out.

Mindy sidled up to me. "You can vote for yourself," she said in an undertone.

"Me?"

"You'd better. My boyfriend Gary said . . ."

"Could we cut the chatter and just get this over with?" Miss Curry said. "The custodian will be around . . ."

I quickly scribbled Mindy's name on the slip and handed it to Miss Curry.

"Leanne," she said, "please write each name I call out on that blackboard, and put a mark for each vote."

Judging by the rapt faces of the girls and the little darting glances, I could see this was more than a mere choosing of captain. There was an undercurrent of something, but I couldn't figure out what.

Liz's name was called out. And then again. Then mine.

Mine! Mindy, probably. But then my name was called again and again. Five times in a row. I felt sort of suspended. No one looked anywhere but at the blackboard, except me.

Mindy's name went up. Whew. Then Liz's.

Mine. Several times in a row. Then Erica's. The girl next to her said something, probably, "You did it," because Erica blushed.

92

When the last slip was read, my name had the most marks behind it, and then Liz's.

"That's that," Miss Curry said, spilling the slips into a wastebasket. "Congratulations, Clara and Liz. You'll have to work extra hard."

Liz wouldn't look at me, but from the glances of some of the other girls, huddling around her, you'd think I'd rigged the election.

"Tough toenails for Liz," Mindy said, putting an arm on my shoulder. "Just don't let her try to take over. Remember, you're number one, first choice."

"I'm kind of scared, Mindy. I don't even know what to do!"

"Ask Angel. She was captain and now you are. I'm going to rush home and call Gary. What a relief!"

Relief? I didn't get it. But I was somewhat in shock at having been elected captain. Liz finally came over and congratulated me and said she hoped I didn't break a hip or anything so she'd have to take over. I made a mental note to watch my step around Liz.

Although the girls begged to be allowed to take stuff home, Miss Curry refused until it was paid for. "I'm responsible. Sorry," she said.

She gave each girl a cost sheet, and when she got to me she said she'd like to set up a conference some day soon. She didn't look too thrilled at having a newcomer elected captain.

I was not only not thrilled but seriously alarmed when I looked at the bill and saw the total amount.

It was like the national debt. I hated to think of Mom's reaction. She was always dead set against spending money for what she called frivolous items. I'd have to convince her that Pom Pon equipment rated as one of life's necessities. It did, to me. After all, I was captain. How many other girls at Harrison Junior High could make that statement?

ELEVEN

When Mom got home I followed her up to her room. While she was changing clothes, I did a replay of the election, leading up to the counting of the ballots.

"And you won," Mom said, slipping into her robe.

My mouth dropped open. "How did you know?"

She laughed. "Look at your face in the mirror."

I glanced above her dresser and saw bright spots of color on my cheeks.

"Mom," I said, jumping up and throwing my arms around her, "it's one of the biggest things that has ever happened to me."

"I'm glad," she said, hugging me.

"It's going to cost a lot," I said, into her shoulder.

"Oh?" She pulled away a little. "What is a *lot?*"

I told her.

"Oh, Clara! Just for . . ."

"It's important to me, Mom! Really important! I'll draw my own money out of the bank to pay for it."

"Clara! That's for your future."

"My future has to start some time." Tears came to my eyes. "I want it to be now. This year is important to me," I repeated.

Mom looked a little disappointed, I thought, but she managed to smile just a shade. "All right, go ahead, if that's what you want."

"Oh, Mom!" I almost squeezed the breath out of her. "I'll work next summer and make it all up after my big year is over!"

I spent almost two solid hours talking on the phone that evening as one member of the squad after another called to congratulate me and talk about the upcoming dance.

"If being elected captain means no other calls can get through in this house, you'd better resign," Mom said. "This is incredible."

"The girls are just excited," I said. "They'll simmer down."

"It's all so boring," Halcyon said. "Listening to the same thing over and over."

I was about to tell her she was free to leave when the phone rang again. Halcyon made a lunge for it. "For you," she said, handing me the receiver. "It's Jay Frank."

"Hi," I said. "What do you want? I can't talk."

I heard Halcyon give a snort as she left.

"Clara!" His voice trembled. "I've just gotta tell you this. Little Clara is eating out of my hand."

"What? Who?"

"I've been putting out bread, and now she takes it right from my hand."

"Jay Frank, what are you raving about?"

"My raccoon. Oh, I guess I forgot to tell you. You said Racky was a dumb name, so I named her after you."

That would teach me to keep my mouth shut. "I'm really honored, Jay Frank," I said.

"That's okay. Want to come over? Maybe my friend will come back."

There was something a little heart-tugging about the way he said *my friend*. "Jay Frank, I'd like to, one of these nights, but I've got to get going right now. I'll see you, though, okay?"

"Okay." He sounded wistful, but also resigned. Well . . . he had to learn sometime to stop leaning on me.

Mom was at her desk in the living room. "I'm off the phone," I told her, as I started upstairs. The front doorbell rang. I got it.

I also got the shock of my young life. It was Skip. Skip Svoboda. He wouldn't come in because a couple of the guys were out on the sidewalk waiting for him.

"Just heard you made captain," he said, with a slow, sweet smile, and his look just resting on my face. "Thought I'd stop by to see how you were taking it."

"In stride." The words came out by themselves.

"That's my girl." He glanced around at the guys who were making with the whistles. "I've gotta leave. See you."

"Sure." It's lucky I was leaning against the door jamb because my legs had gone limp.

I was sort of hoisting myself up the stairs when Mom called me back. "Who was that, and what was it all about?"

"That was Skip. You know. The guy I told you about."

"The one who used to like Angel?"

"Yeh, that's right."

"And what do you have to do with him?"

"Well . . . I guess he likes me, now."

"He . . . what?" Mom had on her principal-type expression.

I decided to try for the light approach even though the situation wasn't ideal for it. "Don't you think I'm likeable?" I smiled and tried to look winning.

Mom didn't react. "Does being head of Pom Pon have anything to do with this sudden switch of *liking?*"

"It's not *sudden!*"

"Answer the question, Clara."

"The Pom Pon girls and the team do sort of hang around together, but no one can make anyone like

98

anyone else. It's not a school code or anything like that."

"It just happens?"

"Sometimes." I felt hurt, I really did. "Mom, you want to know something? You don't give me any credit. Some people like me for who I am."

"That's the point. Who you are is different from what you are. I hope you don't confuse the two."

"Mom, you know what? You're making a big deal over nothing."

"All right. Just don't sell yourself short, Clara."

I said good-night, went upstairs to my room, and closed the door. Why did Mom have to get heavy just when everything was going my way? I guess she just wasn't ready to handle the fact that I had my own ideas. I wasn't like Laurel.

Skip liked me. Really liked me. I guess I could tell, from the way his eyes just practically caressed me. Caressed . . . what a beautiful word! Clara . . . caressed. Clara . . . the caressable.

And then, what he'd said at the last. *That's my girl*. Was I? Could I be? It seemed too good, too sudden to be true.

But it *was* true. Skip *had* meant it. He started hanging around me the very next day at school.

November came, and with it the first snow and frigid air. The Pom Pon girls, out in half-time on the football field, were solid goose bumps from ankle socks to undershorts. I knew it was cold, I could see it on my legs as we got back to the bleachers, but excitement kept me warm. Plus the thought, I'm Skip's girl. I still couldn't fully realize this had happened, even though everyone else took it for granted by now that Skip and I were a twosome.

It had come about so suddenly, without any kind of effort on my part. I didn't let myself question that, but still I couldn't help wondering at times how Angel felt about it. One day I finally broke down and asked her. I knew, being the type of person she is, that she'd level with me.

"Clara, I thought I'd told you," she said. "Skip and I have no interest in each other any more. The field is clear."

"How could you let go of him like that?" I persisted. "He's Number One. A personality."

Angel's eyelids flickered. "Maybe that's it. He used to be a *person*."

"You think there's something wrong with that?"

"Of course not, Clara. I've just lost interest, that's all."

I believed her. But then I had to switch to the other side of it. Had Skip lost interest in Angel, or was he just saving face?

One day after school when there was no practice, Skip and I were sitting at a booth in the neighborhood junk food shop, which for a change was nearly empty. He was going on about all the games our team had lost, and how it didn't mean much.

"No one takes football seriously in junior high," he said, jiggling the ice in his glass. "Except maybe a few who aim for the high school varsity. Not me. I don't want to get mangled."

"I can see why," I said. I meant, *you're so good-looking*. I hoped he didn't think I meant he was cowardly. My mind was really on Skip and Angel and the way they'd liked each other last year, but I said, "Basketball's starting soon now, anyway."

"Yeh, and that's really my game. We're lining up practice now, did I tell you?"

"Yes, you did. I mean, I know. I mean . . ."

"I mean, I mean," he teased. "What do you mean?"

I almost fell apart when he smiled down at me that way, with that lazy, affectionate look in his eyes. "I guess I don't express myself very well," I mumbled. Something inside of me said, *just let it go at that, stop what you're about to say*, but I went on anyway. "I'm not like Angel."

"No, you're not," he said. "And that's in your favor."

I wanted to know why, but couldn't ask.

Skip shifted a little. "Angel's an all right kid, but it's kind of nice to be around someone whose looks are a contrast. Angel and I were too much of a matched pair."

"Oh? I think she's prettier than you." I was teasing, but Skip didn't get it.

"Angel's not all that good-looking," he said.

"Good looking! She's perfect!"

"She just lets on that she is." Skip ran a hand over his own blond hair, shifted again, and then put an arm around my shoulder. "You're the one who's perfect," he said.

He meant it. I just had to believe he meant it.

"Yeh," he said, "you and I are going to look good together at the dance."

I gripped my glass. "Dance?"

Skip laughed. "Come on, you know about it. Two weeks from Friday. Start thinking about what you're going to wear." He laughed again. "Besides that cute look."

Some kids came by then and joined us, and that was that.

I couldn't remember afterwards what anyone had said.

TWELVE

When I got home I saw that the local paper, lying on our kitchen table, was folded to *School News*. The Honor Roll list was circled. My name appeared on the A list and so did Halcyon's. I was a little surprised that my grades had averaged so high, since I hadn't put in too much effort. Halcyon, on the other hand, hit the books every night.

I shoved the paper aside. I didn't want to think about Halcyon. I didn't even want to think about grades. All I wanted to think about was Skip. And what he'd said. And about the dance. It would be our first real date! I'd have to think about what to wear, and cute looks weren't enough. Even Skip had said so. But I guess he was kidding. Even so, I wasn't about to take any chances.

My mind was somewhat muddled during dinner. While Halcyon was rattling on about making the Honor Roll and how it didn't really mean much because this school was so below what she was used to, I thought, *you fake. You want and work for approval*.

Except where I'm concerned. What grudge did Halcyon have against me? And why?

Then my thoughts would switch to Skip and how we were going to the dance together. But how was I going to break the news to Mom? I didn't think she'd be too crazy about the idea. Although I mentioned Skip's name from time to time and got calls from him, I'd never let on that I was his *girl*. Mom wouldn't tune in to that type of thinking. Her life was K-6 where kids were kids. I doubted she realized what a different game it was in junior high. If only Laurel had fallen in love at my age, things would be easier for me now.

"How's Laurel?" I asked, as long as my mind was on her. "What did she have to say in her letter today?"

"Nothing much." Mom leaned her elbows on the table, cupped one hand on the other, and looked at me, smiling. "She didn't need to write much. Because we're going to see her."

"Great! When's she coming home?"

"She's not." Mom smiled even more. "We're going there."

"Really? To New York?"

"That's where she lives now," Halcyon said.

"When are we going?" I asked.

"During Thanksgiving vacation. My friend Annie is taking care of hotel reservations."

I glanced at Halcyon, relieved that we weren't

lined up to stay at her apartment. She had a grumpy look on her face. "Annie's my aunt," she said. "My great-aunt."

So what? Who was making any claims? "I don't know her very well," I said.

"And she really doesn't know you." From the look Halcyon gave me, you'd think I'd pulled a fast one.

"It works out fine," Mom went on, still wrapped in her happy thoughts. "We can all fly out together and back, and yet have our own little separate visits. I wonder if Annie has changed."

"She looks good, considering her age," Halcyon said. "Very elegant."

"Oh, dear. I'd better get something to wear before we go out." Mom's glance fell on me. "And you, too, Clara. A coat, especially. That ski jacket is not appropriate."

"That's for sure," Halcyon said.

"I need other clothes, too," I told Mom. "For school parties. And of course, New York."

"You ought to wait and then hit the shops as soon as you get there," Halcyon said. "My mother can steer you to the best places."

I ignored her. "Let's not wait," I said to Mom. "As you say yourself, if something has to be done, do it."

"We'll see." Mom got up. "Whose turn is it to do the dishes?"

"Mine," I said.

I really didn't mind doing the dishes any more

because Skip usually called around this time, and I hated it when Halcyon picked up the phone.

They had no sooner left than it rang. "Hello," I said, using my soft voice.

"Clara? This is Sheri. Is Jay Frank there?"

"Jay Frank? No, I haven't seen him."

"That kid! Then why doesn't he answer the phone? I'm going to be stuck here at the office for another hour, and I'm worried."

"I'll go check on him for you. And call you back."

"Thanks, sweetie."

I tossed on a cardigan of Mom's that was hanging by the back doorway and then noticed the lights were on in the basement. "Jay Frank, are you down there?" I called.

"Yes."

"What's the idea, hanging around at this hour," I yelled as he came upstairs. "Your mom's worried sick. Why didn't you call her or let us know you were down there in the cellar?"

"I guess I forgot. After Angel and Fergy left, I just kept on holding and petting those little rats. They're all friends with me now."

"Yeh, tell me about it. But first call your mom and say you're okay. Then I'll take you home."

"Will you stay for a while?" he asked, as we started out a few minutes later. "You keep promising to come over, but you never do."

"I have homework every night, remember." I felt

a little guilty, even though my social life and all was none of Jay Frank's business. "You ought to leave on a light when you take off." He was fumbling for the lock. "It gets dark early now. In fact, you ought not to leave, period, when your mother's not home." I sounded like quite the little mother myself, but it was habit.

I threw on a few lights, including the one on the patio.

Jay Frank's dishes, from whatever he had eaten after school, were neatly lined up in the drain rack. "Want some ice cream?" he asked. "We have some thawed raspberries I could put on the top."

"Sure, sounds good. Go light on the ice cream, though. I'm watching my weight." I let him dish it up because it made him feel big. Meanwhile I strolled over to the window by the patio. "What's that stuff out there on the paper plate?"

"I put out food for my night friends."

"Oh. Little Clara and that crowd?"

"Yeh." Jay Frank was digging away at the ice cream container. "Is this enough?"

I turned to check. "Fine." I got a drink of water, then walked back to the window. And then I yelled.

"What's the matter, Clara?" There was panic in Jay Frank's voice.

There was more panic in mine. "That . . . that rat! That giant rat!" I leaped to a chair. "Out there, eating the food!"

Jay Frank crept to the window and looked out. Then he turned to me. "You dummy! That's just an opossum."

"Opossum? Are you sure? It looks like a rat to me!"

"That's just because of his tail. Opossums have very long tails. They can wrap them around things."

I folded my hands under my arms, quick. "Why didn't you tell me you had repulsive animals like that coming around here?"

"I had the feeling you might not come over if you knew."

"You had the right feeling."

"But he's cute, Clara. Come over here and take a close look at those little feet. The back ones have thumbs, just like ours, almost."

"Speak for yourself." I was off the chair by now, but keeping my distance from the window. "Come back and eat your ice cream. It's melting."

Jay Frank sat down and dug in, and I sat opposite. The dinner guest outside had somewhat affected my appetite, but still, raspberries were raspberries, especially in November.

"Did you know opossums travel alone?" Jay Frank asked.

"That doesn't surprise me. If I were one, it's for sure I wouldn't want to look at someone else as ugly as I was."

"Do you know opossums are marsupials?" Jay Frank asked. "That means they carry their babies around in a pouch."

"Could we maybe change the subject? I could read all this in a book, if I was interested."

"That's what I did. Let me tell you just one more thing, Clara. This is really interesting. When opossum babies are born, they're really tiny. I mean, *really*. They're so tiny that twenty of them could fit right into that teaspoon of yours."

Raspberries flew into the air, followed by my teaspoon, followed by me. I ran to the sink and gagged.

"Are you sick, Clara?" Jay Frank sounded really upset.

"No." I pulled myself together. It was just a little retch, nothing more.

"I'm sorry. I keep forgetting how you don't like little animals, but if you'd just . . ."

He looked so guilty and so pleading, I wanted to reach out to hug him, but instead, I stooped to pick up the spoon. Jay Frank bent down at the same time and our heads bumped.

"Oh, sorry," I leaned forward and kissed him lightly on the forehead where we'd bumped.

"Don't do that!" He shrank away.

"Don't do that? A little kiss? How come?"

"I don't like it. Besides . . ."

"Besides what?"

109

"I don't want to be . . . headed for trouble."

I stared at him. "What are you babbling about? What do you mean, headed for trouble?"

"Halcyon said *you* are. She said, 'I know what she's *really* like.' " His look was somewhat accusing. "Well, you do have a boyfriend, don't you?"

"So what! It's none of her business. That low-life creep!"

Jay Frank jumped up. "Don't call Halcyon a creep! She's my friend!"

"Oh, you and your friends! Anyone . . . or anything that pays the least bit of attention to you is your *friend*. Sometimes I wonder about you. I really do."

"Everyone needs friends!"

"Yeh, well, if you're going to palsy up to raccoons and opossums and rats, not to mention that weasel Halcyon, you can just cross *me* off your list!"

I didn't mean it, not seriously, but Jay Frank looked me straight in the eye and said, "I guess I don't like you any more, anyway."

"It's mutual." I snatched up the sweater and headed toward the door, expecting to hear a pleading, *Clara . . . I didn't mean it*, but Jay Frank didn't utter a word.

I went home and upstairs. I wanted to pound on Halcyon's door and ask her if Skip had called, but I didn't want to give her the satisfaction in case he hadn't.

110

Headed for trouble. What a stupid thing to say to a little kid. I knew from experience that Halcyon said anything that popped into her mind, but she ought to learn a little control.

For that matter, I shouldn't have shot off my mouth that way to Jay Frank. But I'd make it up to him.

For now, I thought, as I closed the door to my bedroom behind me, I was just going to concentrate on Skip and what he had said to me in the booth. *You're the one who's perfect. You and I are going to look great together at the dance.*

Two weeks from now! The dance! I'd circle it on my calendar and each day have a count-down.

I found a red pen, found the Friday, and drew a heart around it. And then my fingers stiffened. That was the Friday after Thanksgiving! *The* Friday. The Friday we'd be in New York City!

I threw myself on the bed and banged my feet in frustration. What could I do? I couldn't get Mom . . . no, there was no way I could get Mom to stay home or let me stay home. I had to go. And Skip would be . . . what? Furious? Hurt? He might be so furious and hurt he'd ask someone else. I was so shook up I couldn't even cry. I just began rolling back and forth in misery.

Finally I got up and got ready for bed, but all I could think about later, as I kicked and tossed, was how my life was about to be ruined, and at such an

111

early age. I knew, if I fell asleep, which was doubt-ful, that all I'd dream about was Skip, going to the dance with somebody else.

But strangely enough, the next morning, the only dream I remembered was one about Jay Frank. He was lost, and I could hear him crying. But I couldn't find him.

THIRTEEN

"**D**on't worry about it," Skip said, when I finally got around to telling him. This was two—I repeat two—days before vacation.

"Relax," he said, and he gave a little laugh at what must have been a really blank look on my face. "No sweat."

Of all the reactions I'd expected from Skip, including anger, revenge, disgust (at my waiting so long to tell), this was the one I hadn't even considered. "You're not mad?" I just couldn't believe it.

"Cutie, these things happen. Just have yourself a real good time in New York. And don't do anything I wouldn't do."

I stood, weak with relief, watching Skip shove things into his locker. Gary and Mindy came along.

"Hey, too bad about you guys and the dance," Gary said, as they came close. And then, over his shoulder as they kept walking, he added, "Shake 'em up in Milwaukee."

"What?" I stared after them and then looked down at Skip's back, as he knelt to get something from the bottom of his locker. "What makes them think I'm going to Milwaukee?"

Skip shuffled shoes and notebooks around for several seconds, and when he finally stood up, he didn't quite look me in the eye. "As a matter of fact, my folks are going up to visit relatives and they raised a big stink about my having to go along. So kid, I won't be around, either."

"Oh!" It was like lights coming on after a crime movie and you know you're safe. "Then it works out perfectly. We'll be away together!"

It sounded funny, but we both knew what I meant.

"You're cute, Clara," Skip said with that look that made me weak. "I'll miss you. But it's a load off my mind."

He'd been afraid to tell me, too!

Had Skip thought I'd get hysterical . . . maybe go off to the dance with someone else? How wonderful! Whoever would have dreamed that our being separated during vacation would really bring us closer together like this?

The eight o'clock flight was the earliest we could get on Wednesday night and even so, the plane was jammed. Everyone, though, was in a cheerful holiday mood, except possibly me. I couldn't help wishing that everything had worked out differently and I was going to the dance, with Skip.

I snuggled against my new camel coat and then fumbled around for the seat belt. I flipped Halcyon's furred cuff out of the way. She flipped it right back. "Do you *mind?*" she said. "These window seats are narrow, you know that."

She was the one who'd made a rush for it. "And try to keep your feet off my rat photos. I don't want them all mooshed up."

I pushed them as far away as I could. "Why'd you have to bring them along, anyway?"

"Why? Because my parents are very interested in my talent. Especially my father."

The word *father* suddenly made me feel forlorn. I stared straight ahead. I could feel Halcyon's eyes on me.

Finally she heaved an impatient sigh. "I hope you're not going to be this way all weekend. It's not forever, you know. You'll soon be back in his arms."

"Wh-what?" Really, I was confused.

"Everyone knows what's going on with you two. Except maybe your mother." We both glanced at Mom, who seemed to be dozing. "But if you don't *mind*, I'd just as soon my parents didn't know. I'm certainly not going to tell them."

"Are you talking about . . . *Skip?*"

Halcyon rolled her eyes upward. "As though you didn't know!"

I was so angry I reached forward and grabbed the first thing I could find from the magazine packet. It was a throw-up bag. I shoved it back and took the flyer of all the things you could buy from the airline.

"There's nothing *going on*," I muttered, catching only blurs of merchandise as I turned the pages. "You know, Halcyon, you have a perverted mind." Before she could recover, I added, "And I don't appreciate the little remarks you made to Jay Frank, either. He's just a kid, and you should take that into consideration before you sound off."

Halcyon adjusted her headband, pulled her hair back from her neck, and looked out the window.

The male flight attendant came along with the liquor cart and asked if we wanted cokes or 7-up. We both said, "Cokes," and Halcyon added, "with a twist of lemon."

He gave her a look and handed her a plain coke.

When they brought around the dinner trays, Mom perked up and so did Halcyon. I tried to eat but couldn't get it down.

"If you're not going to touch your dessert, I'll have it," Halcyon said. As we exchanged her empty container for my full one, I marveled at how mere food could bring her around. But maybe she was just easing into a better attitude before we met her parents.

To my dismay, Mr. and Mrs. Hart weren't at the airport to collect Halcyon. Mom explained why.

"We arranged for them to pick up Halcyon at our hotel," she said. "No use for them to battle the traffic all the way out here."

If they had, they could have given us a ride, but we finally got a cab and in due time arrived at the hotel. A youngish couple rushed toward us in the lobby and hugged Halcyon as best they could around all the stuff she was carrying.

Halcyon put on the grand performance, saying how great it was to be back in civilization and how she felt like leaning over and kissing the ground. We were standing on a maroon-colored carpet at the time.

Her father had curly hair and a mustache and was a little bit on the heavy side. As he talked with Mom, he had an arm draped around Halcyon's shoulder. They looked a lot alike.

Mrs. Hart was tiny and stylish in her fur coat and sleek boots. I thought the dark glasses were a bit much at this time of night, and I also couldn't see why such a simple hairdo—free swinging from a center part—called for the services of a top stylist, as Halcyon often saw fit to mention.

While I was sizing her up, Mrs. Hart turned and said, "Clara, you're every bit as pretty as Halcyon said you were. I wish you could get her to wear a touch of makeup." She studied Halcyon. "But of course, the first priority is weight." She sighed.

Mr. Hart came forward, shook hands, thanked

Mom again, and said they should get going. Halcyon hesitated and looked as though she were going to hug Mom, but then she too, shook hands. "See you," she said to me.

I wondered, as I watched them walk away, why she had mentioned my looks to her mother. When Halcyon talked to me, it was always her mother's looks that were so outstanding. I guess I never would understand that girl.

Mom, the bellhop, and I got into the elevator along with some kid of about eight who had stringy blond hair, blue rimmed glasses, and several candy bars in her fist. She leaned toward the buttons, huffed out a breath, and number seven lit up. After she got off, the bellboy told me it's heat, not pressure, that activates the buttons. I wished Fergy and I could be in an elevator some time. I'd like to dazzle him with that inside information. Fergy . . . Angel. They seemed so far away. They *were* far away. I'd rather be there, even in the rat cellar, than here.

"When is Laurel coming over?" I asked Mom, when we were alone in the room. There were two double beds.

"Later. Why don't you take your bath and then get into bed and watch TV?"

"Could I go down and get a candy bar first? I'm starved."

She gave me money and the room key. Going down, there were others in the elevator, but coming back up I had it all to myself. I huffed out my breath on number 9 and sure enough, it lit up.

My spirits lit up, too. You know how that happens sometimes. You're feeling depressed and blah, and then all of a sudden, like a switch being flicked, you see things in a different light. Right now the low feelings that came from being away from Skip and on the plane with Halcyon left me. I began thinking it wasn't bad, being in a hotel and having a holiday in a big city and, of course, seeing my sister after all these weeks.

My plan was to lie in bed, awake, until she got there, but I must have drifted off. I felt Mom lift the pillows from behind my head and shift me down in the bed, and then later I was vaguely aware of voices, and lips brushing my forehead, and another body in the bed.

The next morning when I woke up, Laurel was still asleep, her lovely, slim fingers pressed together as though in prayer, under her cheek. I propped my head on my hand and looked at her.

"Let her sleep," Mom whispered, passing by the bed, but at that instant, Laurel jerked upright and her hand reached to the bedside table for a clock, I guess, that wasn't there.

"Laurel." Mom gave a nervous laugh. "You're with us. No practice today."

My sister slumped with relief, then fully woke up. "Mother!"

Mom sat on the edge of the bed and held Laurel close. "Do you always wake up in such a panic?" She smoothed the long brown hair.

"Always. I'm always afraid I'll be late." Laurel had her arms around Mom, too, and she snuggled her face against Mom's neck. "Oh, it's so good to have you here and to have . . . to have a holiday." She stayed that way for a moment, but then it was like click, click, back to business. She pulled away. "But of course, I love Juilliard. It's a struggle, but worth every minute of it."

"I'm glad," Mom said. Her hands moved to Laurel's arms. "You're thinner than ever."

"You're plain skinny," I said.

Laurel whipped around and with a half-tackle flattened me against the pillow. "Baby Bunting!" she squealed. She kissed me and tickled me the way she used to when I was real little.

I tickled her back, and we were all over the bed, grabbing at pillows for protection. "Don't call me 'Baby Bunting,' " I said, giving her a jab in the ribs. She really was skinny.

"*He's gone to get a rabbitskin, to wrap the Baby Bunting in!*" she said, laughing and dodging the pillow.

"You know I always hated that song," I said. "Wrapped in rabbitskin. Ick."

"Some day, baby, I'll wrap you in mink," she said,

slipping away from me and out of the bed. "Some day when I'm rich and famous."

She stood for a moment in her nightgown, hair tangled over her shoulders. She was quiet now. "I was just talking," she said after a moment, glancing at Mother. "I don't need to be rich or famous. I just need to be good."

I lay back with a pillow cradled to my chest. I hated to think what would happen to my sister if she wasn't good. Good enough, in her opinion. What happened to pianists who didn't quite make it?

To my surprise, after that big bit from Halcyon about *my Aunt Annie*, Mom's friend Annie Schuyler was set to have Thanksgiving dinner with us late Thursday afternoon.

"How come?" I asked Mom. "Why won't she be going with the relatives?"

"She sees Kate and Jeff—Halcyon's parents—often enough. She wants to see *me*. Us. We used to be so close at college."

Boy, that was a million centuries ago. "So Halcyon will be with just her folks, then?"

"Clara, I know this is vacation, but would you still do me the favor of not starting sentences with the word *so*? As for Halcyon, she's going with her parents to the home of friends in Long Island. Isn't that right, Laurel?"

121

"Somewhere like that. Mother, is this going to be a fancy restaurant? I forgot to bring heels."

"You're fine." Mom's look rested on the dress Laurel was wearing. "But is that it? Your best? It's . . ."

"Out-of-date," I said.

"I just don't have time to go shopping. I have the money you sent, Mother. But I don't have the . . ."

"We'll go tomorrow," Mom said. "Laurel, you've got to get some clothes, with recitals coming up and . . ."

"Clothes don't count."

"Even so." Mom's mind was made up. She excused herself to take a shower.

"Laurel," I said, when I heard the water running, "why don't you get what's-her-name—Kate—to take you shopping? She's very *now*." Slight imitation of Halcyon.

"No, if I have to shop, I'd rather it be with Mother. She has good taste, and it's more to my style."

"What do you think of her . . . Kate? Is she stuck up?"

"You ought to call her Mrs. Hart."

"Oh, I will. But *is* she?"

Laurel bit one of her nails. "Not stuck up. But kind of snappish. With other people. Her husband. But not me. She treats me with a sort of . . ."

Laurel gave a tiny, embarrassed laugh. "Awe. You know, as though I weren't quite real."

Laurel did have that effect on people. I guess it was her delicate look. And her talent. Plus, she was so gentle.

"Mr. Hart is more natural," she said. "I don't see a lot of them. They're tied up with the gallery, and they go out most evenings. I have the run of the place when I'm there. It's perfect."

She must have seen something on my face, because almost guiltily, she asked, "How is it for you? With Halcyon?"

"Oh, okay." Mom came out just then, and we got ready to go.

Annie Schuyler gave Mom a grand welcoming embrace, and me a big hug, and a smaller one for Laurel, whom she saw now and then. All the while the maitre d' was making nervous gestures toward the waiting table; the restaurant was packed.

"It's so grand to be with my favorite people," Annie said. "This calls for a drink." She ordered something on the rocks and Mom took the same. Laurel passed altogether, but I ordered a coke. "With lemon." I got it!

Aunt Annie (mentally I kept calling her that, although outwardly I avoided calling her anything) was older looking than I remembered. Or maybe it was just the stress and strain of city life showing up.

Her skin wasn't as smooth as Mom's, but she wore makeup—not too much—to cover. Her hair was waved and a kind of ash-blond, probably tinted. The only woman I saw in all of New York City with gray hair, besides Mom, was a washroom attendant.

Annie and Mom tried to keep the conversation general during the meal, but it kept circling back to college days. I didn't mind. It was great, just being in that fancy place and being able to order anything. "Anything, darling, anything you like," Annie kept insisting. And it was interesting to see Mom from a different view. The drink may have helped, and then the dinner wine, but I think it was mostly the talk that made her seem younger, and more care-free. Even her laugh was lighter.

Laurel must have noticed it too, because she'd look at Mom, then look down, and smile.

"Do you remember me, dear?" Annie suddenly said, leaning toward me. "From the last time I visited you?"

"I remember the cat statue you brought."

"Clara!" Mom's rebuke drifted into a laugh. "Really . . ."

"She's adorable," Annie said. "I've got myself an adorable godchild." Lucky she was looking at Mom when she said that because it's for sure I'd forgotten about the godmother thing. She took my hand across the table. There was a knockout pearl and diamond ring on her little finger. "Could I borrow

124

this child tomorrow?" she asked Mom. "I want to know her. You and Laurel will be busy shopping anyway."

"Well, if Clara . . ."

"Then it's all settled!" Annie said. "We'll have such fun. And I'll tell her all your girlhood secrets, Jessie."

Mom laughed. "Oh, not all. Please, Annie, not all."

As it turned out, the secret told was on Halcyon. But in a way, it was more a plain truth. An answer.

I thought it would be strange, spending most of the day with a woman I hardly knew. Person-to-person, I mean. But Annie Schuyler started talking as though we were continuing a conversation from last week, and I didn't feel uneasy at all.

Her apartment wasn't big, but it had a feeling of comfort, with its flowery, soft-cushioned furniture and a sort of gardeny look.

"Did you do this all yourself?" I asked, and then blushed. She was a decorator, after all. "I love it."

"Take a look at the bedroom. It's in Far East. And I did it before China became the thing."

I liked the lacquered chests, and screen, and oriental rug, but it wasn't a room I'd like to sleep in.

"The kitchen's not much," Annie said. "Cooking's not one of my talents, so that's why we're going out to lunch."

She took me to a place where, like yesterday, the waiters seemed to know her. I guessed she was rich, or at least well off.

"Tell me," she said, after we'd ordered, "does that darling baby still live next to you?"

"Baby? There's no ba . . . oh! You mean Jay Frank?"

"That's the one. Such a pet!"

"Yeah. He gets on my nerves sometimes, but . . ."

"He's like your little brother and you forgive him."

"I guess that's right. We had a run-in about rats not long ago, but we made it up."

"*Rats?* Real rats?"

I told her about the experiments and Angel and Fergy, and then I got around to how Halcyon was photographing the whole schmeer. I tried to make a joke of it, but it fell kind of flat.

"So she's still on that camera kick," Aunt Annie said, disgust showing in her tone. "I've never before known a child with such a one-track mind."

I felt a little defensive toward Halcyon. "She's good at photography, though. And some people have just one interest in life. Like Laurel."

"But music, my dear. That's different."

The waiter who brought our food kept hovering around until Aunt Annie waved him away. "You were saying?" she said, turning back to me.

Instead of going on with the one-track mind topic,

I switched to what I really wanted to discuss. "Could I ask you something? Confidentially?"

"Absolutely."

"Why did Halcyon actually come out to live with us?" I touched the napkin to my lips. "I've heard first one story, and then another."

Aunt Annie moved the anchovies to one side of her salad. "I assumed you knew. Kate and Jeff couldn't swing the tuition at boarding school this year, and they wouldn't let me handle it. And that stubborn girl refused—*refused*—to come down off her high horse and go to public school. So finally, to save the peace, and for another reason, I suggested they send her out to you."

I hesitated, then blurted out, "And what was the other reason?" Had Halcyon really gotten into trouble because of the school pranks? I'd never believed that. She wasn't the type.

"The other reason," Aunt Annie said, "was that I hoped your mother could take that girl and instill some commonsense into her. Jessie's so level-headed, and she's done a marvelous job raising you two girls."

I didn't know what to say to that, so I just started eating my salad.

"Of course," Aunt Annie continued, "I haven't seen a lot of you, darling, but I remembered you as such a nice, outgoing girl and I trusted you still were. And you are." She patted my hand.

127

I forked the lettuce around my plate. "You didn't tell Halcyon that, did you?"

"But of course I did. We had a little chat before she left, and I expressly mentioned she could pick up a few pointers from you."

I felt sick. If Aunt Annie had done a study of the best way to do me in, she couldn't have come up with a better weapon. There isn't a kid alive who likes being compared unfavorably to another. But some grown-ups, especially those who aren't around young people, think it's the sure-fire way to shape up a kid who misses the mark. I could understand that, but it had certainly shot any hope of a decent relationship between Halcyon and me.

"She is getting along, isn't she?" Aunt Annie was almost begging for a pat on the head.

Well, it was done. "Halcyon's doing great in school," I said. And then I quickly changed the subject to Pom Pon.

Aunt Annie tried to be interested, she really did. But after a while, when I was describing our routines and how we were working up to the big playoffs in January, I caught her sneaking a look at her watch.

"I guess," I said with an apologetic little laugh, "I get carried away on the subject of Pom Pon."

"Not at all," she said, trying to make it sound genuine. "Young people have to live in the present. The future's too scary."

"I don't think about the future."

She took my hand. "Neither did I, at your age. But before you know it, it's tomorrow, and the year beyond."

I didn't like that kind of talk. I didn't want to think about years beyond. I wanted things to stay this way forever . . . being captain of the Pom Pon squad and being Skip's girl. That's what was important. The tomorrows didn't matter.

Annie took me sightseeing in the afternoon. The next day—Saturday—Mom, Laurel, and I did a lot of things and before I knew it, Sunday had come and we were all back at La Guardia Airport.

FOURTEEN

Since, in my put-off way, I'd never got around to buying postcards, at the airport I got Jay Frank a little souvenir Statue of Liberty.

"I hate copies of things like that," Halcyon said. "They look too tacky."

"I can't afford the original," I said.

Halcyon walked away, then, to the candy bar section, and I quickly bought a comb shaped like a fish for Skip. It wasn't much, just something to show I'd been thinking of him.

Halcyon's parents were guarding our hand luggage in the waiting area of the airport. I guess they'd convinced Halcyon to leave some stuff at home, since she'd be coming back for Christmas. When they made the boarding announcement, Halcyon's father held out the famous envelope of rat photos. "Here, don't forget this," he said.

"Those are for you!" Halcyon said. "For the gallery!"

He laughed. "Oh, come on. So far we don't show

photographs and even if we did . . ." the way he sort of thrust them toward Halcyon showed what he thought of them.

She snatched them, and her look was a mixture of fury, disappointment, and, I think, a little embarrassment. I turned away but heard her say, "You told me!"

"I told you that maybe . . . maybe some day when you're older and professional enough . . ."

"Yeh, sure, *some day!* What about now?"

"Young lady," Mrs. Hart said, "we're all getting a bit bored with this fixation of yours about cameras. Can't you just be a *child*, doing normal things like . . ." Her voice drifted off. *Like Clara*, she had been about to say. I knew it.

People must have moved between us then, because I heard a blur of other voices, and finally Mom came back from the newstand where she'd bought a magazine. We waited at the corridor, shook hands with Halcyon's parents, and the three of us went on into the plane.

Halcyon was very quiet. She had the look of a dog that had been told to go away and not bother anyone. Not that I thought her folks should have said, "Oh, hey, these photos are great and we'll show them in the gallery." I mean, you can't nauseate customers just to show off your kid's work. But her father could have shown a little more approval. Approval. That's what Halcyon wanted, all right, but she came on so strong, she even put off her own parents.

"You're taking back the photos?" Mom asked, as Halcyon jammed them into the overhead. "I thought . . ."

"She needs them for the science fair," I broke in. I don't know how I happened to come up with that. "They go along with Angel and Fergy's experiment. Isn't that right, Halcyon?"

"Yeah." If she had any feeling about my helping her out, she wasn't going to show it.

"This is really nice," Skip said, when I gave him the comb. "But you didn't need to bring me back anything. Except yourself."

"Did you miss me?" Why did I have to *say* it? I hated myself for letting me say it.

Skip just gave me the look. "Guess."

I still got a tingle when Skip talked like that. I saw him almost every day at practice, at lunch, and at my locker, like now; but I guess I'd never get used to the idea that I was his girl. "I had a good time in New York," I said.

"Yeh? Meet any guys?"

"Skip!" I gave him a playful punch. "We went sightseeing and to plays. We saw a super musical with lots of kids in the cast. It was based on . . ."

I turned to see who or what it was that had caught

132

Skip's attention down the hall. Liz. Liz Halston. She passed out of our view.

"You were saying?" Skip asked, his eyes resting on me again.

"Oh, nothing." What did Skip care about some musical in another town? I had to learn how to keep his interest and hold it. "Tell me about Milwaukee." I said it with a little tease in my tone, the way I'd seen a girl do on a TV show.

"You don't want to hear about Milwaukee." He brushed my cheek with the back of his fingers. I think he might have kissed me, maybe, but just then a custodian rounded the corner pushing a big trash can on wheels and that sort of killed the romantic mood.

I'd noticed in other years that the cold months seem to drag on forever, but December was never like that. This year, it was a whirlwind.

It seemed everyone was caught up in the holiday spirit and there were all kinds of school events crowding the calendar. Most of all, in my life, were the games and practice in between, plus two after-game parties at girls' houses. The parties, I have to say, weren't much in themselves because the parents kept checking to see that the lights were on. No one ever danced, and the stereos blasted so loud you couldn't carry on a conversation. But being close to Skip was all that I asked.

I was really on target with my POPULARITY MUSTS list, which I checked out every now and then. I felt (without trying to be conceited about it) that I was now one of the cutest girls in the school. Not a great beauty like some, but I played up everything I had. I was really in with the Pom Pon crowd and I had the number one boy at school wrapped around my finger. I was on the party list, and while my clothes wouldn't put me in the best-dressed category, I'd learned to switch separates around, and Angel and I traded clothes. My grades so far were keeping up there, and I went out of my way to be friendly to everyone, even teachers.

The next big challenge was to throw a slumber party for the Pom Pon girls at our house, and that I intended to do during the Christmas vacation. It was the perfect time. I'd try to get Laurel to go off somewhere with Mom early in the evening until the party got into gear. Of course, Halcyon would be with her family in New York. That was important. Even though Halcyon had toned down some lately, her kind of talk wouldn't go too well with the Pom Pon crowd.

So everything was going according to plan until late in December, when Mom gave me some really unsettling news.

"I talked with Laurel again," she said, coming into my room one evening. "Her cold isn't any better." Mom frowned. "I think she's more sick than she

134

admits, because she's actually stayed home from classes, and you know your sister."

"She'll feel better once she gets home," I said, checking off a homework assignment.

"If. I'm not going to let her travel in a state of near pneumonia."

"Mom, she'd feel terrible not being with us at Christmas!"

"Then we'd simply go out there."

"We *can't!*" The thought of what the girls would say if I called off the party hit me like a rock. "We were just there a month ago!"

"So . . . we'll go again if necessary. The Thanksgiving trip was a form of vacation and to check out Laurel's situation. And of course, I enjoyed seeing Annie again. But this may be a necessity. I thought I ought to warn you before you made plans."

"I already have," I said, doing graffiti on a pad. "You know about the party."

Mom took a deep breath. "Well, we'll see. It's still a week off." She paused at the door. "You might send Laurel a note." Her look seemed to add, *since you're so concerned.*

The next day I sent Laurel a get-well card. It worked. By the end of the week we got the good news that Laurel was feeling better and would come home as planned. I was glad for her, of course, but I must say I mostly breathed a sigh of relief for myself.

Our plans worked out that we took Halcyon to the airport and picked up Laurel on the same trip.

Laurel looked paler and thinner than before, but she was all hepped up on the idea of coming home. I guess she missed us a lot. Halcyon's parents were so wrapped up in the gallery and social life they weren't much company.

Although Laurel seemed better during the next few days, I could hear her coughing from Halcyon's room at night and sometimes hear her get up and go downstairs. One night I crept down to see what she was doing. I found her wrapped in a blanket in a chair in the living room staring at the lighted Christmas tree.

"Is something wrong?" I asked.

"Oh, no. I just couldn't sleep. She opened the blanket. "Come, bunny, talk to me." I cuddled beside her.

"Want some hot chocolate?"

Laurel laughed. "No. What I need is something to ease my conscience."

"Are you kidding?"

"Here I am, taking it easy, when I should be catching up on work I missed when I was sick. That's silly, I guess. I should just let myself relax and make up for lost time later."

"That's right," I said. "I'm always reading about celebrities hiding out somewhere to recharge their batteries. Now don't laugh," I said, giving her a nudge. "You're going to be famous some day."

Laurel's arm stiffened a little. "Is that all you care about?"

"Well, aren't you going to be a concert pianist, playing in halls everywhere? Even Europe? Maybe Japan?"

"That's the highest rung, all right. But if I don't make it, I'm not going off the deep end."

"Laurel! You'd settle for less?"

"I'd settle for being the best of whatever I can possibly be."

"You can be whatever you want to be." I stared at the tree. "But, of course, it does help to know the right people." Without Angel, I was thinking, I'd never have made Pom Pon.

Laurel turned and looked at me. "Bunny! That's a warped attitude. I'm surprised at you."

"It's the way things work," I said. "Everywhere. You just don't know the ways of the world, Laurel."

We sat quietly for a few minutes, looking at the tree. It wasn't the showy type. It was full and fragrant and familiar, with toyland figures we'd had ever since I could remember. The lights were the old-time ones, too, not miniature, and they didn't flicker. It was very comforting sitting there with Laurel, being close, and not really needing to talk. After a while, though, I got kind of cramped and sleepy. "You ready to go back to bed?"

Laurel stirred, but then her arm around me tensed a little. "Clara?"

"Ummmm?"

"If I didn't really reach the top . . . would you be awfully disappointed? In me?"

"Oh, Laurel!" I leaned my head against her shoulder. "I'm sorry." My lips were against the lace at the neck of her nightgown. "It's you we love. Not what you might be."

She cupped her hand around the back of my head and kissed my hair. "I'm glad. I knew. But it's good to hear."

"Shall we go back to bed?" I covered a yawn.

We went upstairs, and playing the little mother, I tucked Laurel in and kissed her good-night. "Sleep tight, and don't let the bedbugs bite," I said.

Later, lying awake, I got the strange thought, *In a way they're a little alike, Laurel and Halcyon. They both know where they want to go. Only Laurel's like a butterfly and Halcyon's like a bulldozer.*

Christmas was . . . what shall I say? Christmas like always. We had people over, including Jay Frank and Sheri and some of Mom's faculty friends. Jay Frank went bonkers over the toy car wash Halcyon and I had gone in on together (her idea), but for which she still hadn't paid her share (also her idea).

The day after, Angel came over to run her rat

routine. By this time the little critters were onto the trick of racing down the runway, pressing the lever, and getting the goodies.

"Couldn't you just throw them a handful and let them goof off and enjoy the holidays?" I asked.

Angel looked shocked. "And ruin everything we've worked so hard to build up? Oh, Clara, you're kidding."

"Yeh. Hey . . ." I took hold of her hand. "Is that a new ring?"

"It's . . . yes. Halcyon gave it to me."

"*Halcyon?*" She'd given me knee socks. "Is it supposed to be a friendship ring? With that stone in it?"

Angel pulled away and, for once, looked embarrassed. "I didn't want to take it, but she insisted. She said good friends give good gifts. All I gave her was a nice barrette."

I tried to sound unconcerned. "Since when have you two become such good friends?"

Angel hesitated. "We're not really. I mean, I've tried to be friendly to her because she doesn't seem to have anyone. Except you, of course," she added, with a quick look.

"What happened to that crowd she ran with before?"

"I guess she had a falling out with one of the girls, especially. Halcyon's pretty outspoken."

"Don't I know!"

"So lately she's been hanging around Fergy and

me quite a lot. She gave him a pocket calculator for Christmas, but he wouldn't accept it. I wish now I hadn't accepted this ring, but she said it was something of hers that she wanted me to have. I didn't want to hurt her feelings. It's kind of sad that . . ." Her voice drifted away.

Seeing Angel in that mood, it seemed almost as though our friendship had drifted a little, too. "You know what?" I said, leaning forward. "I think you should change your mind and come to the party Thursday night. You know everyone, and you'd fit right into the scene."

"Is the whole Pom Pon crowd going to be here?"

"Liz can't make it, and a couple of others, but most can. Come on, Angel."

"No, I don't think so." She twisted the ring absently and for a moment I thought she'd take it off, but she didn't. "It wouldn't be fair."

Fair? What did she mean? Because she was no longer on the squad? Or did she mean—could she possibly mean—that it wouldn't be fair for her to come when she knew I'd purposely planned the party for when Halcyon wouldn't be here? It seemed incredible, but still . . . had my best friend shifted her loyalty to Halcyon?

That thought bothered me a lot, but it was nothing compared to the jolt I got the next day. Halcyon's parents called to say they'd received an invitation to visit friends on the West Coast. Since they

140

needed to go out anyway on business, they'd like to accept. But here came the big gut-grabber. Could they drop off Halcyon a little early, on their way?

"Mom!" I wailed when she told me. "You didn't agree, did you?"

"Well, yes. Laurel's going back early to catch up on work, as you know, so the room's free. I can't see any conflict."

"I can! My party! This means Halcyon will be here, butting in and probably making cracks about how Pom Pon went out with saddle shoes. You know how she is!"

Mom absently picked up Laurel's bottle of aspirin and set it down again. "Calm down, Clara. You'll manage. It's up to you to do the best you can to make the party a success. It's all in your hands."

As it turned out, my party's success was in the hands of fate. And those hands were lousy with cold germs.

FIFTEEN

I started feeling awful the night before the party. The next morning I wasn't sure I could pull myself together, much less my room where most of the party would take place. It needed rearranging to make room for the girls' sleeping bags.

Feeling feverish and somewhat dizzy, I pushed my bed from the middle of the room over against the wall. The effort made me so weak I wanted to cry. I sat on the floor, my palm against my moist forehead.

Halcyon walked into the room. "What's the matter with you?"

"I don't feel so well."

"I'll go get your mother."

"No!" Mom would take my temperature, and it had to be around a hundred. "I'll be all right. Besides, she's gone to the store for things for the party."

"Oh, that's right, it's tonight, isn't it?"

She knew very well when it was. Halcyon walked

over to my dresser, fingered several things and then sprayed on some French cologne Skip had given me for Christmas. "I used to like this brand," she said, "before everyone started using it."

I was so peeved, along with being feverish, that I blurted out, "What are your plans for tonight? Going out?"

"I *was* going over to Angel's, but now I don't know. She's not very dependable, is she?"

"Angel?"

"So I guess I'll just stick around. I think your mother would feel better, having me sort of on deck, since she's going to the city." Halcyon wandered toward the door. "Why does a woman her age want to see the *Nutcracker?* I mean!" She looked upward.

"Mom bought the tickets for us—Laurel and me— but now she's taking a couple of friends." I got up. "And by the way, Halcyon, you needn't bring my mom's age into every conversation. It's kind of crude."

"Well! Excuse *me!*" she said, and then she left.

I almost called her back. I needed Halcyon in a way. But it would have meant overlooking her attitude, and I just couldn't bring myself to do that.

At our early makeshift dinner, I tried my best to be alert and cheery, but the truth was I was feeling worse by the minute. I had to force down the little I ate.

Mom looked at me. "Are you all right?"

"She's just excited, Mrs. Conrad," Halcyon said. "Aren't you, Clara?"

"That's right."

"And I think she's worried about the weather," Halcyon said. "It's snowing, and you have that long drive into Chicago."

For once, I was grateful for Halcyon's take-over conversation.

"I have snow tires," Mom said, "and anyway, I'll be home before it gets really bad outside. Ah, Chicago weather."

"New York's as bad," Halcyon said.

I couldn't believe she'd actually said that.

By ten o'clock the party was in full swing, and so was my fever. Halcyon, who could really be helpful when she felt like it, got things together in the kitchen. I took up the supplies of soft drinks and bowls of chips and pretzels. I could hardly make my way across the room because of the bodies draped everywhere. Most girls had already changed into their so-called sleeping gear. Beth Meyers had on a tan fuzzy cover-all that made her look like a teddy bear, and Leanne wore a slinky number that brought whistles until she covered up with a robe. Most of the crew, though, lounged around in over-sized T-shirts and underpants. I was still in my jeans and top.

On about my fifth trip upstairs, I couldn't even get

into the room because a few of the extroverts were doing a replay of a really dumb skit from speech class, and there was a lot of milling around. I sprawled in the doorway, leaning against the side. The room seemed to be shifting a little. I closed my eyes. The sounds in the room changed and drifts of conversation came to me, mostly of the and-then-he-said-to-me variety. I edged slightly into the room. My stomach sent up a warning signal.

I heard someone thump-thumping up the stairs and knew it could only be Halcyon. And so it was.

"Dearheart, come on in," I said, waving a limp hand.

She stood eyeing me. "Clara, have you been *drinking?*" I loved that shock in her voice. I'd never heard it before. "You know, your mother . . ."

"Sure, I know my mother." Something told me to crawl out into the hall. Halcyon knelt beside me, probably to smell my breath.

"I'm sick," I moaned. "I think . . ." My stomach gave a lurch.

She grabbed my shoulders and half pulled me into the bathroom. Nothing happened.

Halcyon felt my head. "You're burning up," she said. "You really have got a fever."

I could hear the phone ringing. "Get that, would you? If it's Mom, don't tell her."

"Okay. Just stay there, okay? I'll be right back."

I heard Halcyon thumping down the stairs. The

145

room stopped spinning, and the noise from my room sort of subsided, and then I heard someone say, "Where's Clara?"

"Probably getting more cokes. It's about all she's done all evening. What a bore! I can see why Angel didn't show up."

"I don't think that's it." The voice sounded clear, yet far away. "Why should Angel stay friends with Clara after the way she ripped off her boyfriend?"

"Clara didn't take Skip away from Angel," someone else said.

I didn't, I thought. It just happened.

"That's right," someone said for me. "Don't blame Clara. It could've happened to any girl elected captain. Well, any girl within *reason*."

"I don't believe it could've happened to just anyone," another voice spoke up. "We all know Skip set it up. He passed the word to one of the guys, and he passed it on to someone in Pom Pon that Clara was it. His choice. And so that's why it happened."

You knew, my brain was frantically insisting. You knew all along.

"Sure, Clara's cute, and she was Skip's first choice." It was Mindy's voice. "He told Gary and Gary made me promise to do what I could. But we all know if Clara had lost, Skip would have switched to the winner."

A lot of garbled voices then, with one coming

146

through. "Yeh, probably Liz. But don't tell Clara. That would be mean."

My brain had finally sorted out a message and what it was saying was *Now. Now's the time to be sick.*

I was.

It seemed that everything I'd swallowed, including my pride, was on recall. Afterwards, I felt so weak I could hardly lean over the sink to rinse my face and mouth.

Halcyon came back. "You okay?"

I reached for a towel. "Yeh. Was that my mother?"

"No. It was one of the boys. They're having a party down the street and they might come over."

"No way! Did you say so?"

"Who am I to issue orders? I sent Erica down to try to talk them out of it."

"Tell her to do more than try." The last person in the world I wanted to see right now was Skip. "What time is it?"

"Nearly one."

"One! My mom should be home by now."

"She has to drive those other women home, remember? And it's snowing and blowing outside. You'd better go lie down."

"Okay."

"What if the guys do come over?" There was a worried note in her voice.

"Halcyon, take over! Go get on the phone and tell them not to!" I staggered off to Mom's room.

Lying there, drifting in and out of feverish sleep, I was aware of the girls going up and down the stairs and a lot of squeals and commotion. But through it all what I'd overheard earlier kept going over and over in my thoughts. It was a bad dream come true.

Someone was undressing me. I flung out my arms and fought until I realized it was Mom, and then I asked, "What time is it?"

"Nearly three. The car wouldn't start after the ballet, and I had trouble finding an all-night garage."

"Did you get home okay?" I asked, sitting up. I felt dizzy and disoriented. "Oh. I guess you did. But I was worried."

"I tried to call, but the phone was busy for two solid hours. I'm really annoyed with your friends. Here, let me pull off those jeans."

"You didn't yell at them, did you?" Actually, I didn't care. It was really quiet now. "You didn't send them home, did you?"

"No. I took pity on their parents. But in the morning, out they go. Such carryings on!"

I slept the night with Mom, and the next day, after she'd cleared out the girls and cleaned up the room, she moved me back to my own bed. "I didn't realize that twelve girls could make such a mess," she said. "I even found a peanut butter and jelly sandwich crammed under the cushion of your chair."

"Did they have a good time?" I asked, sinking against the cool pillow.

"You throw a swell party," she said drily. "Even in absentia." She put a thermometer into my mouth. "I described your symptoms to the doctor, and he said it sounds like flu and to do the usual routine. I'm going out for some things and I want you to stay put. Halcyon can take over while I'm gone."

For once, no for twice, Halcyon's take-over qualities were of some use. She hadn't, at least, let the boys come over last night.

I was awfully sick for a couple of days. Mom managed to talk the doctor into stopping by, but all he said was that I should get plenty of rest, drink fluids, and keep on taking the medicine.

It was okay at first, because I was mostly out of it anyway, but when I started feeling better I got restless. I wanted to hear Skip's voice and try to believe that what I'd overheard was all a mistake, that he really liked me for myself. But in a way, I was afraid. I *knew*.

"Mom," I complained one time, as she came in with my juice, "I keep hearing the phone ring, but I don't know what's going on. Can't I go downstairs?"

"The girls just call to see how you are," she said.

Girls. I drank the juice and wiped my mouth. "Have . . . uh . . . any boys called?"

"He's called once or twice that I know of." Mom gave the slightest flicker of a smile. "Didn't Halcyon tell you?"

"No. So that's why I'd like to get up and answer the phone myself."

"In a day or two. In the meantime, I'll ask Halcyon to jot down all messages."

That hit me wrong. Sure, Halcyon had been nice the night of the party, but that didn't mean I trusted her with my personal calls. "Mom, if you appoint her to phone duty, by the time I'm better I won't have any friends left!"

"Now, Clara, that's just silly. Halcyon can't take away your friends. You should know that."

Yeh, Mom, I thought. You don't know her technique. I visualized the ring. That expensive looking ring with the tiny blue stone. "Has Angel called?"

"Every day. I talked to her myself, a little while ago. Since you're no longer contagious, I told her it would be all right if she stopped by this afternoon. If you feel up to it."

"I do!"

Mom took the empty glass and left the room.

I told Angel about the party—what I remembered of it. Next, I wanted to work the conversation around to Skip and ask Angel's opinion of what I'd overheard, but I wasn't sure how to get started. I decided to warm her up first on her favorite topic, rats.

"Two more weeks and then the big event, eh?" I said, sitting cross-legged up in bed. "Think you'll win first prize at the Fair?"

Carefully, Angel selected a chocolate from a big two-pound box Laurel had sent when she heard I was sick. "Fergy and I aren't concerned about winning," she said. "Although we wouldn't blushingly refuse the prize, if offered. The point is, we've proved it can be done."

"What can?"

"Animal behavior can be shaped, Clara. Goodness. What do you think Fergy and I have been doing all this time?"

"Do you like him?"

Angel looked at me strangely, as though the fever had fried my brains. "What do you mean, like him?"

"As a boy."

She put down the candy box. "Fergy's not a *boy*. I'm not even sure he's a *human*. He's a brain, Clara, a brain. A brain that attached itself to a body so it could move from place to place."

"So you don't like him?"

"I like him, I like him. But I don't *like* him."

I knew what she meant. Now we were warmed up. "Did you like Skip?"

151

"Skip?" Angel frowned slightly, as though the name had surfaced from a faraway past.

"That's not really what I want to know." I picked out the empty tissue cups from the box and crumpled them. "Do you think he likes me just because I'm Pom Pon captain?"

"Why, of course."

I'd known, even before the evening of the party I'd known, but the shock still must have shown.

For once Angel looked rattled. "I thought you realized . . ."

"Realized what?"

She shrugged. "The way he is."

"What's that supposed to mean?"

"It means . . . Skip chooses winners."

Winners. Was I a winner? I didn't feel like one at the moment. "So," I finally said, "it's true. If Liz had been chosen, Skip would have . . ."

"He saw to it that *you* were." Angel was trying to be a comfort. "He liked you best, and he arranged it."

After a few swallows, I said, "I guess I should feel honored."

Angel didn't say anything.

"I mean, he did choose me."

"That's right."

"But the girls didn't. Not really. It was a fake. The whole thing was a fake."

Angel was quiet for a moment. "Don't feel bad.

The girls have minds of their own. And you did get the vote."

"But I'm not sure of anything any more. I'm not sure that I have any friends. Real friends." I looked at her. "Even one."

"Clara!" Angel looked shocked. "Could you ever doubt . . .! I mean, we've both been busy, but no matter what, we're still best, true friends."

I knew she meant it. I hated myself for ever doubting.

She leaned forward and touched my hand. I looked at her fingers. "Where's the ring?"

Angel put her hand to her face and laughed. "Halcyon asked for it back. She said her mother had a fit because actually it's a family heirloom. Can you believe it?"

I could. But I didn't understand. "If that's true, why would she give you the ring in the first place?"

"To make a show. Poor Halcyon. She wants so much to be noticed and admired."

"Huh. For sure."

"It would be so much better if she'd just relax," Angel said. "Underneath Halcyon's not all that bad."

"Mmmm." True, maybe, but I wasn't feeling too sympathetic. "So she took it back, just like that?"

Angel nodded. "Halcyon said she'd give me something else instead."

"Well," I said, "you've always looked good in knee socks."

153

SIXTEEN

The question that now loomed in my feeble, fevered little brain was, should I call Skip? But if so, what would I say? *Is it true you set me up as Captain?* I knew it to be true, so the only question was *why*. Dummy, I knew that too. He thought I was the cutest girl on Pom Pon. So let it go. What did it matter? No one knew that I knew except Angel, and she'd never tell. Once I shook off this cold and got the sap running in my system, I'd go out there at half time and prove to everyone that I was a winner—not by election, but naturally.

That settled, I was up the next day and feeling steadier than I'd expected.

"Want to come to the cellar?" Angel asked. "Fergy and I could use your help. We're doing the final run-throughs on the rats. We'll pick the best and put them into heavy training. It's showdown time at the old corral."

I wasn't sure I felt *that* steady. "How about Halcyon helping?"

"She made up with one of the girls and went over to her house. You don't have to handle the rats—Jay Frank likes to do that. Just jot down the times for us on the record sheet."

The cellar was all bright lights and business. Jay Frank was hopping around poking his finger into cages, and Fergy was testing the food-pellet-dropping thing.

"Hello, Sicko," he greeted me. "What brings you to our little laboratory?" (He pronounced it la-*bore*-a-tory.)

"Angel. To help. But I'm not a rat-handler, remember that."

"Don't worry about it," Fergy said. "As a rule, animals don't contract human diseases." He took off his glasses and rubbed them with the bottom of his T-shirt. It looked like an old paint rag. "We started to mix up more dye for the rats—they're fading—but we didn't have all the colors. So, later. Hey, Jay, you ready?"

"I get to bring the rats over to the run, one at a time," Jay Frank told me. "That's my job. They couldn't do it without my help."

I turned to Fergy. "He can't do it during the fair. Who are you going to sucker into doing it then?"

"The job's open," Fergy said. "So if you're interested . . ."

I sneezed. "Let's get going here."

They brought out the rats one by one, set each

behind the starting barricade, then lifted it and set the stop-watch. In spite of myself, I got interested. It was kind of cute, the way each little rat took off down the runway, paused at the end, and pressed the lever. I marked each one's time on the sheet.

"Shall we give Little Blue another chance?" Angel asked Fergy, as Jay Frank handed her the rat with a tinge of blue dye on its head.

"He deserves another chance," Jay Frank pleaded. "He's such a friendly little fellow."

"Amiability cuts no ice in the field of science," Fergy said. "It's the track record that counts."

"Give him a try," Jay Frank still pleaded.

"Yeh, Fergy," I said, "keep an open mind."

"All right, but remember, we're picking the consistently best five performers today for intensive training, and your little pet there is way down on the list, Jay Frank. Put him in position."

Jay Frank did. Fergy raised the barricade and Angel clicked the stop-watch. It ticked on and on as Little Blue sat happily cleaning his whiskers.

"He's hopeless, and never mind prodding with the finger, there, J.F.," Fergy said. "Take him out and, Clara, cross off his name."

"You can't do that to Little Blue!" Jay Frank cried out.

"We're not doing anything to him," Fergy explained. "Just letting him be his own rat-person, as it were. Look at it this way, Jay Frank. Little Blue is not cut out for show biz, but that doesn't make him any less a rat."

"He'll be happier, leading a quiet life, out of the limelight," Angel added.

Jay Frank held Little Blue up to his cheek. "But I love him."

"Then take him," Fergy said. "Compliments of the house."

"Really? For my very own? Oh, Little Blue!" After another round of nuzzling, Jay Frank said, "I need a cage."

Angel sighed. "Take a cage. That small one." From the look she gave Fergy, I could tell that even her super patience was wearing thin.

It wore even thinner as time went on because Jay Frank, engrossed with Little Blue, had to be reminded each time to bring out a new rat for tryouts and then to return it to its cage.

"It's just as well the fair is two weeks away," Angel said.

"There's a lot of work ahead of us," Fergy said, "making the signs and setting up the display and then transporting all these animals and equipment out of here."

"I'm going home now," Jay Frank said.

I went upstairs with him and, when I saw it was turning dark, was about to offer to walk him home. Instead I sneezed. "Tell you what," I said. "You start out, Jay Frank, and I'll dial your number, and then I'll count to see how long it takes you to answer."

He still liked games, anyone could see, by the quick interest in his eyes. "Okay."

"Button your coat. Go!"

I saw him whisk by the window, and then I dialed. The phone rang and rang. Had he dropped the key in the snow? Was there . . . something . . . someone . . .? Finally, he answered.

"What took you so long?"

"I couldn't answer because Little Blue jumped right out of my pocket and ran into a stack of dirty clothes on the floor. He's fast, Clara, when he wants to be!"

"Stupid! Why didn't you carry him in the cage?"

"Because it's cold outside!"

Almost on cue, I sneezed again.

"See," Jay Frank said in triumph. "I don't want him to be like you. Sick."

"Turkey!" I hung up and went back to bed.

By the time school started again, I was feeling better. More or less. There were still times when I'd feel warm and other times cool. I felt the same way about Skip. Cool when I thought of how he'd set me up without saying so, and yet warm when he paid attention to me. There was no denying Skip was cute. But that's what he'd said I was. I was beginning to think of cute as a four-letter word.

158

With the semester coming to a close in three weeks, though, and all the fun things like reviews and tests, I had more than cuteness on my mind. Also, the science fair was scheduled for the same time as the big regional games, which was not a masterpiece of planning on the part of the school.

And as though the tests, science fair, and games weren't enough on their own, Liz suddenly came up with what she called a dynamite variation to one of our Pom Pon routines.

"It's a step I learned at my disco dance class," she said. "Watch . . . let me show you how we could work it right into this number and give it more glitz." She paused. "Miss Curry said it's okay with her if it's okay with all of you."

"We don't have enough time to go messing around. We've got the number down pat, and it's good enough," Erica said.

Liz, who had looked dewy with excitement, faded as more and more comments blasted out.

"Oh, hey, you guys," I heard myself saying. "We're not so hot that we couldn't stand some improvement. Let's see what she has in mind, okay?"

Liz shot me a glance of gratitude. I had to give her a lot of credit. In front of those negative faces, she got up and did some really tricky steps that made the routine come alive.

"Great!" I shouted, as she held the last position, although inside, my thoughts were dit-dash-ditting the message, *Clara, you're putting yourself on the line.*

"Yeh," voices around me were echoing. "That looks glitzy all right. But can we learn it?"

Liz, face flushed, said "The captain has the variations, so she'll need some practice. The squad just does the basic stuff." My heart sank. "I'll show you, Clara, and work with you until you get it down pat, and I'll be with the squad and work with them, too. We can wrap it up in a few sessions."

The squad came along just fine, but I had to work and work. I wasn't a natural the way Liz was.

"Watch," she'd say to me, all patience. "I'll do it in slow motion."

I'd watch and copy. Then we'd speed it up a little and then a little more, until finally I was a repeat pattern of Liz. Still, she was the natural.

"Would you want to lead this one routine?" I asked her. "I wouldn't mind. Honestly."

"You're fine," she said. "Trust yourself." She wasn't such a bad kid.

One night at practice we did the new number when the team and a few scattered parents, come to drive their kids home, were sitting around on the bleachers. As we were trotting off to the locker room afterwards, someone standing behind a pillar grabbed me off to the side.

"Skip, hi!" I hated to think how I looked. Perspiration was actually stinging my eyes.

160

"A real class act you got there," he said. "You looked real cute."

That word did it. "I'm not cute," I said.

"No?" The slow smile built up and his eyes . . . what can I say except that they seemed to caress me more than ever?

"I look lousy, I feel lousy," I said. "But I *am* captain. That's what counts, isn't it?"

"Whatever." Skip's look had shifted to the coach, out on the floor, who was whistling to the team. "See you later."

"Skip," I reached out to grab his sleeve, but since his arm was bare, the grab turned into a pinch. "What if I'd lost the election? That you set up?"

He rubbed the spot on his arm, which was turning a spidery pink. "You're cuckoo. I've gotta go. Coach is . . ."

I reached out to really pinch him this time, only he ducked. "You're cute, Clara, as I said. But don't press your luck." He gave me an almost hostile look, then trotted out to the team.

I stood there thinking, What's your problem, Clara? What are you doing? *Don't press your luck*, he'd said. *You can be replaced*, he hadn't said, though wasn't it true? And so smart, cute Clara had verbally and physically attacked the guy who was only the prize catch of Harrison Junior High. Why, I asked myself? Is it some kind of crime that he likes you and what you stand for?

161

But what is it that I stand for, I thought, as I went back to the lockers. What am I, exactly?

I'm the captain. I'm Skip's girl. The words whirled around in my mind. I wondered if the fever was coming back. There must be something wrong with me, else why would I have lashed out at Skip like that? He'd liked me enough to get me elected captain so he could go out with me. I should be flattered. I should be grateful. Instead, I had a terrible feeling of wanting to punch someone. Mostly myself.

We kept the disco steps in the routine and continued practicing for the first regional game, coming up the next week on Wednesday. Once in a while, leading the variations, I'd get a glimpse of Liz, doing the simpler steps with the rest of the squad, but then I'd look away. Fair is fair, as they say. But not always.

Skip continued to call every night, as though that little scene by the bleachers had never taken place. "I like that dance thing you're doing," he said one evening. "Who came up with that idea?"

I hesitated. *It just developed*, I wanted to say. "Liz," I said. "Liz thought of it."

Now there was silence from Skip's end. "It's great," he said then. "I like it. You look like a real knockout, Clara."

Something inside of me murmured, is that it? Is that where it's at? But all I said was, "Thank you."

162

Meanwhile, back in the cellar, things were moving right along. Fergy and Angel dismantled the run and took it over to the school, along with all the materials for the display set-up.

The rats, meanwhile, were still confined to quarters in our cellar. "We've got to shield them until show time," Fergy explained. "Because all that attention from the crowds might affect their performance."

"Yeh, like they keep rock stars locked in hotel rooms with security guards," I said. "But that's to protect them from the groupies, which doesn't apply in this case."

"Anyway, it's nice of you to offer to feed them tonight while Angel and I are over setting up the display."

"I'm feeding them?"

"Thanks, I accept the offer," Fergy said quickly. "Just what I lay out, though, don't give them any more. We'll pick them up at six tomorrow for the grand opening at seven." He said this with a look at his watch and mine, as though we had to synchronize.

During a free hour the next afternoon, I got a pass to go to the chemistry lab, where the kids were setting up the science fair stuff, on the pretext that I had some vital information for Angel. Actually, I just wanted to wish her luck and to hear her reassure me that I wouldn't louse up the routine during the game. My knees were already shaking, just from my thinking of the crowds that would be there. I mean, this was a killer game.

Angel wasn't around, but there was Halcyon, fastening up rat photos. "How come you're doing that?" I asked.

"Because they go along with the experiment."

It was like my own words on the plane coming back. I'd just meant them as comfort to Halcyon at the time, but boy, she'd jumped on them. When the experiment took first prize, she'd take a lot of credit. Oh, well. "Are you going with Angel and Fergy to pick up the rats?" I asked her. "Or will you give them your key to get in?"

"I'll probably be tied up here. I left the house unlocked. Hold up these two photos so I can step back and see which way they should face."

Face them against the wall was what I wanted to say, but I held them up.

"Higher," Halcyon commanded. "Can't you stop jiggling?"

"I'm jumpy. Our game starts at five. C'mon, Halcyon, decide."

"Oh, all right, go." Halcyon heaved a sigh.

"Listen, this game happens to be . . ."

"Clara, we've heard that so many times. Here, give me those photos."

I tossed them onto the table and left.

After school, the Pom Pon squad gathered in the

locker room and we got into our outfits. Then we went through the routines, with special emphasis on the disco variation. After about the third time, Miss Curry told us to knock it off, we'd peak before our performance.

While the girls were relaxing, she called me aside. "Clara, I guess this is as good a time to tell you as any. I was dubious last fall about putting you on the squad at all, considering your lack of experience. But I decided to play a long shot. Then, when you were elected captain, I confess I had serious doubts." She combed her fingers through her short hair. "It was unusual, to say the least . . . a new-comer. But again, I thought you'd either come through or drop out altogether."

I waited, wondering what she was leading up to.

"Well, you've come through. You've got a spark. The girls have a real live leader, and the crowd out there today is in for a treat." She squeezed her eyes at me. "Give them a good show."

I stood, tugging at my sweater cuffs, not knowing what to say. Someone came to the door and called, "Ten minutes."

Everyone started squealing, checking outfits, knotting shoe laces, looking in mirrors, or making mad dashes to the john. My heart was thump-thump-thumping, and I could feel a trickle of perspiration toward my bra.

"Okay, girls, this is it," Miss Curry said, checking

her watch. "We'll go out and stand in the areaway to be ready. The band plays the national anthem, the principal will say a few words over the mike, then we go on. Let's hit it, girls! Mindy, put that comb away. All out!"

We filed out of the locker room and down a corridor and then into a side door of the gym. Walls of bleachers were on each side. People near the end looked us over.

The band started playing the national anthem. Everyone stood up. We, of course, were already standing, but I want to tell you I thought my legs were going to fold like a card table's any minute.

"Sing," I told myself. "Lose yourself in the anthem." But it was hard to jump in because the people on one side of us were a couple of words behind the ones on the other side, and they were all lagging behind the band.

". . . bursting in air . . . gave proof . . ." I chimed in, just to keep my teeth from chattering.

The girl next to me gave me a jab, and I stopped. I didn't think I'd sounded that bad.

"Clara . . ." she whispered. She pointed back of us, a worried look on her face. I turned. Some boy, with a piece of paper in his hand, was coming forward as the girls stared.

"Clara Conrad?" the boy asked.

Oh, say does th—at star spangled . . . they sang.

"What?" I felt chilled as I stared at the boy.

"There's a phone call for you in the main office."

"I can't leave!" . . . *still wa—ve . . o'er the land* . . . "We've got to go out there in a couple of minutes! Who is it? What is the call?"

The kid hunched his shoulders. "How should I know? They just said to come get you, it's urgent. Yeh, urgent."

Miss Curry had come up and heard the last. She took the paper, put her hand on my shoulder, and said, "Hurry, honey. Go see what it's about. There's time, the principal's long-winded." She was leading me out to the corridor as she talked. "If it's an emergency, do what you need to do. We'll cover all right." She squeezed my shoulder. "But hurry." She rushed back to the girls, and I raced up the steps and down the hall toward the office. Mom . . . I thought. Something's happened to Mom. Or to Laurel. Something awful.

I dashed into the office, and the secretary silently held up the phone. It slipped in my grip, and I steadied my wrist with the other hand. "Hello?"

Nothing.

"Hello? *Hello!*"

And then the voice came through, scared and little. It was Jay Frank. "Help," he said. "Clara, help." And that was all.

SEVENTEEN

"What is it?" I gasped into the phone. "Tell me!"

Silence. Just awful silence.

I took the phone from my ear and stared at it dumbly. And then I looked at the anxious face of the secretary. "I've got to leave," I said through the shaking that had started up in my chest. I slammed down the receiver. "Something . . . terrible . . ." I started for the door. "Tell them," I yelled over my shoulder, "tell them . . . anyone who asks . . ."

"Sweetheart, you can't run out like that. Take this." A coat was flung over my shoulders. "Could I drive you?"

But I was already racing down the hall and out of the building. With the coat flapping at my heels as I clutched it around me, I started running the several blocks home. Jay Frank alone in the house, always scared about monsters and stupid things, but never, never would he call me unless there was a very real kind of danger! A little boy alone, in the gathering dark, and on this day with no one around, someone . . . knowing . . . waiting?

I rounded the corner and ran straight for Jay Frank's house. Sweating, scared half to death, and with no idea of what I'd do once inside, I grabbed at the back door handle. Locked. I shook the door. Locked tight.

I tore around to the front of the house and rattled and jangled that door. Locked like a fort. I rang the bell and yelled, "It's me, Jay Frank! Let me in!"

I tried to look through an opening in the front curtains, but it was dark inside. Why hadn't Jay Frank turned on the light, first thing, like always? *Because there was someone in there with him.* The thought made me pull back and moan with fear. Oh, Jay Frank!

The police! I'd have to go home and call the police. Oh, let me be in time! Gasping for air through my mouth, I cut over toward our back door. About halfway there, I remembered my purse and my key were back at school! But I ran for the door anyway. I'd break it down, or break a window, or . . .

The door was open.

I rushed into the kitchen, dropped the coat, and picked up the phone.

"Oh," a voice said behind me. "You finally got here."

The phone dropped from my hand and dangled

on its coiled cord as I whirled around. "Jay Frank! Jay Frank!" I thought I'd collapse. "Are you all right?" I dropped to my knees and clutched his shoulders.

"Well," he said, "I'm pretty worried."

I felt kind of dazed. *Worried* didn't seem quite the word. "What's happened? Was someone after you? Tell me!" I glanced toward the open door.

"You're so funny, Clara. Who would be after me?"

"You called! You called *HELP!* What's wrong?" I gave him a little shake.

"It's a long story. Why don't we sit down?"

I stared at him, dazed. He was all right. And I'd left everything . . . my *life* . . . and come running.

"It's very confusing," Jay Frank sighed. "Say, why are you wearing that outfit?"

I bent my head and covered my face with my hands. They'd be out on the floor by now. The Pom Pon girls in their short pleated skirts and their sweaters, doing their opening routine. Liz would be leading them, and the crowd would be hyped up and the girls would be even more so. And they'd flash and dip and dance and bedazzle . . .

Jay Frank made a little throat-clearing sound. "Do you want to go back, and I'll tell you about it later?"

I lifted my head. I felt numb. "You might as well give me the story, now that I'm here." I couldn't go back. It was too late. They had gone on without me,

170

and I'd never live it down. "What's happened, Jay Frank?"

"Well." He sat sideways on a kitchen chair and hooked one heel on the rung. "You know Little Blue."

Don't hit him. He's only a child. A child you practically raised, so who's to blame. "Tell me," I said, falling onto the opposite chair and leaning forward on my arms on the table. "Tell me about Little Blue."

Jay Frank licked his thin lips and gave me the kind of look he always gives when he's testing the air, so to speak. "Well," he said, still feeling his way, "he hasn't seemed happy these last few days."

Was I really sitting here in the kitchen, decked out in my Pom Pon outfit, listening to this? *Little Blue is not in a happy frame of mind.* I stared for several seconds, and then in an oh-so-steady voice inquired, "And what seems to be troubling Little Blue?"

Jay Frank's look was still wary. "I had to show him, Clara. I had to show him he could do it if he really tried. But you see, I ran into a problem."

He'd warned me it was a long story. My life was shot. I had all the time in the world now. "You want to take it step by step, Jay Frank? Tell me all about Little Blue and his search for happiness. Don't spare the slightest detail."

He told me. Little Blue, it seems, had been lan-

171

guishing alone in his cage, his little rat-heart despondent, ever since he had been phased out of the semifinals. So in a last-ditch effort to shore up the creature's spirits, Jay Frank had brought him over to our house to do the run again, to prove he still had the stuff. But, lo, the run had been removed. So Jay Frank had had to improvise another, out of bricks and pieces of wood.

"Stop!" I said. "Don't tell me. Your rat jumped the run and now he's loose in our basement!" I shoved back my chair with a sigh. "All right, let's go look." I felt a million years old.

"No! That's not it at all. He's in the cage where I put him."

I was finally getting irritated. No, not irritated. More like rabid. "So! Get to the point! What's the big emergency, huh? You call me at the office, yell *Help!* and get me crazy, and now you tell me what? That your dumb rat's in a cage, where he belongs!"

"Clara, there's a problem. I'm trying to tell you. I put him in a cage with another rat. And now . . . and now . . ."

"And now *what?*"

". . . I can't tell which is which!"

If ever there was a dead silence, this was it.

"You see," Jay Frank said, pulling in on his lips, "they'll be coming to get the five champions pretty soon. And you know how they said they were going to put fresh dye on their heads? Well they haven't, yet . . . and now . . ."

Good-bye Pom Pon, Good-bye Year of the Clara. Good-bye happiness. All done in by an undyed rat.

"Clara . . ." From somewhere beyond my closed eyes Jay Frank's voice coaxed. "Can you help me? Angel and Fergy will be so mad. And they are my friends."

I opened my eyes. "Your friends! And yet, you called *me.*"

He looked at me solemnly. "But you are my first, best friend."

The anger and frustration drained right out of me. He was only a kid, a pesty little kid, but he had a hold on my life. I stood up and held out my hand. I had all the time in the world, now. "Come on, then. Let's go down and see if we can sort them out. You really can't tell which is which, huh?"

"I think I can." He let go of my hand to start down the steps. "But then I think I'm wrong. If I'd only just put him in Little Yellow's cage instead of Little Violet's!"

If only.

If only the phone call had come five minutes later, I would have been unreachable. I would now be radiant, hyped up, wowing the crowds. But here I was instead. In the cellar.

Jay Frank reached into the first cage, took out the mixed up pair, and held one rat in each hand under a bright light. The dye was indistinct. I got a magnifying glass from upstairs and moved it back and forth over each squirmy head. "I'm pretty sure this one's blue," I said finally. "See those hairs there . . . no right here . . ."

"Yes, you're right! Oh, my Little Blue, I love you so." Jay Frank snuggled it to his face. "How could I ever have mixed you up with that regular rat?"

"Will you please shove Mister Regular back into his cage?" I asked. "Hey, when I said shove, I didn't mean literally," I said, as the rat rolled over. "And Jay Frank," I said, latching the cage, "there's an old saying, 'It's a wise mother who knows her own child.' In your case you'd better play it safe with an old felt marker."

"Little Blue doesn't need a mark any more," Jay Frank said. "I know who he is. And he does, too. He'll be all right now."

"Good-bye, then," I said.

"Bye, Clara." He started for the stairs. "Thank you."

Thank you. That was it. *Thank you.* My world shot, and he says *thank you.*

I stared at the five rat cages in a row. They could have been anything. They were nothing to me. Just five rat cages in a row. I stood there for I don't know how long, nothing special in my mind. I felt like nothing.

Suddenly I heard a car door slam, and voices—

Angel, Fergy, and whoever was driving. If they saw me here, in my Pom Pon outfit, there'd have to be all kinds of questions, explanations, and then all kinds of assurances that it wasn't Angel's and Fergy's fault. I wasn't up to it at the moment. Like a flash, I tore upstairs, across the kitchen, and halfway up the other stairs before pausing.

". . . thank goodness Halcyon remembered to leave the door open," I heard Angel say. Then the voices drifted downward.

They were in the cellar for quite a while, probably cleaning the cages and putting fresh dye on the champion rat heads. Little did they dream what the dye delay had done to me, or how close they'd come to carting off a loser because of a happiness crisis.

After the final door slam and the sound of the car leaving, I sank to the steps. It didn't matter that my pleated Pom Pon skirt was too short for that kind of sitting. I was alone in the house. Man, was I ever alone. Like Little Blue, I'd missed out on the main event.

They'd be well into the game by now. I could almost see the team pounding down the court, sinking basket after basket as the crowd went berserk. And the Pom Pon squad, exploding out to the floor in a burst of color and dazzle, whipping the crowd into even further frenzy with its routines.

I shifted, putting my back against the wall and propping a sneakered foot against the banister. I knew I should go back, but what for? They didn't need me. Liz could take over just as well. She already had.

In the dusk, I visualized the court again. Skip . . . dribbling his way down the court, arching his body and sinking another one into the basket. And Liz looking at him. And Skip knowing she was looking. And liking it?

I must not be myself, sitting here on the stairs, not moving, not really caring. The thought of Skip and Liz together interested me. Yes, interested. Like half-watching a TV show while doing math. Everything seemed so distant and far away. I could almost close my eyes here and doze. Except that I'd probably fall down the stairs.

You've got to go back, I told myself. I didn't want to go back. You've got to go back. I didn't want to go back. Clara! Stop putting things off! I'm telling you to get off your duff and go back. I got up, went to the bathroom, fixed up my face and hair, wrapped myself up in the coat, and trudged back to the school.

"Nothing serious?" the secretary in the office asked, as I thanked her for the use of the coat.

"No. Just a family thing. It's okay now. Who's winning the game?"

"Oh, Clara, I don't know. There's so much commotion around this place . . ."

I could hear the crowd yelling as I got near the

176

gym. The game must be really going strong. And then there was a mighty roar, and I heard a whistle, and a voice announce, "Half-time!" Now's when they'd do the disco thing.

I could rush out right now and with a grand flourish take over. One part of me wanted to. But it was as though there was a hand on my shoulder and a voice saying, "Let Liz do it. It's her act." And I was so tired.

Standing barely inside the areaway, in the shadows, I watched as Liz sprinted out front. The music started, and the squad went through the routine without missing a beat. After the crowd cheered, some people started off the bleachers for the restrooms or refreshments, and I took off for the locker room.

In a little while the girls came rushing in, so caught up in the excitement and afterglow that it took a couple of minutes for some of them even to notice me.

"Clara! You missed us! And we were so great!" Liz rushed over and flung her arms around me.

"I saw you! It really was great."

Liz whirled, face flushed, her body still so keyed up she couldn't stop the motion.

Miss Curry came in. "Girls, in one word . . . pow!" she said. "Keep up the pace." And then, "Clara, did something happen at home?"

"Just a family thing. It's okay now."

The girls reclustered around Liz, but she came back to me. "The second half's all yours," she said. She was still breathing in happy little gasps.

"No, Liz," I heard myself saying. "Keep going." She was all revved up and my motor hadn't even turned over. "Finish the game. I'd just like to watch with the others." The standbys, I meant.

Miss Curry hustled them out, then turned to me. "Clara?"

"Would you mind if I dropped out for today?"

A flicker of concern passed over her face before she nodded and left. She probably thought there'd been some really big trauma at home.

The second half of the game seemed to flash by, with the Harrison team sinking so many baskets it was ridiculous. The crowd screamed, the cheers sounded, and finally with a long shot from Skip just before the whistle, it was all over.

Our group of girls poured out into the areaway, and the team came breaking through. I happened to be one of the first ones out, but still with the group. The team came jogging past. The guys didn't touch their girl friends or anything because of the coach, but they called out little things. All of the guys, that is, except Skip. His eyes swept past everyone, including me.

Mindy noticed. "Boy! What's with him!" She glanced at me. "He looked as though he didn't even recognize you."

I didn't know what to say. "Maybe," I said after a moment, "the blue dye on my forehead has faded, too."

Mindy gave a little laugh, the way kids do when they think they should get it but really don't.

To tell the truth, I really didn't get it myself.

Angel did.

I looked her up, manning the booth alone during the dinner lull at the science fair. We sat on matching high stools next to the cages, and I told her about what had happened at home and at the game. And then I mentioned my remark about the blue dye.

"Oh, Clara!" Angel clasped her hands. "You don't really believe you need some special sign or mark to prove you're somebody, do you?"

"I seem to be nobody now."

"You think Little Blue was a nothing rat just because his color faded? A rat like any other rat?"

I shrugged. Who cared, really?

"Listen, I'd have known in a minute if he'd been brought over by mistake. And you know why?"

"Why?"

"Because Little Blue has a mind of his own," Angel said. "I admire that little thing. He decided one day that he wasn't going to race pell-mell down the runway just because of the pellet. It wasn't the most important thing in his life, not at that moment."

179

"Look, Angel, I'm sorry I ever brought up the idea of the blue dye. It was just a remark." I shifted on the stool. "Anyway, as much as you admire Little Blue's independence and all, it has nothing to do with me. You see, I do want the prize. I want to be popular and lead the cheers and be out front more than anything else in the world."

Angel looked at me and slowly smiled. Then in a gentle tone she murmured, *"Help."*

I caught my breath, then I relaxed and slowly let it out. "What could I do?" I said in a small voice. "Jay Frank needed me. I'm his first, best friend." Tears misted my eyes. I looked away.

There was silence. Then ever so softly Angel said, "Clara, you will never need any blue dye. Believe me."

EIGHTEEN

That night Mom was at one of her meetings, Halcyon was hanging around the science fair, and I was hanging around the house waiting for the phone to ring. I didn't know what I'd say when he called. Maybe be cool and let him explain, if he could. Maybe I'd pretend I had someone there and couldn't talk and make him crazy.

The phone didn't ring at seven. It didn't ring at seven-thirty. Or eight.

I started doing a burn. Who did Skip think he was, anyway, to cut me out in front of all the girls, and then not even call to try to explain? Now, when he did get around to calling, I'd have a few choice things to say, myself.

At eight-thirty Halcyon came home. I was sitting at the kitchen table, thinking about but not actually doing my nails.

"How come you're down here?" she asked.

"There's no law against it."

She tossed off her coat, opened the refrigerator,

and took out the milk. "I wouldn't hold my breath, waiting for Skip to call if I were you," she said. She got out a glass and poured the milk.

What could she do . . . look right into my head? "Really." I tried to act unconcerned as I unscrewed the cap of the nail polish.

"He was at the fair. With Liz. Her seventh grade sister has an exhibit."

"Liz!" I looked up and met Halcyon's look. "Liz?"

"Yeh, Liz. She stopped and talked to Angel and Fergy, but Skip just stood off a-ways with that smirk on his face that we all know so well." Halcyon finished the milk and rinsed the glass. "I heard you ducked out of the game. Don't worry, it wasn't on the loudspeaker system or anything like that. Angel told me."

"Oh." I brushed polish on a nail and part of the cuticle, too. Halcyon was hovering somewhere behind me now. I had the feeling she was trying to be decent but couldn't let go enough to face me with it.

"We all . . . Angel and Fergy and I . . . think it was . . ." She cleared her throat. "For Jay Frank . . ." She cleared her throat again. "An okay thing that you did. I mean . . ."

"Thanks." I wanted to turn around, but didn't. I cleaned off the nail with remover. My hand was shaking. "You're sure they were together? Skip and Liz? Not just . . . well . . . ?"

"I'd say they were together. And you know what

else I'd say?" She allowed for some silence. "I'd say let Skip find his own level and go out with Liz, if he wants to. You're too good for him anyway."

By the time I'd recovered enough from shock to turn around, Halcyon was gone. For once, she didn't even elephant-thump up the stairs.

It was too much, all at once. Boyfriend turns traitor, enemy turns ally. What could I make of it? Nothing at the moment.

So much for the manicure. I picked up the bottles, gave the phone a dirty look, and went upstairs.

I was lying on my back in bed, arms folded under my head, when I thought of it. The list.

Springing up, I flung open the desk drawer, found the paper, and tore it into little pieces. As they fell in the general direction of the wastebasket, I said, "So much for list-making."

Feeling free, I climbed back into bed, got comfortable, and was just drifting off when Mom came quietly into the room. "Oh, sorry," she said, as I stirred under her light kiss. "I thought you were still . . ."

"That's okay." I took her hand and eased her to the side of my bed. "How was the meeting?"

"All right. I saw Sheri out by the driveway just now with Jay Frank. He's still quite a chatterbox, isn't he?"

"That kid should be in bed. What did he tell you?" I mumbled into the edge of the pillow.

"Bits and scraps. I'd like to hear the story from you in logical sequence. I got the impression that you've been through a lot lately."

"Yeh, in a way."

"Will you tell me about it?"

"Sure, Mom." I yawned.

"Tomorrow night, after your game? No meetings. No paper work. Just you and me."

"And maybe Halcyon," I said. "She's been in on it, too."

I could almost see Mom's eyebrows lift in the dark, but all she said was, "Whatever." She shifted, touched my hair, and got up.

"Good night, Mom."

"Good night, Clara. Sleep tight."

And together, we said, "Don't let the bedbugs bite."

The next afternoon, I had time before the game to dash into the science fair room again. Angel and Fergy were at the booth together. The judges had been around. There was a red ribbon attached to the display.

"Second place! Oh, no!"

Angel laughed. "Don't look as though we'd been wiped out, Clara."

"But who?" I looked around.

"Tom and Bill did a really great thing on the Voyager I probe of Jupiter," Angel said. "Charts, pictures . . . you should take a look at it."

"But I thought for sure . . ." I went to the cages. "It's not fair. I'll bet those guys had their parents help them."

"Come off it, Clara," Fergy said. "It's not the end of the line. Our show's generated a lot of interest. Some man with college connections even asked us to keep in touch. Right, Angel?"

"Yeh. And Halcyon's floating, too. A *Herald* photographer told her she had the touch."

"Great." I really was glad. "Well, child scientists, I've got to get going. The game . . ."

"Knock 'em out, Captain," Angel said. "Give them the old pizazz."

The word *captain* almost took the starch out of me. "Angel . . ." I motioned her a little away from Fergy. "You once said 'fair is fair.' Remember?"

For possibly the first time in her life, Angel looked uneasy.

"But this whole caper, in a way, wasn't strictly . . . you know?"

"I know." Angel's glance focused somewhere on the floor. "It seemed so reasonable at the time . . . trading what we wanted for what you wanted. But it was a little . . . ummmm . . ."

"Yeh." Everyone had used everyone else. "But, Angel, there's one thing. We did work hard."

"That's right."

"So we shouldn't feel totally bad."

"I don't." Angel gave me a look. "But about Skip . . ."

"Oh, that's something else. I'm going to tell him, but good."

We exchanged girl-type looks. I waved to Fergy and walked out of the room.

And wouldn't you know? Just then I saw Skip coming down the hall. I'm sure he saw me, too, but he turned his head and pretended to brush something off his shoulder as he walked past. He didn't have dandruff. No way. Not with the care he gave his golden locks.

I wasn't going to let him get by. This was my chance. "Hey, Skip!"

He turned and faked a look of surprise.

I hoped my voice wouldn't betray my nervousness. "Nice game you played yesterday," I said, as I caught up with him.

"Oh, thanks." His smile was kind of testing me.

"As it happened, I wasn't around to get the full impact."

Something in my tone faded his smile. "Yeh, I heard. That was a pretty lowdown thing you did, deserting the squad for a nothing reason. And leaving poor Liz . . ."

"Poor Liz did all right."

"Okay, but you're supposed to be captain."

"Yeah. Because you set it up."

His eyes hardened. "I thought you had the stuff."

"Don't give me that *stuff* business. You thought I was *cute*. You thought we'd look cute together!"

"Yeh, well, maybe I've changed my mind."

"No kidding." Boy, my voice dripped with sarcasm.

"Look!" His voice rose with anger. "First you go off during the Thanksgiving dance . . ."

"I! *I* went off! What about . . ."

"And then during Christmas vacation, when we could've got together, you were laying around sick."

"Not *laying*. *Lying*. I was *lying* around sick."

"And then you pulled that little fadeout yesterday. Kid, I've had it with you."

"You've had it! I've had it!" I shouted. "You can go throw *yourself* through a hoop for all I care." And then as a brilliant after-thought I added. "But you might get stuck in the net, with that big head of yours."

Skip's face turned a deep, furious red. "You can try to cut me down all you want, but just keep in mind that I'm still number one on the team. Think of that when you're sitting on the sidelines."

I wasn't nervous any more. Calmly, steadily, I looked him in the eye and said, "But Skip, I won't be sitting on the sidelines. I'm the Pom Pon captain. Remember? And as captain, I'll be right out front, leading the routines."

He seemed to be struggling for a hotshot come-back, but he fell back on a look of complete contempt and a shrug of the shoulders. Then he walked off.

"Don't lose your comb!" I called out.

Instinctively, his hand went back and slapped his hip pocket. Then he really rushed off.

The first half of that day's game didn't go so well for our team. Skip fumbled the ball several times.

As half-time began to loom, I started feeling the old unsureness slip back. What if I led the disco routine and loused it up? Shouldn't I let Liz take over? She was giving me little glances. With a few brief words I could hand it all over. Let someone else do it. Play it safe.

But was this what The Year of the Clara was all about? Wheel and deal, but when it gets really tough, throw in the towel? No, I didn't think so. I'd been on a big popularity binge. Nothing wrong with that. But it had been laid on me. Now was the moment, coming up, to show I'd done at least a little something on my own.

"Clara . . ." Mindy was nudging me. "It's almost half-time. Are you ready?"

"I'm ready, Mindy."

And I was. When the whistle blew, I raced out, pom pons in hand, and the girls raced after me. There was a hush. I smiled, and the team smiled back at me. Every cell in my body was saying, "Let's go!"

The music started, and we went into the routine that had become a part of us. The music quickened, and we swirled, swooped, did the intricate steps all together, all to the beat. And then came the crescendo and the trick finale, and the final beat as we sank to one knee, arms raised toward the crowd, pom pons fluttering. We made it!

We held the pose for the applause.

The cheers felt great, but in a different way this time. I hadn't done it for Skip. I hadn't done it for fame. I'd done it for myself. For me. Clara. And for the school, too. We were all in this together.

With the applause still hanging in the air, the girls rushed off, and I followed. It's all over, I thought, as I watched them disappearing into the locker room. The big ring-a-ding-ding is all finished.

But it wasn't! The basketball season was winding up, to be sure, but what did that count in the grand scheme of things? Another semester, and who knew what? There was a big, exciting bunch of stuff whizzing around out there in the world and just anything could happen. Oh, wow, it was all so stupefying!

There in the hall I tossed my pom pons aside and started turning cartwheels. Then I started twirling. "Watch out, world! I called out, "This time I'm *really* on my way!"

"Clara!"

Hands grasped me. Staggering a little, I saw the wavering figures of Angel and Halcyon.

"What's the matter?" I blinked until they came into focus.

"You're asking *us*?" Halcyon stared. "We came back to say what a smash you were, and here you are, cracking up."

"I'm just . . ."

"Winding down?" Angel asked, helpfully.

"Wrong-o. Winding up."

Halcyon shook her head. "Looney Tunes revisited."

"Oh, well." I picked up the pom pons and slapped one into each of their hands. "A little souvenir," I said.

"What?"

"Why?"

"The season of the Pom Pon has passed. The *year* is just getting underway."

Neither of them got it, I could tell. But as we walked down the hall together, I didn't go on to explain. Some things you just have to know for yourself. Don't you agree?

About the Author

Stella Pevsner lives with her husband and four children in Palatine, Illinois. Her writing career began with a job as copywriter for a Chicago advertising agency, and she has gone on to write books for young people including such Clarion titles as *A Smart Kid Like You*, *Keep Stompin' Till the Music Stops*, and *Call Me Heller, That's My Name*. Her most recent book, *And You Give Me a Pain, Elaine*, was the winner of the 1978 Golden Kite Award for Fiction, and was described in *School Library Journal* as "a popular choice due to its realistic dialogue, likeable protagonist, humor and typical family interactions and crises."

Pevsner, Stella
Cute is a four-letter word.

jW